The Narrative Mediterranean

After the Empire: The Francophone World and Postcolonial France
Series Editor: Valérie Orlando, University of Maryland

Recent Titles

The Narrative Mediterranean

Beyond France and the Maghreb

Claudia Esposito

LEXINGTON BOOKS
Lanham • Boulder • New York • Toronto • Plymouth, UK

Published by Lexington Books
A wholly owned subsidiary of The Rowman & Littlefield Publishing Group, Inc.
4501 Forbes Boulevard, Suite 200, Lanham, Maryland 20706
www.rowman.com

10 Thornbury Road, Plymouth PL6 7PP, United Kingdom

British Library Cataloguing in Publication Information Available

Library of Congress Cataloging-in-Publication Data
Esposito, Claudia.
The Narrative Mediterranean : Beyond France and the Maghreb / Claudia Esposito.
pages cm.—(After the Empire: The Francophone World and Postcolonial France)
Includes bibliographical references.
ISBN 978-0-7391-6821-9 (cloth : alk. paper) — ISBN 978-0-7391-6822-6 (ebook)
1. North African literature (French)—History and criticism. 2. Postcolonialism in literature. 3. France—Foreign relations—Africa, North. 4. Africa, North—Foreign relations—France. I. Title.
PQ3980.5.E73 2014
840.9'96—dc23
2013035499

ISBN 978-1-4985-2125-3 (pbk : alk, paper)

∞™ The paper used in this publication meets the minimum requirements of American National Standard for Information Sciences Permanence of Paper for Printed Library Materials, ANSI/NISO Z39.48-1992.

Printed in the United States of America

Contents

Acknowledgments

My utmost gratitude goes first and foremost to those who most inspired me to pursue literary studies; Réda Bensmaïa and Pierre Saint-Amand, as well as Robert Schwartzwald and Patrick Mensah. Reaching back that far I also thank Laura Reeck for her shared enthusiasm upon discovering new writers, new texts and new paths to follow, and for her witty but always grounded approach.

Particular appreciation and admiration go to all of the writers in this book, but specifically to those who generously discussed their work with me; Mahi Binebine, Amara Lakhous, Abdelmalek Smari, and Mohsen Melliti. Along with them I thank Editions Gallimard for giving me permission to reprint passages from Albert Camus's *Essais* (Editions de la Pléiade, 1965). I am grateful to the Editors at the journal CELAAN for allowing me to reprint parts of my article "Neapolitan Baroque: Tahar Ben Jelloun's Italian Works" in Vol IV No.3 (2006) that appear in chapter 5. A section on chapter 2 appears as "Translating the Self: Amin Maalouf's Léon l'Africain," in *Comparative Literature and Translation/Littérature Comparée et Traduction,* Conference Proceedings (Rabat: MJB, 2006). I truly appreciate the efficiency and guidance of Lindsey Porambo and Kelly Shefferly at Lexington Press.

I would also like to wholeheartedly thank all my colleagues in the Department of Modern Languages, Literatures and Cultures at the University of Massachusetts, Boston for their rare and wonderful sense of collegiality and warmth, in particular Antonio Carrara, as well as my daily interlocutors Pratima Prasad, Thierry Gustave, and Kristina Kalas.

Inestimable thanks go to numerous friends both near and far; Allison Gross, Edwige Tamalet-Talbayev, Hakim Abderrezak, Pamela Pears, Alessandra Di Maio, Alexandra Offiong, Abdellah Baida; but special appreciation goes to those who, in various ways, also actually had a hand (and keen eyes) in the fine-tuning of this book; Lindsey Moore, Elizabeth McCahill, Jenny Volkert, Stéphanie Ravillon, Mokhtar Bouba, Heidi Brevik-Zender, and David Leyenson.

Finally, my deepest sense of gratitude and love goes to Marco, to Lea, to Silvia and to my parents.

Note on Translations and Transliterations

All quotes in languages other than English have been translated. If a published translation of the work I cite exists in English, I have used it and referenced it in the bibliography. All other translations are my own. Words and names in Arabic have been either reproduced as they appear in the texts I discuss or transliterated using a simplified version of the *International Journal for Middle East Studies* IJMES transliteration chart. I have left the words that are commonly used in English (such as *casbah,* for instance) in their Anglicized form, assuming the reader will be familiar with such terms.

Introduction

Walking through the chaotic streets of Palermo one day, eyes skyward, I came upon three small but striking pink domes. As I turned into Piazza Bellini, two adjacent churches stood before me, one of them crowned with the three pink cupolas. The other, more sober, was capped with only one small dome. The pink trio stands atop the unadorned façade of the Chiesa di San Cataldo while the single dome, which carries traces of Arabic calligraphy, belongs to the Chiesa della Martorana, a church extolled by the twelfth-century poet from al-Andalus Ibn Jubaīr as the most beautiful monument in the world. The dome of the Martorana was built in 1143, commissioned by George of Antioch, whose official Arabic title, Emīr al-baḥr, translates as admiral, or commander of the sea. Both churches have changed denomination numerous times over the centuries—San Cataldo even served as a post office in the nineteenth century—and today stand as architectural and cultural testaments to the Greek, Arab, Norman, and Byzantine presence in Sicily. It struck me, standing in that small piazza, how many emirs, ideas, materials, and philosophies have crossed the Mediterranean in both directions, and how much the emphasis has shifted today with the continual resurgence of Club Meds on the one hand and drowning refugees on the other. What has become of yesterday's transcultural crossings today? This book investigates the space of the contemporary Mediterranean from the perspective of writers who draw individual and textual trajectories to and from the Maghreb. My analysis is determined by a crucial moment in the history of the Mediterranean: the long aftermath of the French colonization of North Africa. More specifically, I examine literary texts written in French and Italian by writers from former North African colonies in direct relation to today's increasingly tempestuous debates on the shifting identity of the modern Mediterranean.

Literature written in French by writers of North African origin saw its inception in the early twentieth century as a direct result of French imperialism and linguistic colonialism. Maghrebi literature in French fully came into being in the 1950s and 1960s in conjunction with various national struggles for political independence (achieved in Tunisia in 1954, Morocco in 1956, and Algeria in 1962). Hindered by colonial laws, which often included prohibition of Arabic, and suffering from what the Moroccan writer Abdellatif Laâbi called "aliénation linguistique," or "drame linguistique" in the words of the Tunisian writer Albert Memmi, numerous writers left the Maghreb for France, and repeatedly thematized—often with great disquiet, as the words "drame" and "aliénation" indicate—what it means to live a double belonging. Torn between two languages, two nations, and two allegiances, they have written, to different degrees and in myriad forms, the hardships and possibilities of such a predicament. It has followed, well into the postcolonial period, that criticism of Maghrebi literature written in French has tended to focus specifically on this double bind and double belonging.

While this has undoubtedly been a fundamental, formative, and enduring constituent of North African Francophone literature, studies of such texts seldom consider what lies around, between, outside, and beyond France and the Maghreb. I join the critic Winifred Woodhull in challenging "the interpretive frame that is adopted [and that] rarely relates North African texts to any socio-cultural reality beyond the France-Maghreb nexus" (2003: 211). This book brings together widely read writers such as Albert Camus and Tahar Ben Jelloun alongside lesser-known authors such as Fawzi Mellah and Mahi Binebine in a transnational rather than dichotomous interpretive frame, and thus moves beyond the colonial and postcolonial bind where France is the dominant point of reference. Instead of treating Maghrebi literature written in French as a kind of subordinate literature, this approach allows us to read a number of writers outside of their strict affiliation with France within what Pascale Casanova calls a "world literary republic," where literatures shape a cultural form across national borders. This does not imply the neutrality or universality of literary spaces; on the contrary, it places texts in relation to one another rather than in relation to a center or to a single nation. In effect, as Casanova affirms, "[l']éclatement géographique des espaces littéraires les plus éloignés des centres et le système de leurs dépendances multiples est peut-être l'un des signes majeurs de la non-coïncidence de l'espace littéraire et de la nation politique, c'est-à-dire de l'autonomie rélative de l'espace littéraire mondial" (1999: 285)[1] [the cleavages characteristic of literary spaces that are the furthest removed from the center and the pattern of their multiple dependencies furnish perhaps the surest sign of the incongruence of literary space and the political nation, which is to say of the relative autonomy of world literary space]. It is with this incongruence of literature and nation in mind that I deal with writers who aim to operate between and outside the confines of several nations, toward imagined affiliative horizons, and who consequently address questions of multiple forms of cultural, political, sexual, and existential belonging. In a Mediterranean context, moving across nations means to be in both foreign and familiar physical, affective, and intellectual spaces and thus often precludes any sense of permanence.

While French, along with Arabic, remains one of the main languages of Maghrebi literature, both the thematic and linguistic diversity of North African literature is becoming increasingly difficult to overlook.[2] For if diversity has been eclipsed by the domination of such major languages, and therefore by critical attention to those attendant cultural influences, it has remained a steadfast, even growing, attribute of writers and their texts. Studies of the enduring roles of French and Arabic have been indispensable, crucial and certainly justified, but they do not sufficiently account for the multiplicity of contacts with other parts of the world, especially with those neighboring countries in the Mediterranean.[3] The Maghreb—a region that is internally very diverse—has historically been defined by cultural admixture, just as its diaspora has participated in the formation of national cultures across the Mediterranean; one thinks, for instance, but not exclusively, of al-Andalus, of the Spanish enclaves in Morocco of Ceuta and Melilla, of the notable Italian presence in Tunisia throughout the centuries, not to mention the current and vast migratory phenomenon from the Maghreb across the Mediterranean.

This book examines the works of writers who, through their texts and often their personal trajectories, draw upon the long-standing cultural points of imbrication between the Maghreb and the larger Mediterranean; I draw particular attention to connections with Italy as Maghrebi writers continue to turn to it, their texts suggesting such incentives as historical interest, the search for another home and Italy's "uncanny familiarity," desire, discovery but also need and occasionally chance.[4] Many of these same incentives indeed subtend the France-Maghreb relationship, yet in the context I provide, produce new identitarian configurations which are not strictly bound by (post)colonial conditions. The modalities of cultural crossings, as I discuss later, form the second objective of this book, which argues for a cultural and literary Mediterranean as a counterpoint to its invention in the disciplines of history and the social sciences. This book focuses primarily on only part of the Western Mediterranean; in doing so, it, like most other works on the Mediterranean written after Fernand Braudel, recognizes the impossibility of doing full justice to all the areas touched by the legendary sea. More importantly, it is in specific places that important local sites of expression can be found that are related to, but also disengaged from, France's (post)colonial influence.[5] Camus's Algiers, Ben Jelloun's Naples, Maalouf's Fes and Bouraoui's Rome, to name only a few, bring new languages and original modes of thought to the Francophone literary corpus.

I delineate a distinct literary corpus around a number of writers who fundamentally critique narrow identitarian labeling, warn against sectarianism, and announce the necessity of multiple forms of translation and historical rewritings. Their modes of expression differ as they range from poetic to baroque to realist, as do their concerns which include existentialism, gender identity, and emigration, for instance. A transnational purview makes visible not only what these writers have been living and creating all along, but also suggests an epistemological object of inquiry that might extend beyond them, sharpening our critical sense of what being in this specific part of the world entails. The Mediterranean, then, can function as a heuristic device, as Sharon Kinoshita reminds us, enabling continual inquiry into ways of thinking of the present. Mine is not an attempt to affirm an authentic or essential Mediterranean identity, but rather to engage in a series of close readings in order to reveal the instances and differential moments where writers have re-created and invented their Mediterranean(s) often at odds with dominant historical and political discourses. Despite the fact that the Mediterranean may be seen as a "third space" that comprises both France and North Africa, it is never neutral. Nor is it a haven of uncompromised universalism; it is a space which allows and offers the potential to "transformer les souffrances et humiliations et dépressions dans la relation aux autres" [transform suffering, humiliation and depression when it comes to our relation with others] as Abdelkébir Khatibi put it, in ways that reach beyond a facile multiculturalism (1983: 7). Indeed, Khatibi adds, "quoi qu'il en soit cet intime de notre être, frappé, brutalisé par l'Occident, ne peut être résorbé par une naive déclaration du droit à la différence" [be that as it may, this intimate part of our being, that is injured and battered by the West, cannot be healed by a naive affirmation of our right to be different].[6] The contemporary space I am referring to, then, is not the portrait of a felicitous multiculturalism, a simple assertion of the plurality of monolithic cultural forms.[7] What affords the Mediterranean unending interest is precisely that it is a space of contestation and infinite translation. As one of the most incisive contemporary thinkers of the Mediterranean, Franco Cassano, observes, it is also a space with global implications: "il Mediterraneo è ancora oggi una linea di confine proprio tra nord-ovest e sud-est del mondo, e quindi, per certi versi, pur essendo un mare locale, è l'epicentro di un problema globale" (Fogu 2010: 4). [The Mediterranean is, still today, a border between the northwest and southwest of the world, and thus in a certain sense even though it is a local sea, it is the epicenter of a global problematic.] I situate postcolonial Maghrebi-Mediterranean literature within this global problematic in an attempt to amplify a field of study which currently remains focused on center-periphery interpretive practices.

Providing a relational interpretive paradigm is a move away from the verticality of a France-Maghreb relationship in order to think toward and back to multiple connections between Francophone writers and other spaces and languages of enunciation. As Woodhull aptly puts it,

> why should we persist in segregating the Francophone world from the rest of the planet in our thinking about literature and culture, particularly when the most interesting North African writers of our time are expressly drawing connections between North Africa and other parts of the world, and when so many North African literary scholars are

living and writing in countries outside the French speaking world? (2003: 217)

A decade after Woodhull's discerning remarks, several studies have successfully wrested Francophone literary texts from a perceived insularity.[8] Furthermore, on the heels of the *Pour une littérature monde en français* manifesto of 2007, such methodologies are all the more urgent given the added voices of disquiet, this time of the writers themselves, calling for a "Copernican Revolution."[9] Reading writers who identify with the Maghreb in relation to the Mediterranean rather than in opposition to France allows not only for more wide-reaching, broader and deeper transversal understandings into the after-effects of colonization, it also presents new iterations of a millennial space. And at a time when identitarian dogmatisms risk turning the Mediterranean into a theater for what Samuel Huntington named a "clash of civilizations," it does indeed behoove us to read between the lines of those marginal characters—writers, that is—who reveal the tenuousness of origins, of cultural identity, of historical fashioning of geographic spaces, and of the fine line between the foreign and the familiar.

(CON)TEXTUAL BEGINNINGS

Before outlining how this book unfolds, a brief analysis of France's relationship to the greater Mediterranean and to its varying definitions is in order. From the eve of the Napoleonic conquests to today, France has played a critical role in these debates by defining itself within the history and identity politics of the larger Mediterranean. From the time of the Roman Empire, the Mediterranean, or *Mare Nostrum*, has existed as a distinct historical and political space, most often written about—beginning in the sixteenth century when the term *Mediterranean* came into common use—by French thinkers.[10] If, in the past, identification with the Mediterranean provided France with a useful justification for imperial expansion, the argument being one of geographical proximity between France and North Africa, today this same identification serves the followers of former French president Nicolas Sarkozy and his proposed agenda for a Mediterranean Union (*Union pour la Méditerranée*).[11] This projected political alliance, in effect, serves as a palliative to a much feared clash of civilization between "Islam" and "the West" on European ground. To be sure, there is a traceable continuity of a Mediterranean ideal, one that appears instrumentalized, in political and historical discourses, in order to maintain ties with former colonies in the Maghreb and, more subtly, to conceal neocolonial practices.[12] In the words of former French Foreign Minister Bernard Kouchner, as recently as 2008, "La Méditerranée est au cœur de toutes les grandes problématiques de ce début de siècle. Développement, migrations, paix, dialogue des civilisations, accès à l'eau et à l'énergie, environnement, changement climatique : c'est au sud de l'Europe que notre avenir se joue."[13] [The Mediterranean is at the heart of all the major issues of the beginning of this century. Development, migrations, peace, dialogue between civilizations, access to water and energy, the environment, climate change: our future hinges on what lies south of Europe.] Alongside the historical, political, and geographic Mediterranean, there exists a vital literary space that provides alternative histories and imagined possibilities, necessary devices that reveal the ruptures and discontinuities of a reductive rhetoric of willed unity. Within this literary space, other possible histories are told, often by subjects in a position of perpetual translation and between nations. It is in particular those texts that carry with them colonial and postcolonial experiences that bring to light the double phenomenon occurring in the Mediterranean, between migration and transnational movements on the one hand, and dogmatic and identitarian fundamentalisms on the other.

Historians, anthropologists, and geographers have written extensively on this area of the world, fixing and describing events, dates, and landscapes. Yet this is neither the whole story nor necessarily its most illuminating aspect; woven into these histories, there must exist what Gilles Deleuze would call the "intensities," affects and singularities that only art—here literary texts—is able to reveal. Affect, or feeling, that is stirred by art dislocates the commonsense associations we make between words and experience, and effects changes in consciousness. In this sense affect is a force. Continuously pushed to define and redefine meaning, varying intensities, or degrees of feeling, we are led to reach a wider and more insightful understanding of what the Mediterranean is, and to redraw the lines of a space unceasingly reinvented and reterritorialized.[14]

It is to this multiplicity of affects and intensities that I point when I employ the term *Mediterranean*, and not only to a strictly geographic, physically localizable space. A proper name—"the Mediterranean"—conjures up fixity, a totalizing, presumably knowable whole, while obscuring the inherent complexity that lies within any denomination. As critic Pierre Jourde put it, "le nom propre donne au signifié une cohérence, une unité profonde parce qu'il fait appel à l'imagination: il rassemble—fictivement—la diversité du réel dans un signe unique et dense" (1991: 288). [A proper name gives the signifier coherence and a profound unity because it calls upon imagination: it brings together—fictively—the diversity of the real in one unique and dense sign.] Paradoxically then, the names indispensable to identify people, things, and geographies hide the multiple realities to which they refer. It makes sense, thus, to consider what the term *Mediterranean* places under erasure, and to be cognizant, as we use the term in reference to a specific geographical and historical space, of its incompleteness or inadequacy. It may not come as a surprise, for example, that Leopold Sédar Senghor (1906–2001), Senegalese writer and first president of independent Senegal, evokes a Senegalese Mediterraneity. Nor is it incongruous that Kenneth Brown, sociologist and founder of the journal *Méditerranéens/Mediterraneans* considers Iraq to be Mediterranean.[15] Furthermore, as Edward Saïd reminds us, "Words are not passive markers or signifiers standing in unassumingly for a higher reality; they are, instead, an integral formative part of that reality" (2004: 58). Continually taking on new meanings, its name slipping and sliding with every turn, this space paradoxically has become associated with historical fixity; labeled the "cradle of civilization," the "birthplace of philosophy," and etymologically defined as the very center of the earth, it has indeed been synonymous with permanence and continuity. As Jacques Derrida puts it:

> En parlant du lac de la Méditerranée, que nommons-nous? Comme tous les noms dont nous parlons, comme tous les noms en général, ceux-ci désignent à la fois une limite, une limite négative et une chance, la responsabilité consistant peut-être à faire du nom rappelé, de la mémoire du nom, de la limite idiomatique, une chance, c'est-à-dire une ouverture de l'identité à son avenir même. (1992: 37)

> [When speaking of the Mediterranean lake, what are we naming? Like all the names we are invoking, like all names in general, these designate at once a limit, a negative limit, and a chance. For perhaps responsibility consists in making of the name, of the idiomatic limit, a chance, that is, an opening of identity to its very future.]

In other words, to want to ascribe a single meaning to the Mediterranean would be a futile attempt, and in Derrida's estimation, irresponsible. Instead it offers a "chance" and an "opening," grounded in history but yet to come.

To take the Mediterranean as both an epistemological object of inquiry and an analytic tool is to encounter a number of clichés and paradoxes; clichés that tend to revolve around food, sea, sex, and sun, together with stereotypes of exoticism and the tourism-driven complexes that dot the coastlines. The paradoxes, which necessitate fertile and creative investigations, can be articulated around a tripartite nexus: first, the Mediterranean is both a real space and an imaginary one, actual and virtual, historical and fictional. Second, it is at once considered a single geographic space and a heterogeneous constellation of nations, thus characterized by unity and difference. Lastly, given the economic disparities between the Northern and Southern shores, a drastic discrepancy simultaneously makes the Mediterranean a playground for tourists and a graveyard of clandestine immigrants who attempt the crossing of the straits from Africa to Europe in subhuman conditions. The complexity and perpetual shifting of perspectives and the debates around these contradictions have made for an object of inquiry that defies any single definition and escapes circumscription.

The difficulty of definition has led a number of critics, for instance the historian and journalist Paul Balta, to suggest that the Mediterranean—as an entity—is an impossibility. Yet other scholars, including the anthropologist Michael Herzfeld, argue that the concept of the Mediterranean is here to stay: "In an age where just about every other category has been deconstructed and reconstructed, or at least has self-destructed, 'the' Mediterranean has shown a remarkable tenacity in the face of a barrage of critiques—indeed, that barrage has at times seemed simply to confirm its general importance" (2005: 46). It is perhaps this very impossibility and its unceasing importance that has led to what Kinoshita in a 2009 issue of the *PMLA* calls "an explosion of interest in Mediterranean Studies" over the last decade.[16] In this book the general importance of the Mediterranean conjoins with its particular relevance in a new perspective that relates it to Maghrebi literature. Already in 1997, Khatibi called for such an interpretive framework in an effort to look beyond cultural nationalisms: "nous sommes aujourd'hui au Maroc devant une civilisation dont on ne peut nier ni l'identité, ni la permanence, ni la singularité, ni le brassage. Elle est appelée à jouer son rôle dans la nouvelle Méditerranée" (1997: 86). [What we have today in Morocco is a civilization whose identity, permanence, singularity and mixity cannot be denied. It is incumbent upon such a civilization to play its role in the new Mediterranean.] The Mediterranean, Khatibi insists, must be reinvented anew and not as mere geography.[17]

THE INVENTION OF THE MEDITERRANEAN IN HISTORY

Historiography of the twentieth century emphasized and, in large part, created the idea of the Mediterranean as a space of continuity. Capital in this determination was the historian Fernand Braudel (1902–1985), whose name is inextricably linked both to the history of the Mediterranean and to histories of French identity. Braudel taught in Constantinople and in Algiers for a number of years in the 1930s and was deeply influenced by the history of French colonialism which, in part, shaped his perspective on the Mediterranean. On the one hand, colonial policy pushed for a unifying Mediterranean whereby France and the Maghreb were part of the same geopolitical space. On the other hand, there was a strong sense that the region was divided along cultural and religious lines. In Algiers, Braudel worked with the Belgian historian Henri Pirenne, who claimed that the Arab conquests of the Mediterranean in the eighth century had created an irreversible schism between East and West, putting a definitive end to Mediterranean unity. Rather than positing unity or disunity and treating the Mediterranean from a single perspective, Braudel's work draws on numerous disciplines.

This multidisciplinary methodology stemmed from Braudel's affiliation with the historians of the *Annales*, a group that believed that history should not be isolated from the disciplines of geography, economics, anthropology, and the social sciences more generally. Braudel's seminal work, *The Mediterranean and the Mediterranean World in the Age of Philip II*, published in 1949 and revised in 1966, was groundbreaking and revolutionary in that in it he proposed to regard history not only in terms of grand events, battles, and stories of heroes, but from a much larger perspective, one including, indeed dominated by, geography, peasant activity, trade, and ecology. Through this interdisciplinary approach, he sought to develop a *histoire totale* that would account for his three concepts of historical time: the *longue durée* (most often translated as "long perspective") in which geography acts as a determinant of history; *conjonctures* or the social, impersonal collective aspects of historical change (economic and socio-political history); and a time of the *histoire événementielle* of battles, dates, and stories of heroes. The latter were, for Braudel, mere moments inscribed upon the two deeper, more permanent layers, and by far the least privileged form in his work; the slow-changing and structurally stable aspects of history gave it its lasting importance. This three-layered approach to the history of the Mediterranean was unquestionably revolutionary in that it attempted to write a *people's* history, and not (only) one "of a few princes and rich men, the trivia of the past," but one of peasants and farmers, nomads and wanderers and their relationships to the earth and to geographical space (2001: xiii).

Braudel affirms that the Mediterranean is not a space of unity, but one created by the movements of men, the relationships they imply, and the routes they follow. However, he also asserts its continuity:

> We may be tempted to linger over its picturesque aspects, to accompany Cervantes along the Spanish cart tracks from *venta* to *venta*, to follow the voyages of merchant or pirate vessels as we read their log books, to go down the Adige aboard the *burchieri*, the heavy cargo boats working below Verona, or to embark "upon the water to go to Venice" at Fusina on the edge of the lagoon, with Montaigne's belongings. But the essential task before us is to measure the relationships this network implies, the coherence of its history, the extent to which the movement of boats, pack animals, vehicles and people themselves makes the Mediterranean a unit and gives it a certain uniformity in spite of local resistance. (1972: 277)

Despite his focus on movement and connectivity, Braudel insists on the importance of defining a historical coherence, as the cited passage indicates, that is articulated primarily in terms of geography. By considering geography as the basis of history and civilizations, he suggests that the latter are static. If geography can account for human action, then how do "civilizations" change? Without ignoring the human element of history,

Braudel fails nonetheless to nuance the profound, dramatic transforma-
tions upon which entire "civilizations" are built. His is not a traditional
history; nor is it complete in any sense. Yet it was the first and only
history to treat the Mediterranean as a unified space with a threefold,
long relation of time.[18]

Intent on writing histories that were supposedly scientific, the Annalistes found narrative histories excessively novelistic and dramatic. As
Hayden White affirms, "One suspects that it is not the dramatic nature of
novels that is at issue but a distaste for a genre of literature that puts
human agents rather than impersonal processes at the center of interest
and suggests that such agents have some significant control over their
own destinies" (1987: 33). Remaining attached to the role of human
agents, but in an altogether different vein, in their Braudel-style history
of the Mediterranean *The Corrupting Sea: A Study of Mediterranean History*
(2000), Peregrine Horden and Nicholas Purcell allege that Braudel's work
is over-determined by geography, accounting for geography's effect on
humanity but ignoring the reverse. Perceptions, attitudes, beliefs, and
symbols, they assert, are reduced to a relatively few pages. Braudel's
subjects are environmentally determined, thus leaving little room for, as
Horden and Purcell state, an understanding of mentalities. Of his work
on the Mediterranean, Braudel affirms that "the final effect is to dissect
history into various planes, or, to put it another way, to divide historical
time into geographical time, social time, and individual time. Or, alterna-
tively, to divide men into a multitude of selves" (1972: 21). But, like
Horden and Purcell who claim, but fail, to deal with "unintended patterns of behaviour," Braudel does not take into account subjectivity in
those "unintended patterns" that literature and the imaginary so effectively reveal. Their men—and they are mostly men—despite their physical movements, are static and, to some extent, empty.

THE SMOOTH PAGES OF FICTION

Seen through the lens of history and of stability the Mediterranean has
been dominated, for the most part, by what Deleuze and Guattari would
call its striated dimension. In *A Thousand Plateaus*, a text that draws on
numerous geographical concepts, the authors identify what they consider
marked and unmarked space, distinguishing them as striated and
smooth. In a section entitled "The Maritime Model," they propose that
smooth spaces—according to them the sea is a smooth space par excellence—or those that have yet to be mapped are open to intensities and
affects. Striated spaces, however, marked by fixed structures and reference points, both confine and restrict. In the case of the Mediterranean,
the interplay between the two spaces is clearly defined by, on the one
hand, the smooth space of the sea and *unwritten* spaces—open to infinite

passages, markings, inscriptions—and on the other, the "constructed" entities such as nations, cities, political structures, state regulations and so forth. This model allows us to conceive of a framework within which to understand the difference between the roles of literature and history; where striated space is characterized by history, smooth space is characterized by fiction. While telling two very different stories, the two are not in opposition, but rather operate in relation to one another and co-exist by a mutually defining bond.

What are the stories that fictions are able to tell? For Paul Ricoeur, narrative is what allows mediation between the world and its meaning as well as the meaning of self and subjectivity. Literature opens up possibilities and allows us to understand the world not only in terms of our direct experience but in terms of the imaginary as well. Taking on Heideggerian terminology, Ricoeur writes that "par la fiction, par la poésie, de nouvelles possibilités d'être au monde sont ouvertes dans la réalité quotidienne; fiction et poésie visent l'être, non plus sous la modalité de l'être-donné, mais sous la modalité du pouvoir-être" (1986: 115). [Through fiction and poetry, new possibilities of being-in-the-world are opened up within everyday reality. Fiction and poetry intend being, not under the modality of being-given, but under the modality of power-to-be.] Literature can reveal or shock; it can alter our ways of understanding geographies; it is interdependent with "reality" so that the Mediterranean is invented or produced by writers as much as it produces them. The *Iliad*, the *Odyssey*, Paul Valéry's poems, Camus's essays and hosts of others have been instrumental in the mapping and understanding of such a space. As Jean-Marie Schaeffer affirms,

> ce qui explique, selon moi, l'importance des arts dans la vie des hommes depuis que les hommes existent, c'est justement le fait qu'il n'y a pas d'un côté la vie que nous menons et de l'autre les pratiques artistiques. Il existe un lien indissoluble entre les deux et ce lien tient notamment au fait que les pratiques artistiques tirent profit de ressources mentales qui, par ailleurs, ont aussi des fonctions non artistiques. (1999: 2)

> [I believe that it is precisely the fact that there is no separation between the life we live, on the one hand, and artistic practices on the other, which explains the importance of art in life, and has explained it since the existence of mankind. The inextricable link between the two comes from the fact that artistic practices draw on resources of the mind which in turn also have non-artistic functions.]

In *Pourquoi la fiction?* Schaeffer argues that literature exposes a space of experimentation that can lead us to a practical, cognitive understanding of reality and occupies a crucial function in the cultural sphere; it is, in effect, a cognitive practice. Literature, affirms Schaeffer persuasively, acts on our lives and consequently on the world.

Indeed, in light of texts such as Edward Saïd's *Orientalism* and *Culture and Imperialism*, it has become even more patent that representations of cultures fashion modes of apprehension; the "Orient," Saïd argues, has been grossly objectified, misunderstood, and co-opted by texts claiming to characterize its makeup as well as by fictional texts that effect comparable outcomes. Writers like Camus and Gide are included in Saïd's critique as paradigmatic models of such representation. Such texts, then, create a presumed object of knowledge. Literature, this suggests, has fashioned beliefs about certain cultures and their histories. Indeed, it has the power, the possibility, to change our perceptions and modes of behavior, in other words, our ethos. If this is indeed the case, then literature has had, and will continue to have, a capital role in the definition of a Mediterranean space and of mentalities. In effect, if "ethos," as Michel Foucault explains in *What Is the Enlightenment?* has to do with personal attitudes, beliefs, and predilections rather than with principles, arguments, and proofs, then what better medium than literature to guide us in understanding such a space?

TEXTUAL MEDITERRANEANS

"Comment ne pas revenir à la Mediterranée?" [How can we not come back to the Mediterranean?] asks the Algerian writer Maïssa Bey, "à cette 'immensité obsédante, omniprésente, merveilleuse, énigmatique' telle que la définissait Fernand Braudel. Une définition qui, me semble-t-il, contient aussi tout le mystère de la création littéraire" (2009: 10).[19] [How can we not come back to this captivating, omnipresent, marvellous and enigmatic immensity defined by Fernand Braudel. Such a definition, I think, also carries within it the very mystery of literary creation.] The Mediterranean becomes, for Bey as for other writers, a metaphor for literature, and for narrative.[20] Like a metaphor which stems from creativity and the imagination, it refers back to an imagined community like those that Benedict Anderson and Homi Bhabha envisioned in relation to the nation. The transnational—even supranational—and regional configuration of the Mediterranean, however, makes for an imagined community that is centrifugal rather than centripetal as borders are crossed in the hybrid creation of new narrations. "Metaphor, as the etymology of the word suggests, transfers the meaning of home and belonging, across the 'middle passage,' or the central European steppes, across those distances, and cultural differences, that span the imagined community of the nation-people" (Bhabha 1994: 291). Like Bhabha's "middle passage," the Mediterranean stands as a space across which new iterations of belonging are formed and in which writers make the invisible visible.[21]

The first part of this book is articulated around questions of humanism and history. The opening chapter contextualizes colonial relations between France and the Maghreb during the late nineteenth and early twentieth century when Algeria, in particular, was divided into French departments, comparable to Normandy or Brittany. At the same time colonial discourse described the Mediterranean as being no different than the Lac Léman that separates France from Switzerland, and it was out of this climate that Albert Camus's notion of a Mediterranean Humanism was born. Mediterranean Humanism allows an examination of the link between nation and nature, which in turn brings to the fore the discovery of a strong tension between a pre-discursive metaphysical Mediterranean and a Mediterranean overrun by political calculations. Considered by many (Sartre first and foremost) as a traitor to the Algerian cause for independence, his relationship to the space of the Mediterranean, which played out mainly in Algeria, has been overshadowed by his political positioning. As a pied-noir born to a Spanish mother and a French father and who grew up in Algeria during the height of French colonialism, Camus lived on the margins of society as well as on the liminal space of the seashore. This juxtaposition, that may at first appear negligible, determined his philosophy of the Mediterranean. As a witness to the divisiveness of colonial Algeria, Camus's early philosophy called for a Mediterranean free of divisions along national and cultural lines, and for a return to Greek notions of measure and beauty. Alongside his political perspectives, Camus cultivated a profound affinity for the Ancient Greek philosophy of the Stoics and for the natural universe. His texts demonstrate the depth and force of a pre-discursive space where intellect gives way to instinct, and where sound or sunlight can offset reason.[22] My analyses of *Noces, L'exil et le royaume, Le premier homme* and Camus's early non-fiction affirm a Mediterranean that, despite the fact that he has rarely found a comfortable place when juxtaposed with Maghrebi Francophone writers, subtends all the works considered in this book; that is, a Mediterranean at the crossroads between instinct and intellect.[23]

In part, Camus's brand of humanism is a critique of excess. Following the Enlightenment, he suggests, the focus on reason has created immoderate beings prone to dictatorships, totalitarianisms, and rigid ideologies. This position is echoed, albeit in vastly different form, in the texts of Amin Maalouf and Fawzi Mellah, which are all set in the Mediterranean basin.[24] Chapter 2 builds on the position that the Mediterranean has been overrun by a rationale of imperialism and disparity. Rewriting and rethinking the historical narrative of the Mediterranean—through literature—counteracts a fallacious tendency toward a Huntingtonian model of interpretation and a teleological view of the region. Where Camus sees an excess of reason, Maalouf writes of a lack; a "clash of civilizations," he implies, is happening in the contemporary Mediterranean *because* there is a lack of awareness and knowledge of history. Maalouf and Mellah's works of historical fiction resurrect and (re)fashion defining moments in the history of the Mediterranean (such as the siege of Carthage and eighth- to fifteenth-century Andalusia) as a means of denouncing present-day practices of exclusion and essentialism. Moreover, they model the rewriting of individual as well as collective histories in order to point to the urgent necessity of linguistic and self-translation. Maalouf's and Mellah's historical novels blur the lines between history and fiction and open up new possibilities for reading the past, which I call alternative histories. They also point to a continual pursuit of self-knowledge across cultures as well as to the dangers of collective identification. Maalouf and Mellah champion a common Mediterranean belonging between and among different nations, which, however utopian it may seem, is implicit in the perspectives of all the authors in question in this study. In discussing the present and future of the region it becomes clear that rewriting and remapping turn out to be necessary alternatives to stultified and teleological narratives of the past. This chapter presents new histories and imaginary cartographies of the Mediterranean, ultimately positing history as interpretation and concluding that the role of individual subjectivity is central to the creation of alternative histories.

If the Mediterranean is understood as a space of conflict, as evidenced by many of the works just discussed, it is largely due to a tendentious prism of opposites that tends to frame its representations. Part II addresses modes of dismantling such dichotomies through writers who effect a reversal of this approach. Nina Bouraoui and Tahar Ben Jelloun break down binaries of geography and gender, challenging divisions between North and South and probing the separation between man and woman. In chapter 3 I argue that works by Tahar Ben Jelloun that are set in Italy, a country itself internally split, demonstrate how contemporary geographical divisions are rendered inoperative. A distinctly baroque ethic and aesthetic emerge from these works as Ben Jelloun pushes readers outside of restrictive geographical and aesthetic paradigms, revealing a tragic Mediterranean in ruins, overrun by twenty-first-century "progress" and glaring abuses of power. While evoking the economic disparities, he delves into racial and gender inequalities, at times directly condemning both governments and patriarchal structures.[25]

Is the Mediterranean an intrinsically masculine space? Based on the prevalence of histories written by men and of literature that places women in secondary roles, I ask this question in chapter 4. Nina Bouraoui's novels guide us towards several possible answers as she calls into question the profound heteronormativity of the space of the Mediterranean, where gender roles tend to be dictated by latent patriarchy and thus seen as traditional and static. Rather than simply supplying a feminist perspective, Bouraoui's works point to the troubles and constructedness of gender identification that is often over-determined in restrictive societies. Her Franco-Algerian protagonists, who live on the margins of the nation both in Algeria and France, are often further outcast for expressing same-sex desire. Her own female positioning becomes an object of analysis in

her 2005 novel in which the protagonist—who, she admits, bears an uncanny resemblance to Bouraoui herself—recounts her "mauvaises pensées" (the title of the text) about her same-sex desire to a psychoanalyst.
What emerges, in examining her work, is how subjectivity is constructed
in a very specific locus that is the postcolonial Mediterranean, between
Algeria and France, and how that construction stands in violent opposition to the practice of categorization. Ultimately Ben Jelloun and Bouraoui, like all those present in this book, write performative encounters
that challenge the dyadic positions to which they, as postcolonial subjects
born of the colonial encounter, are relegated.[26]

Building on the premise of a Mediterranean traversed by heterogene-
ity and multiplicity, Part III examines the movements across the sea of
Maghrebi writers and their subjects to non-hexagonal spaces and idioms.
Narratives of emigration across the Mediterranean further reach beyond
dyadic positions and suggest explicit and implicit transnational practices.
Tahar Ben Jelloun and Mahi Binebine present migrant, emigrant and/or
immigrant subjects, often literally at sea or on its shores, moving from
South to North across the Mediterranean, or from South to South, to
return to the problematic cardinal designations challenged in the previous chapter. These individuals reverse the standard colonial trajectory of
North to South, to arrive in countries such as Italy and Spain, themselves
internally divided between an industrialized and slightly more homogenous North and a disadvantaged South. Chapter 5 examines how
through these works the role of imagination—of both authors and characters—becomes all the more crucial given conditions of extreme repression, enforced borders, and conditions where first- and third-world divisions continue to oblige contestation and redefinition. First denouncing
the very real preconditions of emigration (such as lack of opportunity,
corruption and poverty) and then creating narratives that I call dissonant,
Ben Jelloun and Binebine bring together the role of illusion, fantasy and
imagination as counterpoints to national narratives of purity. Both authors underscore the discrepancies between emigrant subjects whose imagined geographies of an ideal Mediterranean north of the Maghreb
stand in stark contrast to the sociopolitical and economic hardships of
discordant and dysfunctional European and Eurocentric societies. Now
more than ever, in a climate of increasing conservatism and austerity
measures, these regions appear hostile to newcomers and foreign workers.

The last chapter collocates writers from the Maghreb with Italy; in it, I
identify a transnational Maghrebi-Mediterranean literary landscape
where the hegemony of the French language is displaced and no longer
occupies the center of the postcolonial debate. Here I consider the works
of Mohsen Melliti, Amara Lakhous, and Abdelmalek Smari, three authors
fluent in French but who live in Italy and have chosen to write in Italian,
a language that, unlike French, labeled by Khatibi as "une fatalité histo-

rique" [a historical inevitability], does not carry the weight of a colonial burden. Although remaining within the France-Maghreb axis, Alec Hargreaves predicted, as early as 1996, that a move away from French and France was a likely possibility.[27] Melliti, Smari, and Lakhous distance themselves from France through direct and indirect thematic and textual strategies that take the form of what I call an urban-centered accented literature. Further, drawing on what Smari calls *letteratura d'impatto* [literature of impact], I move toward an interpretive reading that extricates such texts from their national moorings, both European and Maghrebi. In effect, these texts signal a new aesthetic by a young generation of writers who write beyond resentment and beyond an uneasy conscience (Khatibi) and whose focus on language—both elected and imposed—advances theories of plurilingualism crucial to a Mediterranean ethos. Closing this chapter with a discussion of multiple idioms, both national and textual, brings this book back to the beginning, given that one of the principal preoccupations in postcolonial Francophone literature of the Maghreb is precisely the dilemma of language. More importantly, however, it draws connections outward, beyond the Franco-Maghrebi nexus, and thus functions as a kind of case study of the types of literary connections happening between the Maghreb and other places in the Mediterranean.

For the writers in this study, the Mediterranean is produced as much as it is explored; each of them directly affirms a belief in the existence of a Mediterranean that signifies beyond its geographical sense, yet never emerges as entirely intelligible, circumscribed or attainable.[28] The notion of quest indicates a degree of impossibility and the act of experiential investigation; the object of a quest is always absent or at an insurmountable distance. Juxtaposing the [medieval] *quest* to scientific knowledge, Giorgio Agamben notes, "la *quête* è . . . il riconoscimento che l'assenza di via (l'aporia) è l'unica esperienza possibile per l'uomo" (1978: 24) [the quest is . . . a recognition that the *absence* of a path (aporia) is the only experience possible for man]. The writers studied in this book confirm this aporia, defying definitions and tracing, most often through first-person narratives, a lived present that appears different with each enunciation. Their texts underscore the pivotal importance of subjectivity in the trajectories of narrative; first-person, frequently homodiegetic narrators draw our attention to self-conscious subjects who reflect upon the very practice of narration. As the characters emplot their experiences and their encounters, they become their own objects of critical analysis, revealing the ways in which they are both constructed—by language, colonialism, patriarchy, even the Mediterranean climate—and at the same time active agents. A Mediterranean ethos, thus, is a constituent of identity that is both tacitly created and actively engaged. It is a sense of ontological being in a specific part of the world that is characterized by historical tensions as well as productive encounters. It is also distinctly different from the Mediterranean ethos commonly evoked by many historians and anthropologists (Peristiany, Pitt-Rivers, Pirenne), that is to say, a Mediterranean dominated by codes of honor and shame, kinship and family, and alimentation. These "gatekeeping concepts," as Arjun Appadurai calls them, tend to limit and restrict knowledge, and to homogenize rather than valorize, a space that must be conceived of in its diversity rather than its sameness.[29]

ENDNOTES

1. The translator leaves out the important qualifier "géographique" [geographic] in the description of those cleavages between center and margin. If a work I cite has been translated into English, I have used the published translation. All other translations are my own.

2. Tamazight (in its different variants) and vernacular Arabics, such as *Darija* in Morocco, for instance, have only recently become more commonly used as literary languages. The IRCAM (Institut Royale de la Culture Amazighe) and various scholars worldwide are spearheading several research projects on these works.

3. Numerous Maghrebi writers have drawn connections to parts of the world that extend beyond the Mediterranean, of course. A few notable examples include Abdelkébir Khatibi's *Un été à Stockholm,* Mohammed Dib's trilogy *Les terrasses d'Orsol, Le sommeil d'Eve* and *Neiges de marbre,* as well as Youssouf Amin ElAlamy's *Un Marocain à New York.*

4. I am not fully proficient in other Mediterranean languages, and while one can undertake a study on works in translation, this would require a separate investigation given the crucial importance of language. It would require a study of a different order, with a focus on the actual processes of translation. For studies on Maghrebi literature in Spanish and Catalan, for example, see Adolfo Campoy-Cubillo's *Memories of the Maghreb: Transnational Identities in Spanish Cultural Production* and Cristián Ricci's "La literatura maroquí de expresión castellana en el marco de la transmodernidad y de la hibridación poscolonialista," in *Afro-Hispanic Review,* vol. 25. No.2.

5. That is not to say that these are the only sites of encounter and contact; numerous other sites such as Palestine or Egypt, and many other writers such as Albert Memmi and Malika Mokeddem, for instance, merit analysis in an analogous context.

6. Although this dates back to 1983, it still has purchase in today's divided Mediterranean, where the Maghreb and Maghrebi writers still remain disadvantaged in relation to European power structures.

7. It is a space that in Bhabha's terms can be qualified as hybrid, inflected by cultural *difference* rather than cultural *diversity.* In *The Location of Culture* Bhabha conceptualizes "an *inter*national culture based not on the exoticism of multiculturalism or the *diversity* of cultures, but on the inscription and articulation of culture's *hybridity* . . . by exploring this Third Space, we may elude the politics of polarity and emerge as the others of ourselves" (1994: 56).

8. For a thorough assessment of the state of Francophone studies and the need for new paradigms see Tamalet Talbayev (2012).

9. In a manifesto published in the French newspaper *Le Monde* on March 16, 2007, forty-four authors who write in French, among them Tahar Ben Jelloun and Amin Maalouf, announced a new Copernican Revolution; they affirmed the center is no longer "fin de la francophonie." Referring to the recent attribution of a number of major French literary prizes to writers of non-French origin, they declared that preserving the notion of Francophonie—and thus a binding relationship with the "center," France—is the last avatar of colonialism.

10. Most prominently André Thevet, Antoine Furetière, Fernand Braudel, Alain Corbin, and Edgar Morin.

11. François Hollande's government has taken over this initiative with little change in rhetoric.

12. Iain Chambers maintains that "planned imperialism" in the Mediterranean began with the Napoleonic conquests and ended with the Algerian war of independence (2008: 144).

13. Bernard Kouchner, "Europe: l'avenir passe par la Méditerranée," *Le Monde*, July 10, 2008, accessed March 24, 2013, http://www.lemonde.fr/idees/article/2008/07/10/europe-l-avenir-passe-par-la-méditerranée-par-bernard-kouchner_1068626_3232.html.

14. According to Deleuze and Guattari, "a great novelist is above all an artist who invents unknown or unrecognized affects and brings them to light as the becoming of his characters" (1994: 174). They cite Madame de Lafayette's creation of "catatonic rest" and Proust's invention of a unique form of jealousy.

15. Senghor's poem entitled "Méditerranée" (in the collection *Hosties noires*) evokes a unified Mediterranean. This was much in the spirit of supporting cross-cultural alliances like an institutional "Francophonie" as well as evoking a time when Egypt and the Greco-Roman world came together.

16. This is noticeable in multiple disciplines that treat the modern Mediterranean (rather than the Classical era); in history (*The Corrupting Sea*, Horden and Purcell, 2000, *Rethinking the Mediterranean*, Harris, 2005; Kinoshita, 2009), cultural studies (*Mediterranean Crossings*, Chambers, 2008), literature (*Mediterranean Passages*, Cooke, Göknar and Parker, 2008) as well as in sociology (*Southern Thought*, Cassano, tr. Bouchard, 2011), politics and the media. In North American colleges and universities we are beginning to see departments such as Francophone and Mediterranean Studies Department (Colorado College), degree programs such as a Masters in Mediterranean Studies (Middlebury College) as well as research initiatives like the Mediterranean Studies Forum (Stanford) are becoming increasingly common.

17. Cultural expressions of the Mediterranean emerge outside its geographic borders, thus it is useful to consider it the way Immanuel Wallerstein envisages an "extended Caribbean" that he describes as "geographic linkages of the U.S. South, the Caribbean islands, and the coastal areas of Central and South America all the way down to Brazil; areas where societies supported by enslaved labor developed and thus share strong commonalities" (1974: 25).

18. It was also the first to make such a lasting mark, to the point that few studies of the Mediterranean are undertaken without reference to Braudel.

19. Maïssa Bey's works also provide fruitful insights into a Mediterranean ethos. The intertextuality with Camus's works is particularly interesting.

20. The countless works on the Mediterranean in most major fields of study inevitably take this space to signify [something] beyond its geographical borders. According to Claudio Fogu, "Contrary to the clearly marked geographical boundaries of the Mediterranean Sea, the flow of metaphors around the theme of Mediterranean-ness is virtually infinite, and may indeed be without parallel in other cultural contexts" (2010: 2).

21. The Mediterranean may also be seen as a postcolonial middle passage for those who set out across the sea in subhuman conditions in hopes of finding a better future in Europe. (See chapter 4.)

22. One need only think of how Meursault explains his homicide as a consequence of being blinded by the sun.

23. See Azzedine Haddour, *Colonial Myths, History and Narrative*. Edward Saïd, *Culture and Imperialism* and Emily Apter, *"Out of Character."*

24. Although Maalouf is not, strictly speaking, from the Maghreb, I consider his works for their theoretical import and for the ties to the Maghreb that emerge from them.

25. For an anthropological perspective of the role of women in the Mediterranean see Germaine Tillion, *Le harem et les cousins*. Tillion maintains that the subjection of women in the Mediterranean, and in the Maghreb in particular, is not tied to Islamic

practices as it is often thought, but actually pre-dates the advent of Islam in the Mediterranean and goes back to Ancient Greece and paganism.

26. Mireille Rosello defines a performative encounter as what occurs when two presumably incompatible cultural entities come together to create "a new subject-position, a new language and a new type of engagement" (2005: 2); for example, she analyzes the Moroccan writer Fouad Laroui's relationship to French and demonstrates how he makes use of an ideologically fraught language for humorous ends.

27. "As the colonial period recedes into history and the reading public within the Maghreb grows in size, authors based on the southern shore of the Mediterranean may feel less inclined to direct their writings towards the former colonial motherland" (Hargreaves 1996: 40).

28. For example, Albert Camus saw in it the possibility for a new *humanism*, Amin Maalouf affirms a Mediterranean *belonging*, Tahar Ben Jelloun writes about Mediterranean *affinity*, and Nina Bouraoui associates it with a *feminine* space, a *mère méditerranée*, as she puts it.

29. For Appadurai, a "gatekeeping concept" is a concept that refers to ossified regional characteristics and that is often used metonymically and indiscriminately to describe a region.

I

Humanism and History

ONE

A Humanism of the Sun

Albert Camus between Nature and Politics

In 2010, the fiftieth anniversary of Albert Camus's death was marked by a series of controversies on both sides of the Mediterranean; one set off by French president Nicolas Sarkozy's proposal to move Camus's body from the Provençal village of Lourmarin to the Panthéon in Paris, the other unfurled by the "Caravane Albert Camus 2010," an itinerant literary project throughout France and Algeria conceived to celebrate the anniversary. Sarkozy's proposal sparked several quarrels but then was quickly turned down by Camus's heirs. The debate surrounding the literary project polarized opinions and turned predictably polemical. Supported by Algerian intellectuals and the Centre Culturel Algérien in Paris run by Yasmina Khadra, and opposed by a group of Algerian professors, it was reminiscent of the *casus belli* that notoriously put an end to the friendship between Camus and Jean-Paul Sartre. For Sartre, the discord came down to Camus's criticism of Communism and his conception of a Mediterranean Humanism. Despite this being somewhat reductive, for their disagreement reached into numerous other domains as many critics have shown, it nevertheless signals the complexity, contradiction and the wide-reaching effects of Camus's Mediterranean thought. With regard to French and Algerian national sentiment, evoking Camus invites, still today, impassioned political, cultural, academic, and personal disputes.

In this chapter I examine the way in which Camus created a singular and original Mediterranean, both through his essays and his fiction. I argue that although his vision of the Mediterranean is utopic and ultimately impracticable, his politics for the region illuminate the difficulty, that still persists today, of defining such a space. I further suggest that his affective response to the sentient and the natural create unprecedented

3

ways of apprehending the Mediterranean in its physical dimension. As the author himself states: "je n'ai jamais rien écrit qui ne se rattache, de près ou de loin, à la terre où je suis né" (1965: 1892). [I have never written anything that was not, either directly or indirectly, linked to the country in which I was born.] I thus lay bare the connection between nation and nature that Camus's texts invite us to consider, a conjuncture that in turn brings to the fore a strong tension between a pre-discursive metaphysical Mediterranean and a Mediterranean overrun by political calculations. Camus's embattled personal and political situation can be drawn back to the land from which he comes. I thus begin my analysis through a brief discussion of the formative cultural and political climate of Algiers in the 1930s, and trace the continuity, but also the evolution, of Camus's Mediterranean vision through his early essays and his posthumous novel *Le premier homme*.

During the early years of the Cold War, Sartre lashed out at Camus, accusing him of being weak-willed, unrealistic and entirely too moderate on espousing firm political beliefs. Bringing the virulent controversy surrounding Camus's position on Communism, the Cold War, Algeria and Algerian independence to its apogee, Sartre and Camus parted ways, leaving many intellectuals and critics to take up where the two left off. In August 1952 Sartre wrote to Camus: "Un mélange de suffisance sombre et de vulnérabilité a toujours découragé de vous dire des vérités entières. Le résultat c'est que vous êtes devenu la proie d'une morne démesure qui masque vos difficultés intérieures et que vous nommez, je crois, mesure méditerranéenne" (1952: 82). [The mixture of dreary complacency and vulnerability that typifies you always discouraged people from telling you unvarnished truths. As a result you have fallen prey to dismal extremes that hide your inner problems, and that you call, I think, Mediterranean moderation.] Sartre's somewhat self-contradictory words—conflating dismal extremes and Mediterranean moderation—point both to the beginning of the thorny debate around Camus and Algeria and to the weightiness of Camus's Mediterranean thought. This debate, along with Camus's infamous comments on the heels of his Nobel Prize speech regarding justice in Algeria, gave rise to the highly contentious and increasingly uncomfortable position in which he found himself towards the end of his life. When an Algerian student asked Camus about his position on Algeria, he answered that if the indiscriminate bombing by the pro-independence FLN in the streets and trams of Algiers was to be seen as justice he would rather defend his mother (who could easily have been a victim of those random bombings) over justice. Often taking this statement out of context, critics were quick to condemn Camus and seal his fate as a *persona non grata* in the Paris of the 1950s. Already cast out from Algeria by pied-noir militants, Camus found himself in physical and affective exile.

Conor Cruise O'Brien, Edward Saïd, and Emily Apter have assertively argued that Camus suffered from a blindly colonialist mentality, if not from outright racism, whereas others, such as John Foley, David Ellison and Amina Bekkat have closely examined Camus's positions on Algeria and conclude the contrary. But what emerges as certain is that Camus's case is far more complex than the either/or dichotomous positions that have been ascribed to him. The Tunisian writer Albert Memmi weighs in on this quandary as he famously calls Camus a "colon de bonne volonté" ["well-meaning colonialist"] but ultimately writes, referring to Camus's conundrum "Il y a, je le crois, des situations historiques impossibles, celle-là en est une" (Memmi 1965: 39). [There are, I believe, impossible historical situations and this is one of them.] To be sure, Camus's Mediterranean Humanism reflects not only an "impossible" historical situation but also a somewhat neglected ontological closeness with this geographical space.

Criticism of Camus abounded both on the French and the Algerian sides, and at the time of the Nobel Prize speech the media launched sensational invectives around the mother/justice comment pronounced in Stockholm. Given that these matters were salient and garnered considerable attention, the specificity of Camus's concern with, and love of, Algeria were quickly elided. More importantly, Camus's thought must be situated in the context of the status of the Mediterranean in Franco-Algerian relations between the 1930s and the 1950s. By tracing the evolution of his thought through certain works of fiction and his essays, a move that neither accuses nor absolves him, we gain a deeper understanding of Camus's Mediterranean Humanism. A wider viewpoint invites us to consider a modern Mediterranean whose identity, although grounded in the political, reaches well beyond such discourses to encompass an ethos of nature and of the sentient.

A CO-OPTED SPACE

According to the historian Alain Corbin, during the eighteenth century the Mediterranean came to be perceived not as a dangerous and hostile sea dominated by rivalries between Islam and Christianity, or by the ancient division between a Greek Orient and a Latin Occident, but rather as a desirable, politically advantageous, and exciting destination. In literary texts, this is patently clear during much of the following century when writers such as Eugène Fromentin and Gérard de Nerval idealized an Oriental Mediterranean or embarked on grand tours of Italy. In effect, French authors increasingly crossed the sea pursuing adventures or self-discovery, planning new routes and charting untraveled paths. Revolutions in the transportation industry undoubtedly contributed to the frequency of these crossings as well as to drawing France closer to what would soon become one of its major strategic focal points.[1] Napoleon's Egyptian campaign marks the beginning of a French mission across the sea, and with it, an attempt to form or forge mentalities, to co-opt and dominate territories deemed advantageous. Not long after the expedition to Egypt, France embarked on a similar political and ideological appropriation of the Mediterranean, this time through the violent colonization of the Maghreb.

Throughout more than a century of colonization, France ideologically appropriated part of the Mediterranean, privileging a striated, regulated, and organized perception of this space. The political situation in this region was particularly complex during the whole of the colonial period; this played itself out most notably in the struggle between France and Italy for conquerable lands in the Mediterranean. Until the 1880s France considered Italy a minor power, yet even when the former entered the Triple Alliance (1882), France's politico-imperial rhetoric remained steadfast and aggressive.[2] Given the close proximity across the sea, French control of the Maghreb, particularly of Algeria, was one of intense interest and steady investment. In 1930, in honor of the centennial celebration of France's presence in Algeria the official program stated:

> La grande affaire, c'est de montrer qu'il existe, à côté de la France millénaire, à vingt heures de Marseille, sur l'autre rive de cette Méditerranée qui berça de son flot l'hellénisme et la latinité, une autre France, âgée de cent ans à peine, déjà forte, pleine de vie et d'avenir, unissant dans sa formule heureuse les races latines et les races indigènes, pour en faire des races également françaises.[3]

> [The important thing is to show that on the other shore of the Mediterranean, which cradled Hellenism and Latinity, and alongside a thousand-year-old France another France exists, only twenty hours from Marseille. Another France that is just one hundred years old, but already strong, full of life and future prospects, and in its felicitous disposition unifies Latin and indigenous races, to turn them into races which are French as well.]

The Mediterranean, according to official discourse, simply united the age-old motherland, France, with its much younger offspring, Algeria, which as stated in this excerpt, appeared to be a felicitously homogeneous area. Algeria becomes merely "une autre France" just one hundred years old, where "indigenous races" and "Latin races" came together to form a new French "race." Included in this dubious recipe of indigenous and Latin-based peoples that physically and morally decimated millions, there existed numerous groups that were occluded in official discourse. Among them were a number of pied-noirs, such as Albert Camus, who drew their origins back to different Mediterranean places such as Spain, Italy and Malta, and who took an active role in resisting the polarization of colonial politics in the 1930s. Such a political climate could hardly be kept out of the literary circles, and indeed fostered two distinct schools of thought; one that adopted an outlook that fit the official discourse and another that proposed an alternate way of conceiving the France-Mediterranean relationship. Camus's Mediterranean Humanism was born in such a climate.

A LITERARY MEDITERRANEAN

The reference to a Latin race can be traced throughout the works of a group of organic intellectuals, as political analyst Thierry Fabre puts it, known as the *Algérianistes*. Spearheaded by writer and academician Louis Bertrand, this conservative literary and cultural movement was primarily composed of white French settlers. Early members of the *Algérianistes* justified their colonial presence in Algeria by the fact that the latter, having been part of the Roman Empire, had a Latin heritage and consequently was part and parcel of *la plus grande* France.[4] Bertrand and his followers attempted to veil the French imperial project by manipulating historical claims so as to unite France and Algeria within a teleological, homogenous, long-standing civilization. But Algiers in the 1930s was also rife with a different group of pied-noir writers and thinkers such as Gabriel Audisio, Emmanuel Roblès, and Jules Roy.[5] Like the *Algérianistes* they broke with the tradition of French Orientalist writers such as Fromentin and Nerval, finding it necessary to observe not how the "oriental" lived, but rather how they themselves—the settlers and their descendants— belonged to Algeria. However, unlike the *Algérianistes*, they pushed further, grappling with questions about belonging to the world, beginning with Algeria and the Mediterranean, but in fact reaching into larger ontological questions of being *tout court*.

In reaction to the *Algérianistes*, Albert Camus and Gabriel Audisio founded another literary group, *l'Ecole d'Alger*, where instead of tracing Algeria back to Rome—because Rome, as Audisio writes in *Documents sur l'esprit méditerranéen*, "a donné ses lois au monde, pas son sang . . . Rome ne fut qu'un moment de la Méditerranée" (1936: 12) [gave the world its laws, not its blood . . . Rome was but a moment in the Mediterranean]—they opted to draw on a rather more imaginary Mediterranean that was driven by an attempt to formulate a universal, apolitical humanist discourse. Audisio, whose early poems, novels, and essays preceded Camus's works by a few years, often featured ideal Mediterranean Men. In his novel *Héliotrope*, the main character named Sauveur is youthful, idealistic, and indifferent to socio-political concerns.[6] He finds fulfillment in nature and in his passions and generally lacks the introspection or scrutiny of a dark side of humanity that we later find in Camus's fictional works.

Given the intense involvement of many pied-noir writers in the political arena, the distinction between a geopolitical Mediterranean and an imaginary one was frequently slippery and at times ill-defined. Through an approach that erased differences in race, class and nationality, most of the works by l'Ecole d'Alger writers tended to eschew the political calamities playing out in colonial Algeria, even though this may not have necessarily been their strict intention. Evidence of the predominance of the Mediterranean as well as its elusiveness is clear in the numerous failed attempts, in colonial Algeria, to set up institutions, journals, and organizations centered on the idea of a Mediterranean identity; in the capital, these literary journals were, for the most part, published by Edmond Charlot, Camus's first publisher. Charlot, through his bookstore "Les vraies richesses,"[7] was a key figure in the lives of pied-noir writers. In 1936 he founded a collection which went by the name of Méditerranéennes, in which Camus's L'envers et l'endroit was first published, and in 1938 he launched the journal Rivages, for which Camus wrote the opening statement and subsequently worked on the editorial board. Other members included Jean Grenier, Gabriel Audisio, and Claude de Fréminville.[8] From the mission statement it was clear that there was no precise idea of what the Mediterranean was to this group of writers and intellectuals: "Il est difficile à Rivages d'apporter avec elle sa définition puisque aussi bien son but est de se définir, et avec elle le visage d'une culture dont nous savons seulement qu'elle est et que nous l'aimons sans pouvoir encore en classer les résonances" (Camus 1965: 1330). [It is difficult for Rivages to provide a definition since its aim is also to define itself along with the portrait of a culture which we know exists, and which we love but whose character we cannot yet describe.] The only thing they could articulate about the Mediterranean, at that stage, was that "elle est" [it is], that it existed, and that they loved it. The journal was forced to cease publication after only two issues, when the Vichy government destroyed the third and last issue devoted to Federico Garcia Lorca.[9] Camus also founded La Maison de la Culture in Algiers, for which he created a monthly bulletin entitled Jeune Méditerranée. Here too, despite the strong and passionate commitment of its contributors, the periodical's purpose was somewhat ill defined. Two more journals, Sud and Prométhée also sought to define themselves as Mediterranean. However, while Sud[10] remained in existence for twenty years, Prométhée never went beyond the planning stages.[11] The difficulty in defining the notion "Mediterranean" was symptomatic of the troubled place occupied by a number of French Algerians.

Both the Algérianiste writers and those of the Ecole d'Alger elaborated distinctly utopian views of what living in the Mediterranean meant, although in the case of the former, the blind Francocentric rhetoric is far more short-sighted and limited than the idealistic and naïve positioning of authors like Audisio and Camus in their early years.[12] In the last interview before his death, a journalist asked Camus, "Que croyez-vous que les critiques français aient négligé dans votre oeuvre?" [What do you think the French critics have overlooked in your work?] to which he answered, "La part obscure, ce qu'il y a d'aveugle, d'instinctif en moi. La critique française s'intéresse d'abord aux idées. Mais, toutes proportions gardées, pourrait-on étudier Faulkner sans faire la part du Sud dans son oeuvre?" (1965: 1925) [The hidden side, what is blind and instinctive in me. French criticism is first and foremost interested in ideas, but all things considered, can one study Faulkner without distinguishing the role of the South in his work?] Returning to the opposition between intuition and reason, Camus emphasizes the importance of the former in his work. He also underlines how geography leaves indelible marks on the writing of certain authors, including his own. Discerning Camus's own "southernness" and his attachment to the Algerian soil is crucial in coming to an understanding of his conception of a new humanism.

Born in 1913 and raised with very modest means in a working class suburb of Algiers, Camus developed a profound affinity with nature and with the physical universe of man.[13] This is particularly striking in his early works where he reflects on beauty, measure and freedom, although traces of this *weltanschauung* exist throughout his oeuvre. Critics of his "mediterraneity"[14] have mostly focused on his early short stories and lyrical essays such as *L'envers et l'endroit*, *Noces*, and *L'été*, in which he most patently exalts the relationship between the senses and the mind. However, *Le premier homme* written towards the end of his life is equally steeped in what he calls his "Mediterranean thought." In considering this temporal aspect of Camus's work, we are fittingly drawn to both the young and the late Camus, *at the limits of his life*, a notion perfectly in concert with his Mediterranean thinking. More than twenty years after writing *L'envers et L'endroit* (1935), Camus wrote in the preface to its re-edition: "Chaque artiste garde ainsi, au fond de lui, une source unique . . . pour moi je sais que ma source est dans *L'envers et l'endroit*" (1965: 6). [Every artist carries a unique source within himself. . . . I know that my source is in *L'envers et l'endroit*.] In this essay, his purported "source," he writes, "et jamais peut-être un pays sinon la Méditerranée ne m'a porté à la fois si loin et si près de moi-même" [and perhaps never did a land such as the Mediterranean bring me so far and so close to myself]. Well-known for his many dualities (here, far/close, right side/wrong side), for the many opposites that traverse his work, Camus was a thinker eternally in search of a middle ground and of an interior balance: "que d'heures passées à . . . tenter d'accorder ma respiration aux soupirs tumultueux du monde! . . . j'ouvre les yeux et mon coeur à la grandeur insoutenable de ce ciel gorgé de chaleur. Ce n'est pas si facile de *devenir ce qu'on est*, de retrouver sa mesure profonde" (1959: 14). [How many hours I have spent . . . trying to match my breathing with the world's tumultuous sighs ! . . . I open my eyes and heart to the unbearable grandeur of this heat-soaked sky. It is not so easy to become what one is, to rediscover one's deepest measure.] Along with being in search of a middle ground, he also strove to question the nexus between being and becoming.

The paradox in Camus's words above might better be articulated as a question: how does one become what one is, and how does one find one's measure? It is likely that the notion of being and becoming came to Camus through Pindar (whom he cites), and Nietzsche, whose philosophies of Being were founded on principles of infinite becoming. Yet Camus's conception of Being is singular and specific and is dependent first and foremost on two major mutually defining concepts that are indeed capital throughout his work: the Absurd and Revolt. In the context of this framework, becoming what one *is* is the ultimate challenge and tension of life, where man is forever confronted with a renewed sense of self yet conceives of himself as the same throughout time. Camus looks to the present and to revealing potentialities; this "virtuality" of Being subtends the Mediterranean ethos of each of the writers in question in this book.

THE ABSURD, REVOLT AND THE "OCEANIC FEELING" OR "LE SENTIMENT MÉDITERRANÉEN"

The fundamental philosophies of the Absurd and of Revolt lie at the genesis of Camus's Mediterranean thought. Beginning with *L'envers et l'endroit* and *Noces*, and subsequently in his plays (*Caligula, Le Malentendu, Les Justes*), Camus insists on the non-rational aspects of being; here he addresses affective responses of instinct and sentiment. These issues are less prominent in his other works, such as *Le mythe de Sisyphe* and *L'homme révolté*, which instead tend toward a philosophy of reason. Given the basic premise at the heart of the absurd-revolt problematic, that in the face of the absurdity and meaninglessness of the world man must find a way to revolt and to affirm life, Camus insists on the responsibility of taking destiny into one's own hands. But, a particular tension defines the discrepancy between man's tendency towards rationality and a non-rational natural world. In *Le mythe de Sisyphe* he affirms "ce qui est absurde, c'est la confrontation de cet irrationel et de ce désir éperdu de clarté dont l'appel résonne au plus profond de l'homme. L'absurde dépend autant de l'homme que du monde" (1965: 113). [But what is absurd is the confrontation of this irrational and the wild longing for clarity whose call echoes in the human heart. The absurd depends as much on man as on the world.] If we understand "désir éperdu de clarté" [wild longing for clarity] as synonymous of a tendency toward reason, we can gather that, for Camus, the absurd is also characterized precisely by the rational-irrational opposition and is thus a universal condition of man. Camus calls for action and affirmation and at the same time embraces a

Nietzschean *amor fati*, looking neither into the future nor toward the past but intent on being alive to the present.

With an analogy that is particularly pertinent to this argument in its evocation of the Mediterranean, John Cruickshank writes of the intellectual odyssey that Camus undertakes in coming to terms with the Absurd: "The open sea, as well as the prison, is a major symbol in his work. The dynamic of revolt, which is produced by the absurd, possesses sufficient force to carry him beyond negation to affirmation" (1968: 11). The dynamic of revolt also allows him to live daringly in opposition to a nihilistic despair of death. In this case, the sea may be taken as a metaphor for sentiment and the prisons as being reflective of reason at its most restrictive and potentially dogmatic. In *The Sea and Prisons* Roger Quilliot writes, "Sans doute, cette audace s'allie-t-elle à une sorte de d'inconsciente foi méditerranéenne en l'ordre du monde, au sentiment aigu de la nécessité de l'homme dans le monde, et, pour tout dire, de sa primauté, fût-elle contestée" (1970: 121). [Doubtless, this daring [to revolt] is allied to a sort of unconscious Mediterranean faith in the order of the world, to the acute sense of man's necessity in the world, and, in sum, of his primacy, contested though it might be.] Underlying his sense of revolt Camus exhibits a form of faith that is not specifically religious or transcendental but is unconscious and inextricably tied to the Mediterranean.

Cruickshank emphasizes that to revolt against the absurd "is to rediscover oneself. Rebellion reveals to a man the existence of a part of himself which he holds to be important, by means of which he identifies his essence as a human being, and in the name of which he confronts the absurdity of existence" (1968: 97). Beyond the absurd-revolt question, well-rehearsed by many critics, and the suggestion of a Mediterranean faith, there exists a more hidden relationship between the Absurd and a *sensitivity* or *feeling*, that one might call *le sentiment méditerranéen*. I adopt this thought from Romain Rolland's "sentiment océanique" [oceanic feeling]; in his correspondence with Freud in 1927, Rolland describes the expression as being all-encompassing. Freud begins *Civilization and Its Discontents* with this same notion, which he explains as

> a feeling which he [Rolland] would like to call a sensation of "eternity," a feeling as of something limitless, unbounded, something "oceanic." It is, he says, a purely subjective *experience*, not an article of belief; it implies no assurance of personal immortality, but it is the source of the religious spirit. . . . One may rightly call oneself religious on the ground of this oceanic feeling alone, even though one rejects all beliefs and all illusions. (1962: 11; my emphasis)

Rolland, who used many oceanic metaphors, notably when he became interested in Hindu mysticism, emphasized the importance of such a feeling in uniting the Orient and the Occident. The oceanic feeling transcends particularistic, circumscribed thought, and finds its expression in both Oriental and Occidental theories of the self. In another letter to Freud he writes, "j'étais frappé de constater, une fois de plus, qu'il n'est pas du tout vrai que l'Orient et l'Occident soient deux mondes à part l'un de l'autre, mais tous deux sont bâtis du même fleuve de pensée" (Vermorel 1993: 309). [Once again, I was struck by the fact that it is not true at all that East and West are two separate worlds. Both are built on the same current of thought.] At the source of this feeling, that, Freud admits, left him "aucun repos" [no rest], is the primacy of the self and the reconciliation of opposites (Vermorel 1993: 308). Where Freud drew his understanding of the oceanic feeling back to psychoanalysis, Rolland remained in the realm of the psychological. For Freud the sensation of infinity pointed to the return of an infantile sensation where mother and child are one and where the child has no sense of his or her boundaries. Quite differently, and rather more consonant with a Camusian Mediterranean feeling, Rolland writes to Freud in a letter dated May 1931: "Je distingue très nettement en moi: 1) ce que je *sens* 2) ce que je *sais* 3) ce que je désire. Ce que je sens . . . c'est l'Océanique, ce que je *sais*, c'est le 'Que sais-je' de Montaigne" (Vermorel 1993: 45). [Within myself I clearly distinguish 1) what I *feel* 2) what I *know* 3) what I desire. What I know is . . . the Oceanic, what I know is Montaigne's "What do I know"]. Insisting on the indecipherable nature of "truth," Rolland and, I suggest, Camus after him, question objective certainties, clearly distinguishing reason ("what I know") from sentiment ("what I feel").

The "oceanic feeling," which can be summarized as an expansion of the boundaries of the self and the feeling, beyond rational comprehension, of being part of a totality, is transformed, by Camus, into something specifically related to the Mediterranean. Furthermore, it is consonant with an ethos which he chooses, rather than a psychological condition that he has to endure. The experience in which it is grounded comes from sensory attributes that include perceptions of particular (sun)light, smells, and landscapes. "Mediterranean feeling," like the oceanic feeling, is triggered by a moment of awe followed by a sense of infinity, of being overwhelmed by something larger than life, and impossible to comprehend.

Freud adds that with the "oceanic feeling" Rolland "means the same thing as that consolation offered by an original and somewhat unconventional writer to his hero, contemplating suicide: 'out of this world we cannot fall.' So it is a feeling of indissoluble connection, of belonging inseparably to the external world as a whole" (Freud 1962: 76). In his elaboration of the Absurd, Camus states that man's only choice, if he does not revolt against it, is to extricate himself from the world through suicide. Insistence on the revolt rather than on suicide underscores his unwavering "Mediterranean feeling," that it is to the cosmos that man belongs, first and foremost, and that separating oneself from the physical world is virtually impossible.

A powerful sense of affiliation with the world and the earth takes on a certain poignancy when placed in the larger context of a modest upbringing. Camus's material conditions played a significant role in the development and articulation of his thought, and in examining his first and last works, it is crucial to understand how his environment shaped him. Both his early lyrical essays and his unfinished novel *Le premier homme* are highly autobiographical; in his essays he often writes in the first person, or as a collective "one," and in *Le premier homme* he recounts the early years of Jacques Cormery, a character whose life recognizably mirrors his own. Having grown up in extreme poverty, Camus sought pleasure in what was naturally given to him; the earth and its landscapes. In *Noces* he writes about his first encounters with the shores of Algiers, where his very existence, his breathing are at one with the earth: "J'apprenais à respirer, je m'intégrais et je m'accomplissais" (1959: 14). [I was learning to breathe, I was fitting into things and fulfilling myself.] Algerian landscapes and the Mediterranean sea compose such an integral part of him that it does not come as a surprise that both are present throughout nearly all his works of fiction, testifying to the inseparable correlation between his mind and his body: "Il me faut être nu et puis plonger dans la mer, encore tout parfumé des essences de la terre, laver celles-ci dans celle-là, et nouer sur ma peau l'étreinte pour laquelle soupirent lèvres à lèvres depuis si longtemps la terre et la mer" (1959: 15). [I must be naked and dive into the sea, still scented with the perfumes of earth, wash them off in the sea, and consummate with my flesh the embrace for which sun [*sic*] and sea, lips to lips, have so long been sighing.] Camus's communion with the earth, his naked plunging into the sea, points to an effacement of the separation between man and nature, placing him in a virtually timeless, ethereal world. "Et jamais je n'ai senti, si avant, à la fois mon détachement de moi-même et ma présence au monde" (1959: 26). [And never have I felt so deeply and at one and the same time so detached from myself and so present in the world.] Nature—Mediterranean nature—takes him out of his consciousness to place him in a world of earthly flux where sensations precede thought. For Camus, "il n'y a rien dans l'intellect qui n'ait d'abord été sensuellement senti" (Chabot 2002: 25). [There is nothing in the intellect that has not already been felt through the senses.]

With the connection between the intellect and the senses in mind it is possible to propose that Camus's Mediterranean thought, in its inception, grows out of a geophilosophy, a philosophy that privileges geography and contingency. Thus, it is of greatest import to identify the conditions of possibility for an event, thought, or concept to emerge.[15] Just as Braudel shifted the focus of history from the stories of heroes and battles to one that integrated geography and a long view of time, Deleuze and

Guattari—drawing on Braudel directly—envisage a philosophy of deterritorialization. In *What Is Philosophy?* they write: "Thinking is neither a
line drawn between subject and object nor a revolving of one around the
other. Rather, thinking takes place in the relationship of territory and the
earth" (1994: 85). Thinking, or reason, as Cartesian philosophers had it, is
not disembodied from an objective world, and Camus's being is a being-
in-the-world. His subjectivity and lived experiences, and those of many
of his fictional characters as well (one thinks immediately of Meursault),
are embodied.[16] He thus equates human nature to Mediterranean nature,
where "intelligence," or thought, cannot be conceived without its surrounding light, sounds, smells, and sensations: he is fully part of
"l'exigence invincible de la nature humaine dont la Méditerranée, où
l'intelligence est soeur de la dure lumière, garde le secret" (1965: 702) [an
irrepressible demand of human nature, of which the Mediterranean,
where intelligence is intimately related to the blinding light of the sun,
guards the secret]. Camus's early Mediterranean thought is holistic; man
is historically and corporeally situated, so that consciousness and the
world (or the environment) are intertwined. Put another way, consciousness and the body are imbricated and act upon one another. What we
think often comes from what we see. Camus writes, "A Tipasa, je vois
équivaut à je crois, et je ne m'obstine pas à nier ce que ma main peut
toucher et mes lèvres caresser" (1959: 18). [At Tipasa 'I see' equals 'I
believe,' and I am not stubborn enough to deny what my hands can touch
and my lips caress.] For Camus, like for phenomenologist Maurice Merleau-Ponty, we *are* our vision and our bodies. These are not separate from
our consciousness, and one cannot exist without the other. "The visible
about us seems to rest in itself. It is as though our vision were formed at
the heart of the visible, or as though there were between it and us an
intimacy as close as that between the sea and the strand" (Merleau-Ponty
1968: 130). Tracing this to his fictive protagonists Janine in "La femme
adultère" or Meursault in *L'étranger* or even Rieux in *La peste*, it is evident
that for Camus, sensations also account for action. Nothing, Camus
seems to say, can affect us and disturb our complacency of thought as
much as the blazing sun, the cold night desert air, or an unusual sound.

   Camus's "solar thought," as it is often called, is also ruled by a dark
side: the tragic fate of man, caught between the awareness of his own
mortality and a world in perpetual renewal. To Camus, Mediterranean
landscapes are signs of the beauty of the world that contrast starkly with
the bitterness of death. In *Noces*, he writes "Quel accord plus légitime
peut unir l'homme à la vie sinon la double conscience de son désir de
durée et son destin de mort? On y apprend du moins à ne compter sur
rien et à considérer le présent comme la seule vérité qui nous soit donnée
par 'surcroît'" (1959: 64). [What more legitimate harmony can unite a
man with life than the dual consciousness of his longing to endure and his
awareness of death? At least he learns to count on nothing and to see the

present as the only truth given to us "as a bonus."] The only way to live is in the present, in an *eternal present* that cannot, however, imply only the here and now. For Camus is well aware that, regardless of one's will to live in the present, time is not an isolated phenomenon that can be stopped and started. In the plenitude of the present, where there is no higher being such as a God and no transcendence, one is always aware of the horizon in the distance that impedes seeing or thinking further than one's own immediacy. Yet, this is the effort man has to make in order to live fully, to live in concert with the world. We are thus not surprised to read the same Pindaric ode that Valéry cites in his poem *Le cimetière marin* in the epigraph to Camus's *Le mythe de Sisyphe*: "O mon âme, n'aspire pas à la vie immortelle, mais épuise le champ du possible" (1965: 96). ["O my soul, do not aspire to immortal life / But exhaust the limits of the possible."] In other words, he suggests, it is unsound to wish to live forever and sensible to live fully in the possibilities of the present. The dualisms between joy, or happiness, and the tragic that subtend a great majority of Camus's works are largely due to his passion for Ancient Greek thought and its dialectical nature. Citing Valéry once again, he implies that the necessary equilibrium can only be attained by resuscitating our ability to recognize our one-ness with the earth: "Nous possédons, en quelque sorte, une mesure de toutes choses et de nous-mêmes. La parole de Protagoras, que l'homme est la mesure des choses, est une parole caractéristique, essentiellement méditerranéenne" (1957: 1092). [In some way, within ourselves, we possess a measure of all things and of ourselves. Protagoras' statement that man is the measure of all things is characteristic and essentially Mediterranean.] Valéry, like Camus, traces the standard of measure to Protagoras, suggesting that it is in fact to Greek thought that one must return in order to understand Mediterranean distinctiveness.

Camus had a profound affinity for Greece and for the pre-Christian civilizations of Algeria and Italy. The ethic of freedom that he attempted to create was inspired in great part by his reading of Presocratic philosophy, which, some critics such as Paul Archambault conclude, were simply interpretations of Nietzsche's reading of Heraclitus and Empedocles. But this should interest us less than the system of belief that Camus gleaned from Nietzsche and the Presocratics, namely a vision of the world and of man that was built upon constant movements of chaos and order, measure and hubris, form and function. These are notions that indeed are operative throughout Camus's early works and illuminate his philosophy in his later years, as can be seen in *Le premier homme*. His answer to a question once posed to him in an interview reveals his profound attachment to the Presocratics and to Greece: "La bonne explication est du moins toujours double. La Grèce nous l'enseigne, la Grèce à laquelle il faut toujours revenir. La Grèce, c'est l'ombre et la lumière. Nous savons bien, n'est-ce pas, nous autres hommes du Sud, que le soleil a sa face noire?" (1965: 1343). [The right explanation is always double, at least. Greece teaches us this, Greece to which we must always return. Greece is both shadow and light. We are well aware, aren't we, if we come from the South that the sun has its black side.] There is evidence of Camus's proclivity for Ancient Greece in his citation of Pindar and in his choice of Sisyphus and Prometheus as primary protagonists of his works. Yet, as Camus himself acknowledges, "La Grèce" or "Hellenism" are complex terms that obtained different meanings at different points in his life.[17]

At the source of the philosophies of many of the thinkers Camus refers to is the Heraclitean idea, contained in the famous aphorism "from all things one and from one thing all," that a cosmic vision of the universe is defined by the unity of opposites and the constant flux of matter. Camus strives for the unity of opposites and their presumed balance and advocates such a paradigm as being the most fundamental aspect of his Mediterranean thought: "Cet esprit qui mesure la vie, est celui-là même qui anime la longue tradition de ce qu'on peut appeler la pensée solaire et où, depuis les Grecs, la nature a toujours été équilibrée au devenir" (1965: 701). [This spirit which takes the measure of life, is the same that animates the long tradition that can be called solitary thought, in which, since the time of the Greeks, nature has always been weighed against evolution.] Following Heraclitus, Camus also read a number of Stoics such as Epictetus and the Roman Marcus Aurelius and reasserted that despite the different schools of interpretation, Stoicism was a practical, prescriptive mode of philosophy which held, most importantly, that Man must live in accordance with nature and be cognizant of his relationship to the cosmos.

Reflected in the philosophies of Camus, Merleau-Ponty, and Deleuze and Guattari, the opposition between Man and nature is conjugated, and the place of the former is without special privilege. The critic John Sellars writes that the stoic thinker Marcus Aurelius "proposes what might be called a point of view of the cosmos, a Braudelian perspective of geological time from which the apparently rigid organism and self are merely momentary pauses in the flows of matter that constitute the infinite and eternal cosmos" (1999: 14). The self is seen as a pause in the flow of the cosmos, and the quasi-stillness of Stoic thought reflects the moment of acceptance of the forces of nature and a preparedness to experience or to the event. A Stoic ethos accepts the event, freeing it from moral judgment, but subjects it nonetheless to evaluation. Although Camus did not preach or prescribe any transcendental moral law per se, he fought ardently for justice and universal human rights.

In his lyrical essay L'exil d'Hélène, included in Noces, Camus presents a criticism of Europe's bellicose conduct and issues an appeal for a return to the Greek values of beauty, measure and nature. He forges a space for art and thus for literature: "L'esprit historique et l'artiste veulent tous deux refaire le monde. Mais l'artiste, par une obligation de sa nature, connaît ses limites que l'esprit historique méconnaît. C'est pourquoi la fin de ce dernier est la tyrannie tandis que la passion du premier est la liberté" (1959: 138). [Both the historical mind and the artist seek to re-make the world. But the artist, through an obligation of his very nature, recognizes limits the historical mind ignores. This is why the latter aims at tyranny while the passion of the artist is liberty.] The freedom that comes with art, as suggested by Camus, thus acts as an alternative to history and to historical refashioning in favor of worlds built on affect and perceptions. Drawing on the mythical figure of Helen of Troy, he condemns the excess in war and the loss of beauty. His frequent refer-ences to Greek gods lead us to question the interplay between past (An-cient Greek thought but also past experiences of beauty, for example) and present (modern warfare, Western rationalism and the immediate senso-ry perceptions of nature). They also point to something otherworldly and beyond human understanding.

Camus's concern for Europe's past and present political relationships with the rest of the world clearly grew out of an opposition established a few years earlier in a speech he gave at the Maison de la Culture, which he founded in Algiers in 1937. In his speech, entitled "La culture indigène-la nouvelle culture méditerranéenne" [The New Mediterranean Culture], Camus, who was only twenty-three years old, puts forth a con-ception of Mediterranean Man that is still vague; here the slippage be-tween a political philosophy and an existential one begins to surface. It is in this speech that Camus calls for a Mediterranean free of nationalistic tendencies, be they the old imperial pursuits of the Ancient Roman Em-pire or the more recent ventures in European colonialism. "Les nation-alismes apparaissent toujours dans l'histoire comme des signes de déca-dence" [Nationalisms always seem like signs of decadence in history], he affirms, and although he never mentions France's specific role in Algeria, he does take Italy's role in Ethiopia as an example. [18] Interestingly he does not mention Italy's colonization of Libya, however, which was the most successful of the Italian colonial conquests and in that sense perhaps most similar to France's role in the Maghreb. Just as for most of the colonial period France perceived the Mediterranean as the link to its other "coast" in the Maghreb, Mussolini called Libya Italy's "quarta sponda" [fourth shore]. Conflating past and present and reacting to the discourses on a Latin Mediterranean, Camus expresses an idealistic hope in the coming together of East and West:

> Bassin international traversé par tous les courants, la Méditerranée est de tous les pays le seul peut-être qui rejoigne les grandes pensées orien-tales . . . L'Afrique du Nord est un des seuls pays où l'Orient et l'Occident cohabitent. Et à ce confluent il n'y a pas de différence entre la façon dont vit un Espagnol ou un Italien des quais d'Alger, et les Arabes qui les entourent. Ce qu'il y a de plus essentiel dans le génie

méditerranéen jaillit peut-être de cette rencontre unique dans l'histoire et la géographie née entre l'Orient et l'Occident (1965: 1325).

[The Mediterranean, an international basin traversed by every current, is perhaps the only land linked to the great ideas from the East. . . . North Africa is one of the few countries where East and West live close together. And there is, at this junction, little difference between the way a Spaniard or an Italian lives on the quays of Algiers, and the way Arabs live around them. The most basic aspect of Mediterranean genius springs perhaps from this historically and geographically unique encounter between East and West.]

Camus's speech is rife with puzzling statements; for instance, he affirms that there is no difference in lifestyle between an Arab, a Spaniard or an Italian, when in fact they differed. Moreover, he suggests that the unity of Mediterranean people is based, among other things, on linguistic similarities because Latin-based languages resemble each other. Finally, he altogether ignores Berber languages, but also Maltese and Spanish, spoken by many pied-noirs, not to mention other languages also spoken throughout the Mediterranean. But perhaps most difficult to identify is what, if anything, beyond the simple fact of being geographically close, brings people from the Mediterranean together. "L'unité n'est plus dans la croyance mais dans l'espérance" [its unity no longer lies in faith but in hope], he states. In fact, if on the one hand his discourse has strong naïve ideological undertones, on the other hand it is defined by less rational qualities, grounded in sensations, as we saw earlier, rather than in historical explanations or religious beliefs. After all, he gave this speech merely two years after he wrote *L'envers et l'endroit*, in which he states "le soleil m'a appris que l'histoire n'est pas tout" (1965: 5–6). [The sun taught me that history was not everything.]

In his 1937 speech Camus claims: "Ce n'est pas le goût du *raisonnement* que nous revendiquons dans la Méditerranée, mais c'est sa vie—les cours, les cyprès, les chapelets de piments—Eschyle et non Euripide" (1965: 1324; my emphasis). [What we take from Mediterranean culture is not the taste for reasoning and abstraction but the life—the streams, the cypresses, the bouquets of color. It is Aeschylus, not Euripides . . .] [19] But it is his reaction to fascism and colonialism that stands out in his speech as the catalyst of his profound hope in—the possibility of—a Mediterranean Man and his revolt against nationalism and dogmatism. What also emerges from this speech is his belief in nature as a unifying factor. Is it really around cypress trees and courtyards that one can be united? Is Camus not espousing the same notions Braudel did in uniting Mediterranean people around courtyards and cypress trees? In a short chapter, entitled "The Landscape, Still Recognizably the Same," of his epic work on the Mediterranean, Braudel supports his point that "geography helps explain many things" by stating that wheat, vines, and olive trees "have been rooted since the beginning of time on the shores of the Mediterranean" and are, in part, responsible for economic and social relations in the region (1972: 84). Camus's relationship to nature differs significantly from Braudel's, however, as it is grounded in inner spirit and the senses rather than in nature's materiality.

Finally, it is in the last section of *L'homme révolté* entitled "La pensée de midi" [Thought at the Meridian] that a more mature Camus articulates a less naïve ideological perspective. In "La pensée de midi" he takes the notion of unity further. For Camus there lies a clear distinction between what he calls Mediterranean thought and German thought—predominantly that of Hegel and Heidegger. Where the former is built upon a Greek conception of the world, with a vision of a cyclical cosmic unity and an aspiration towards balancing opposing forces, the latter is steeped in excess, *démesure*, stasis and rootedness. His "pensée de midi," as the name suggests, is the quest for a balance between nature and history, past and present and a criticism of absolutes. With this he calls for man to seek within himself, and again not in history, a singular existence founded not on any religious or intellectual doctrines but on a human spirit that would harmoniously reach an equilibrium and situate him in the world. He saw what he defined as Mediterranean Man as the example to follow: youthful and full of life, able to reconcile the tensions between past and present, nature and history and therefore close to freedom. This idealistic and at times hazy vision of existence is crucial here because of its conception of man's place in the world. More specifically, it is a reflection on a world that was growing increasingly hostile and dependent on scientific reasoning and dogmatic doctrines, clearly evident in the Soviet Purges, the beginning of the Cold War and colonialism. Camus's vision called for a form of revolt that would lead to an understanding and praxis of measure. Returning to a point made previously, it is in response to the absurdity of existence but even more so to the excess of fundamentalism and oppression, that Camus writes of man's only choice (other than suicide), that is to revolt. To do so necessarily involves an "other"—it is intersubjective—and thus it inevitably draws one out of solitude. The concept of Revolt enabled Camus to elaborate a critique of absolutes, a notion that indeed underlies the construction of Mediterranean Man. It allows Camus to go from a singular subjectivity to a collective conception of man: as he puts it in *L'homme révolté*, "je me révolte donc nous sommes" [I rebel therefore we are]. Mediterranean Man's *being* is, for Camus, grounded in a strong sense of humanistic kinship despite the extreme solitude of the individual's non-privileged position in the cosmos. His "pensée de midi" exists between the tension of being and becoming and is, as Raymond Gay Crosier writes, a "pensée ouverte par excellence, la mesure interdit la fermeture d'une conclusion proprement dite" (Gay-Crosier 1998: 107). [An open system of thought *par excellence*; measure prohibits an actual conclusion.] But even if this system of thought is open and changing, can a point of departure be identified? Camus states, "On ne peut dire que l'être n'est qu'existence. Ce qui devient toujours ne saurait être, il faut un commencement. L'être ne peut s'éprouver que dans le devenir, le devenir n'est rien sans l'être" (1965: 699). [But nor can it be said that being is only existence. Something that is always in the process of becoming could not exist—there must be a beginning. Being can only prove itself in becoming, and becoming is nothing without being]. Indeed Camus leads us to a beginning, one that steers us back to the primordial moment of birth as well as to allegorical origins of the world.

MEDITERRANEAN ROUTES/ROOTS AND *LE PREMIER HOMME*

One point of departure, in its symbolic dimension, is the first man, and Camus's novel *Le premier homme*. Camus's elaboration of a Mediterranean Humanism in his lyrical essays and in *L'homme révolté* is characterized both by a phenomenological conception of being as well as a political response to Europe's increasingly dogmatic conduct. Increasingly appalled by the waves of Nazism and Fascism that swept through Europe, Camus went so far as to consider Communism and Marxism equally restrictive and dangerous. *Le premier homme* goes beyond these notions, through a problematization of roots, nation, and nature, fully illuminating Camus's philosophy of Mediterranean Man. Unlike the previous works considered, *Le premier homme* is a work of fiction, although it is closer to autofiction and, in numerous instances, autobiography.[20] Found in manuscript form at the moment of Camus's untimely fatal car accident, *Le premier homme* is an unfinished work and perhaps the reflection of what was most impulsive in Camus.[21] It has no clear beginning, middle, or end and can be read, on one level, as being closer to his sensory inclinations and perceptions than to polished intellectual reasoning.

Nevertheless, the novel has been organized into a coherent order and opens with the birth of the protagonist, Jacques Cormery, in Algeria. The narrative follows the protagonist through adolescence and into early adulthood. Referring to Jacques Cormery soon after his birth as JC, and setting the scene in a barn reminiscent of another Mediterranean site, Bethlehem, Camus brings us to reflect, from the very first pages, upon the origins and limits of man. This is at odds—if indeed he alludes to Jesus Christ as critics have suggested—with his Greek affiliations, but not contradictory to a larger Mediterranean ethos, where in fact the two systems of belief co-exist. Is Camus pointing to the notion of origins through the figure of Jesus Christ, or is there a looser nexus with the *first man* and Adam? Why would a thinker such as Camus, so steeped in Hellenic thought and so close to nature, choose to draw on this image? A possible answer may simply lie in the suggestion that the space of the Mediterranean is at once unitary and multiple: it is a site of origins (Greece is the site of the birth of philosophy, Christianity and Judaism originated in the Mediterranean, for instance), but it is at the same time a place where various origins overlap and where purity is compromised. By equating the protagonist with the first man, Adam, we are drawn to making the distinction between a prelapsarian world where purity and the One prevailed and a world after the fall, where man is thrust into multiplicity.

Le premier homme implicitly pushes us to question the origins of man through the protagonist's search for his own roots, both natural and national. In the opening chapter entitled "Recherche du père," Cormery searches for traces of his deceased father; standing at the site of his tomb in Saint-Brieuc, he is overcome by the realization that his father died at twenty-nine, eleven years younger than Cormery's present age as he stands in quiet contemplation of death: "Quelque chose ici n'était pas dans l'ordre naturel et, à vrai dire, il n'y avait pas d'ordre mais chaos et folie là où le fils était plus âgé que le père . . . les années cessaient de s'ordonner suivant ce grand fleuve qui coule vers sa fin . . . elles n'étaient plus que fracas, ressac et remous" (1994: 35). [Something here was not in the natural order and, in truth, there was no order but only madness and chaos when the son was older than the father . . . and the years no longer kept to their places in the great river that flows to its end. They were no more than waves and surf and eddies.] Cormery's conception of time is destabilized, and he decides to make the journey from France (where he now lives) to Algeria in pursuit of any traces of his family. However, from the very beginning of his journey, he is projected into a desperate remembering of his past in a poor neighbourhood of Algiers ("l'île pauvre du quartier" [the neighborhood's island of poverty]), and what begins as a search for his father in fact turns into an existential search for himself. Not surprisingly, the first two-thirds of the book entitled "Recherche du père" and the last, "Le fils ou le premier homme"(of particular interest is a chapter entitled "Obscur à soi-même"), mark the conflation of the search for origins and a search for self. Despite the logical link made between father and son, it is rather a feeling of chaos and disarray that strikes Cormery as the true order of time; if, as he maintains, time no longer flows like a river to its end, to the sea, it is characterized by the ebb and flow of a vast and open expanse, metaphorically akin to the sea rather than to a river. From Jacques Cormery's perpective the relationship between father and son is horizontal, rather than steeped in verticality as one might find in the typical conception of a family tree.

Cormery's initial investigation proves fruitless as there are no records of his father's death, and his mother, the only person who really knew him, is illiterate and virtually mute. With few traces and having virtually not known his father, Cormery understands that it is not necessarily genealogy that defines one's roots and oneself, but a multitude of different physical and intellectual sensations and affiliations. Camus writes, "Les traditions familiales n'ont souvent pas de fondement plus solide, et les ethnologues me font bien rire qui cherchent la raison de tant de rites mystérieux. Le vrai mystère, dans beaucoup de cas, c'est qu'il n'y a pas de raison du tout" (1994: 130). [But family traditions are often no more soundly based, and ethnologists certainly make me laugh when they seek the reasons for so many mysterious rituals. The real mystery, in many cases, is that there is no reason at all.] Often steeped in mystery, roots and rites are secondary to what exists in the present and in the material world.

Cormery experiences the search for his father and his pursuit of self-knowledge through a sense of place and timeliness in the tragic landscapes of his poverty-stricken existence. Wealth comes not from heritage, nor birthright, nor material possessions but from the earth itself. In their childhood, Cormery and his peers "régnaient sur la vie et sur la mer, et ce que le monde peut donner de plus fastueux, ils le recevaient et en usaient sans mesure, comme des seigneurs assurés de leurs richesses irremplaçables" (1994: 64). [Reigned over life and over the sea, and, like nobles certain that their riches were limitless, they heedlessly consumed the most gorgeous of this world's offerings.] In a country devastated by the effacement of a pre-colonial history, a nation not yet independent that France viewed as a mere child of the motherland, Camus turns to what is not contingent upon man. And yet, as Cormery moves into adolescence and lives through those formative years during which sensations translate into ideas and reason comes to offset intuition, he becomes aware of the need to further understand his place in the world. "Il lui avait fallu . . . trouver seul sa morale et sa vérité, *naître* enfin comme homme pour en-suite *naître* encore d'une *naissance* plus dure, celle qui consiste à *naître* aux autres, aux femmes, comme tous les hommes *nés* dans ce pays qui, un par un, essayaient d'apprendre à vivre sans racines et sans foi . . ." (1994: 214; my emphasis). [He had to learn by himself, to . . . find his own morality and truth, at last to be born as a man, and then to be born in a harder childbirth, which consists of being born in relation to others, to women, like all the men born in this country who, one by one try to learn to live without roots and without faith.] For Camus, birth is strictly tied to the Mediterranean. The recurring references to Dionysus, the God twice born, in Camus's early works find their echo in *Le premier homme*, the first man, who is born again and again, further complicating the notion of roots. Here birth is a multiple signifier: first as the passage into adult-hood, then as a symbolic re-birth to others, and finally as the symbol of a country (Algeria) forced into an involuntary rebirth (by colonial France). If our origins cannot be traced back to *an* original birth then we are inevitably brought to consider ourselves as multiple and, as such, part of a cosmic flux. Man is then part of a larger living entity, one subject among many. Camus insists that man comes from the earth before he comes from another human being:

Cette nuit en lui [Cormery], oui ces racines obscures et emmêlées qui le rattachaient à cette terre splendide et effrayante, à ses jours brûlants comme à ses soirs rapides à serrer le coeur, et qui avait été comme *une seconde vie, plus vraie* peut-être sous les apparences quotidiennes que de la première vie et dont l'histoire aurait été faite par une suite de désirs obscurs et de *sensations puissantes et indescriptibles*, l'odeur . . . des jasmins et des chèvrefeuilles sur les hauts quartiers . . . (1994: 303; my emphasis)

[This night inside him, yes these tangled hidden roots that bound him to this magnificent and frightening land, as much to its scorching days as to its heartbreakingly rapid twilights, and that was like a second life, truer perhaps than the everyday surface of his outward life; its history would be told as a series of obscure yearnings and powerful indescribable sensations, the odor of . . . jasmine and honeysuckle in the upper neighborhoods . . .]

It is the tangled and mysterious ties, the horizontal, rhizomatic roots that account for his origins; the lost traces of his father—his *per(t)e*—and the solace he finds in the presence of the silent sea—the *mer(e)*—make sense of his very existence but cannot ultimately account for the discrepancy between the idea he has of himself and the slow recognition, as the novel progresses, of someone else, another Jacques Cormery. What he has lived is what Jean-Jacques Gonzales in an essay entitled "Dissonance de Camus" calls the "expérience d'un décalage originaire, que rien ne pourra jamais combler, faillite définitive de l'illusion identitaire, des identités meurtrières, du mirage de la coïncidence de soi avec soi" (2004: 76). [The experience of an original chasm, that nothing can ever fulfill, a definitive collapse of the illusion of identity, of murderous identities and of the false impression that the self coincides with the self.] In his French-style school Jacques is surrounded by French children in contrast to whom he tries to establish his own sense of belonging and singularity, but

Jacques se sentait d'une autre espèce, sans passé, ni maison de famille, ni grenier bourré de lettres et de photos, citoyens théoriques d'*une nation imprécise* où la neige couvrait les toits alors qu'eux mêmes grandissaient sous un soleil fixe et sauvage, munis d'une morale des plus élémentaires . . . incapables de concevoir la vie future tant *la vie présente* leur paraissait *inépuisable* chaque jour sous la protection des divinités indifférentes du soleil, de la mer ou de la misère . . . (1994: 227; my emphasis)

[Jacques, and Pierre also, though to a lesser degree, felt themselves to be of another species, with no past, no family home, no attic full of letters and photos, citizens in theory of a nebulous nation where snow covered the roofs while they themselves grew up under an eternal and savage sun, equipped with a most elementary morality . . . unable to imagine a future life when this life seemed so inexhaustible each day under the protection of the indifferent deities of sun, of sea or of poverty.]

Camus underscores the dangers of too narrow an explanation of oneself. In a [geological and] geophilosophical sense, roots are inextricably linked to nature, which is, in turn, as their etymologies indicate, tied to issues of nation.[22]

What is the epistemological value of the nexus between nature and nation? Camus's Mediterranean Humanism allows us to discern an ethos that is both universal and specific; in other words, not only can we, through Camus, examine a part of the world that is singular, we are also drawn to consider an ontological model that reaches beyond geographic and spatio-temporal borders. How is this humanistic model configured? Drawing on what I have exposed thus far we can begin by saying that Being is not to be understood as fixed or rooted in verticality but rather as immanent, and first and foremost grounded in pre-discursive experience. As part of a larger living entity of the cosmos, man's place and perspective is just one among others.

Camus's Mediterranean thinking can be situated within the line of Merleau-Ponty's rejection of a subject-object dichotomy in which Man (and his rationality) is incorporated with the world and not separate from it. This is apparent in the title of one of his very first works, *Noces*, which points to a marriage of man and Earth. The Earth is not only there to be perceived, it *interacts* with the perceiver:

> Il n'est pas toujours facile d'être un homme, moins encore d'être un homme pur. Mais être pur, c'est retrouver cette patrie de l'âme où devient sensible la parenté du monde, où les coups du sang rejoignent les pulsations violentes du soleil de deux heures. Il est bien connu que la patrie se reconnaît toujours au moment de la perdre. Pour ceux qui sont trop tourmentés d'eux-mêmes, le pays natal est celui qui les nie. (1959: 48)

> [It is not always easy to be a man, even less to be a man who is pure. But to be pure means to rediscover that country of the soul where one's kinship with the world can be felt, where the throbbing of one's blood mingles with the violent pulsations of the afternoon sun. It is a well-known fact that we always recognize our homeland at the moment we are about to lose it. Men whose self-torments are too great are those whom their native land rejects.]

It is striking that Camus, who was so critical of absolutes, would write about the purity of man, yet the above passage suggests that "purity" seems to go hand in hand with realizing one's relation to the Earth and finding the proper measure of oneself to one's world. This is not to say that there is a pure being, but that those who are too "tourmentés d'eux-mêmes" [self-tormented] are rejected by the Earth, beginning with their very birthplace. In this way, nature becomes a protagonist in Camus's works, recalling once again the infamous murder in *L'étranger* where the sun acts as the catalyzing agent of a killing.

MAKING SENSE OF SCENTS

Le premier homme is saturated with references to sensory perceptions, most strikingly with Camus's fifty-eight allusions to smells, odors or scents. Let us look at one of Camus's most revealing of the fifty-eight mentions: "Chaque livre, en outre, avait une odeur particulière selon le papier où il était imprimé, odeur fine, secrète, dans chaque cas, mais si singulière que J. aurait pu distinguer *les yeux fermés* un livre de la collection Nelson des éditions courantes que publiait Fasquelle" (1994: 270; my emphasis). [Moreover each book had its own smell according to the paper on which it was printed, always delicate and discreet, but so distinct that with his eyes closed J. could have told a book in the Nelson series from one of the contemporary editions Fasquelle was then publishing.] Here smell is the key factor in distinguishing one text from another and may even be considered a means to understanding the world, or an epistemological tool. Smells, according to Fiona Borthwick in a critical essay on the philosophy of olfaction and taste, "Lack meanings based in reason. Thus, in Western culture olfaction was marginalised in the push towards rationality" (2000, 3). It is not surprising then that Camus attempts to recuperate the olfactory over the other senses.

Plato considered smell an ignoble sense as opposed to sight and hearing, and, according to Borthwick, a number of other philosophers have placed it in the realm of the negligible. However, in carefully considering the above quote, it would appear that to Camus the sense of smell takes on even more importance than the sense of sight. Further, he writes: "Ce que contenaient ces livres au fond importait peu. Ce qui importait était ce qu'ils *ressentaient* d'abord en entrant dans la bibliothèque, où ils *ne voyaient pas* les murs de livres noirs mais un espace et des horizons multiples qui, dès le pas de la porte les enlevaient à la vie étroite du quartier" (1994: 269). [Actually the contents of these books mattered little. What did matter was what they first felt when they went into the library, where they would see not the walls of black books but multiplying horizons and expanses that, as soon as they crossed the doorstep, would take them away from the cramped life of neighborhood.] Indeed the sense of smell may be considered subjective, and the sense of sight somewhat more objective. In the last chapter of *Le premier homme* entitled "Obscur à soi-même," Camus abandons himself to a three-page-long sentence in which he lists a number of smells, despite the fact that to him these are "sensations [puissantes et] indescriptibles" [strong and indescribable sensations]. These invisible bearers of effects are representative of the very mystery that is present in every life and that, following Camus, needs to be heeded rather than questioned. Camus's numerous references to the wind as well as to the air may well translate his insistence on the ethereal and the transitory.[23]

Why such a preponderance of the olfactory? Proust's evocation of his *madeleines* set a strong literary precedent whereby memory has been the most common trope associated with smell in literature, and indeed given the fundamental element of retrospection in *Le premier homme*, this may also account for Camus's use of smell. After all, the novel is an autobiographical recollection of his own past. Lastly, smell may be privileged specifically in its opposition to the other senses in that it, more than touch, sight, the auditory, or taste, can be instrumental in defining a place or a mood. Wittingly or not, this is precisely what Camus does in *Le premier homme*: he conveys a pre-discursive Mediterranean that is a site of affects, memory and unity with nature. This was already apparent to him in 1937: "La Méditerranée c'est cela, cette odeur ou ce parfum qu'il est inutile d'exprimer: nous le sentons tous avec notre peau" (1965: 1323). [That is what the Mediterranean is—a certain smell or scent that we do not need to express: we all feel it through our skin.]

Following Husserl, Merleau-Ponty calls sensory forms of experience "la vie antéprédicative de la conscience" [the pre-predicative life of consciousness], which are always that of one who is in a finite and limited situation but where the possibilities of its effects are infinite. Dermot Moran writes:

> Our bodies and the specific formation of the sense organs reveal the world for us in a very special way. Merleau-Ponty invites us to consider what our notion of the world or of external objects would be like if we had eyes in either side of our heads rather than mounted so they both see the same things. Our whole understanding of the world is grounded in our corporeal nature." (2000: 418)

Merleau-Ponty's emphasis, throughout his work on perception, is on the status of the sense of sight. Indeed the sense of smell is *the* sense, of the five, that has been largely neglected in the philosophy of aesthetics, most commonly in favor of sight and touch.[24] Kant and Hegel dismissed it altogether as the site of base, animalistic instincts and as disconnected from materiality: "Things are only available to smell in so far as they are in process and dissipated through air" (Hegel 1975: 622). Smells cannot be turned off and cannot be "shut out" the way one can close one's eyes or cover one's ears.

True to his philosophy of measure and tension between opposites, Camus contrasts the predominance of a self fashioned through affective states with one constructed through reason and knowledge. For the protagonist of *Le premier homme*, experience of the world and of oneself, located in the middle ground—the "Mediterranean" of Man—between mind and body, cannot be fully elaborated in strictly rational terms. The frustration of not being able to make sense of himself plunges him into a mad desire to defy the order of time and to know what lies beyond the linear narratives one creates for oneself.

> Il n'était plus que ce coeur angoissé, avide de vivre, révolté contre l'ordre mortel du monde qui l'avait accompagné durant quarante années et qui battait toujours avec la même force contre le mur qui le séparait du secret de toute vie, voulant aller plus loin, au delà et savoir, savoir avant de mourir, savoir enfin pour être, une seule fois, une seule seconde mais à jamais. (1994: 35)

> [All that was left was this anguished heart, eager to live, rebelling against the deadly order of the world that had been with him for forty years, and still struggling against the wall that separated him from the secret of life, wanting to go farther, to go beyond, and to discover, discover before dying, discover at last in order to be, just once to be, for a single second, but forever.]

Le premier homme is especially interesting as it is doubly incomplete. The existential quest leads us to the last part of Camus's Mediterranean Humanism that is also, and paradoxically, determined by questions of national belonging. As this chapter demonstrates, there is also a deep political scar that inevitably plays into his conception of self and that subtends his identification with the space of the Mediterranean.

FROM NATURE TO NATION

One of the most poignant and complex facets of Camus's thought pertains to his sense of place and to the question of nationalism. Although *Le premier homme* is highly personal and subjective, it could be argued that it tells the story of the existential predicament of a whole generation of pied-noirs. Neither fully French nor fully Algerian, Camus is caught in a double-belonging that he attempts to resolve by affirming that his *patrie*, his homeland, is the larger transnational space of the Mediterranean. Thus it is not a question of either/or, either French or Algerian, but a double belonging where the two, for once, exist in a complementary relationship rather than an oppositional one. In *Le premier homme* he writes:

> La Méditerranée séparait en moi deux univers, l'un où dans ces espaces mesurés les souvenirs et les noms étaient conservés, l'autre où le vent de sable effaçait les traces des hommes sur de grands espaces . . . il savait . . . que la mort le ramène dans sa vraie patrie et recouvre à son tour de son immense oubli le souvenir de l'homme monstrueux et [banal] qui avait grandi, édifié sans aide et sans secours, dans la pauvreté, sur un rivage heureux et sous la lumière des premiers matins du monde, pour aborder ensuite, seul, sans mémoire et sans foi, le monde des hommes de son temps et son affreuse et exaltante histoire. (1994: 214)[25]

[The Mediterranean separates two worlds in me, one where memory and names are preserved in measured spaces, the other where the wind and sand erases all trace of men on the open ranges . . . he knew . . . that death would return him to his true homeland and, with its immense oblivion, would obliterate the memory of that alien and ordinary man who had grown up, had built in poverty, without help or deliverance, on a fortunate shore and in the light of the first mornings of the world, and then alone, without memories and without faith, he had entered the world of the men of his time and its dreadful and exalted history.]

His protagonist, much like himself, envisions France on the one hand, with its measured spaces and systematic ways of committing names and events to national memory, and on the other Algeria, where history is lost in the vast expanse of space and swept away by the wind. However, Camus may also be suggesting that it is colonization that swept away traces of the past and that in fact, for the pied-noir, the division between two presumed homelands is not quite so clear. As he gains awareness of himself and of his "people," Cormery realizes that it is loss and anonymity that define his *patrie*, beginning with the example of his father:

Inconnu des siens et de son fils, rendu lui aussi à l'immense oubli qui était la patrie définitive des hommes de sa race, le lieu d'aboutissement d'une vie commencée sans racines . . . comme si l'histoire des hommes . . . s'évaporait sous le soleil incessant avec le souvenir de ceux qui l'avaient vraiment faite, réduite à des crises de violence et de meurtre, des flambées de haine, des torrents de sang vite gonflés vite asséchés comme les oueds du pays. (1994: 212)

[Forever unknown to his people and his son, he too was returned to that immense oblivion that was the ultimate homeland of the men of his people, the final destination of a life that began without roots . . . as if the history of men . . . was evaporating under the constant sun with the memories of those who made it, reduced to paroxysms of violence and murder, to blazes of hatred, to torrents of blood, quickly swollen and quickly dried up like the seasonal streams of the country.]

He, the first man, hails from a forgotten land. There is a bitter sense of irony in this, as Camus knows all too well that another Algeria existed long before 1830. But above all, there is, through the melancholy of a people stripped of its land, not only a reflection upon the French Algerians but recognition of the existential loss suffered by Arabs, Amazigh people (Berbers), and *other* Algerians as well.

As for his own sense of place, Cormery clearly cannot belong to any nation. Instead, he positions himself at the liminal space of the shores, on the edges of the Mediterranean which he often refers to as pays or patrie.[26] The liminality and the dividedness of Cormery's "two universes" point to a split in him that ultimately fails to be completely resolved by his conception of Mediterraneity. The "two universes" are actually multiple, once again recalling the words of Valéry, "Notre vie . . . n'est que l'une des vies innombrables que ce moi identique eût pu épouser . . . un regard sur la mer, c'est un regard sur le possible" (1957: 1093). [Our life . . . is but one of innumerable lives that the identical self could have embraced . . . looking onto the sea is looking onto the possible.] In terms that are rather more concrete than Valéry's, Camus's desire is one of possibility and new beginnings, both inextricably linked to the very place from which he comes.

In the very first note of the manuscript, which follows the dedication "à toi qui ne pourras jamais lire ce livre" (1994: 5) [to you who will never be able to read this book], Camus writes, "ajouter anonymat géologique. Terre et mer [add geological anonymity. Land and sea]." From the very beginning of the novel, this "citoyen théorique" [citizen in theory] draws us into a "nation imprécise" [nebulous nation], whose contours are barely defined by the earth and the sea. Indeed if "the first man" is to be truly first, his past must be obscure or altogether non-existent: he is a man without a past in an anonymous setting, an Algeria ravaged by colonialism and characterized by generations without a past. To some extent, this depiction characterizes generations of pied-noirs estranged in an Algeria itself in tension with the nation of their forebears. Numerous critics have commented on the "unapologetic defense and illustration of French Algerians," as Edward Hughes (1999) puts it, that *Le premier homme* offers, affirming that Camus attempts to rehabilitate a colonial mentality, or unconsciously allies himself with the wrong people.[27] Yet there exists another, even more important anonymity in the "first man." A phenomenological perspective of being allows us to posit that what Camus is ultimately calling for is a disposing of assumptions, the *epoché* or bracketing off of presupposed ideas.

If we closely examine Camus's notion of anonymity in *Le premier homme*, we discover that it is "le mystère de la pauvreté qui fait les êtres sans nom et sans passé" (1994: 213) [the mystery of poverty that creates beings without names and without a past]. With no riches to contend for, the underprivileged in *Le premier homme* resemble each other regardless of their nationality and, Camus seems to suggest, are those whose being is closer to nature and further from historical determinism. This is not to say that only those who are underprivileged accede to a proximity to nature but that they in particular may be characterized by a unique sensitivity. Camus's great disdain for History and "heroes" grows out of this very opposition with nature.[28] The "first man" is not unique and he is not a hero; he happens to be born in "la terre de l'oubli où chacun était le premier homme" (1994: 180) [the land of oblivion where each one is the first man]. Put this way, Camus may rather be suggesting a quasi imperceptibility of man so as to, again, do away with a subject-object dichotomy and resituate him within a larger cosmic space. Unlike Meursault, who with great indifference floats from incident to incident like an atom in space and kills an (anonymous) Arab because he was blinded by sweat in his eyes and the sun, Jacques Cormery is passionate. His "folie de vivre" [mad passion for living] is driven by "le sentiment soudain terrible que le temps de la jeunesse s'enfuyait" (1994: 260) [the sudden terrible feeling that the time of his youth was slipping away], by his desire to hold on to a time when man is closer to his instincts and farther from his reason, where he is in some sense more *anonymous*. The "first man" is a Nietzschean being, with no origins, no religion and no fixity. Foucault, who in the same vein as Deleuze and Merleau-Ponty worked toward decentering the subject, writes in *The Order of Things*:

> Nietzsche took the end of time and transformed it into the death of God and the odyssey of the last man; he took up anthropological finitude once again, but in order to use it as a basis for the prodigious leap of the superman; he took up once again the great continuous chain of History, but in order to bend it round into the infinity of the eternal return. (1973: 263)

Working toward the possible and the measured, and against the idea of finitude, Camus almost resembles a Nietzschean superman in that life is to be affirmed, revolt is necessary and moral judgment is to be suspended. It is this model of man that is the principal actor in Camus's conception of a Mediterranean Humanism.

CAMUS'S MEDITERRANEITY: CASTLES MADE OF SAND?

It has been argued elsewhere that Camus's Mediterranean Humanism was a valuable but failed utopia.[29] Far from being a metaphor for joy or for transnational unity, the Mediterranean—in its physicality—fuels Camus's thought, his intellect and his very living and breathing. His place is firmly established on earth, his gods the sun and the sea, his most ardent wish: measure. Camus's Mediterranean is marked as much by pain as by pleasure. Like Jacques Cormery, Camus was doubtless eternally in search of "la part obscure de l'être, ce qui en lui pendant toutes ces années avait remué sourdement comme ces eaux profondes qui sous la terre, du fond des labyrinthes rocheux n'ont jamais vu la lumière du jour et reflètent cependant une lueur sourde" (1994: 300) [the secret part of his being, something in him that through all those years had been blindly stirring like those measureless waters under the earth which from the depths of rocky labyrinths have never seen the light of day and yet dimly reflect a light], and yet despite the very specific situated socio-historical context in which Camus was writing, his Mediterraneity ultimately calls for a universal model of being. He specifies, "Pour parler de tous et à tous, il faut parler de ce que tous connaissent et de la réalité qui nous est commune. La mer, les pluies, le besoin, le désir, la lutte contre la mort, voilà ce qui nous réunit tous" (1965: 1085). [But in order to speak about all and to all, one has to speak of what all know and of the reality common to us all.

The sea, rains, necessity, desire, the struggle against death—these are the things that unite us all.] Further on in *L'envers et l'endroit* he affirms, "À cette heure tout mon royaume est de ce monde." [At the moment, my whole kindgom is of this world.] Here it is clear how his profound attachment to the Mediterranean land allowed him to espouse a perspective of his place in a world that reached far beyond his own. Thus, Camus's Mediterranean man lives between the waves of a poetic practice, and the storm of political positioning that he, in his early years, undeniably oversimplified. For this very reason we might ask if Mediterranean Man's dwelling, in his "kingdom," is not in fact a castle made of sand and, as several critics have already suggested, a utopic ideal whose contribution to our way of understanding human existence is circumscribed. But this would mean falling prey, once again, to the political dimension that haunts the Mediterranean. In fact, despite the instability of Camus's multi-layered, or stratified model of Mediterranean Humanism, one aspect is unwavering: "L'essentiel: ne pas se perdre, et ne pas perdre ce qui, de soi, dort dans le monde" (1962: 38). [The essential thing is not to lose oneself and not to lose that part of oneself that lies sleeping in the world.]

It is not only *Le premier homme* that remains unfinished, in manuscript stage; one might say that Camus's Mediterranean man is also incomplete. But like the framework of another typology that Camus seemed to hold in fascination—Don Juan—even our situatedness is always in process. What stands out as most singular, in Camus's Mediterranean thought, is man's ontological relationship to the earth and to the senses and consequently his sense of place. Camus creates a *sui generis* humanism that echoes Greek and Roman philosophers and Nietzsche among others, and that inscribes itself within a line of philosophical thought that privileges stratification and a decentering of the subject. Was Sartre wrong in his famous condemnation of "Mediterranean moderation?" Drawing the contours of Mediterranean Humanism around the dissolution of subject and object, the primacy of the sensory, experience over reason, and an affinity for an ethos that privileges continual regeneration, allows us to rehabilitate a mode of thinking that opens onto empathy and tolerance. Put this way, the eternal return of difference also safeguards something that can still, decades later, be called a Mediterranean humanism.

ENDNOTES

1. "The development of steamships revolutionized travel in the Mediterranean, and the construction of railroad lines between Oriental cities by European colonizers . . . furnished western European travelers with the comfort indispensable in encouraging them to make the long journey across the Orient" (Behdad 1994: 35).

2. Italy's incursion into Africa was hindered by France's occupation of Tunisia in 1881; this was one of the factors that led to an Italian alliance with Germany and Austria. This agreement stipulated mutual protection should Italy be attacked by

France and was ill received by the Italians as Austria and Germany had, only twenty years earlier, been opposed to the unification of Italy.

3. *Le centenaire de l'Algérie française. Programme,* Alger, numéro spécial de la "Presse nord-africaine," 10 décembre 1929: 10.

4. See Peter Dunwoodie's *Writing French Algeria* for an in-depth discussion of the differences between members of this group.

5. Seth Graebner's *History's Place* explains Emmanuel Roblès's singular and less idealistic view on the possibility of a Mediterranean identity, thanks in part to his status as a Spanish subject. "By beginning to understand his own subject position as Spanish and Mediterranean, but *foreign to the French*, Roblès can better comprehend his relationship with both French and Arabs. He can also work to create the sort of links with Arab and Jewish characters that neither Audisio nor Camus were able to portray" (2007: 240).

6. In his epic work *The Mediterranean and the Mediterranean World in the Age of Philip II*, Braudel mentions Audisio's essay "Sel de la mer" as an illustration of the unity and constancy of man. In the Mediterranean, Braudel writes, "One can find Ulysses himself, man unchanged after the passing of many centuries" (353).

7. The name of the bookstore is inspired by Jean Giono, yet another writer who weighed in on a definition of the Mediterranean. He writes, "Les vraies richesses, celles qui permettent la générosité parce qu'elles sont *inépuisables*" (1954: 251). The notion of "infinite possibility," which is crucial in defining the space of the Mediterranean, will be taken up in chapter 2.

8. The importance of Jean Grenier in Camus's life is significant; originally his teacher, spiritual and philosophical mentor, and then close friend, Camus explains that he owed him much of his success. About Grenier Camus writes, "Je lui dois un doute, qui n'en finira pas et qui m'a empêché, par exemple, d'être un humaniste au sens où l'on entend aujourd'hui, je veux dire un homme aveuglé par de courtes certitudes" (1965: 1159). [It is thanks to him that I have a doubt that will always be with me, and that prevented me from being a humanist in the way that people mean it today. That is to say, a man who is blinded by narrow-minded certainties.] Grenier taught him about the dangers of dogmatism, the importance of doubt and the necessity of questioning the world. He symbolizes Camus's double persona, first as the subejct of a poor environment and later as a prominent intellectual. This dualism was forever a source of anguish for Camus. Lastly, there is a strong intertextual alliance between Paul Valéry, Jean Grenier (who used Valéry's title for a speech *Inspirations Méditerranéennes* for one of his works), and Camus.

9. Garcia Lorca was shot to death by Franco's soldiers for his stance against Fascism.

10. For more about *Sud* see letters between Camus and Grenier in *Correspondance 1932–1960. Camus & Grenier.*

11. It is clear that Camus was greatly inspired by Paul Valéry, who himself had founded, in Nice in 1933, an institution by the name of Centre Universitaire Méditerranéen. "C'est ici [en Méditerranée] que la science s'est dégagée de l'empirisme et de la pratique . . . que la philosophie, enfin, a essayé à peu près toutes les manières possibles de considérer l'Univers et de se considérer elle-même" (1957: 278). [It is here (in the Mediterranean) that science was freed from empiricism and practice . . . that philosophy finally found all means possible to examine the universe and to examine itself.] At the root of this endeavour was the rehabilitation of an area of the world through a less empirical and practical lens in favor of a questioning of Being and the value of philosophy. Valéry's mission statement, or "charte" as he called it, for the center, includes sub-sections such as "Action du milieu sur l'homme," "Action de l'homme sur le milieu" and "Édification de l'homme." The center is still in existence today although its mission has changed.

12. Although the *Algérianistes* saw themselves as regionalists, and set themselves apart from French national culture, their rhetoric still appears dominated by colonial discourse.

13. Camus does tend to use this term normatively. Chapter 3 takes up the question of gender and the Mediterranean.

14. Many books and articles refer to Camus's "mediterraneity"; a selective list includes: Jacques Chabot's *Albert Camus: la pensée de midi,* Franco Cassano's chapter on Camus in *Il pensiero meridiano,* Emile Témime's *Un rêve méditerranéen,* proceedings from a conference in Jerusalem in 1997 "Albert Camus: parcours méditerranéens."

15. Deleuze and Guattari provide the following example: "Philosophy appears in Greece as a result of contingency rather than necessity, as a result of an ambiance or milieu rather than an origin, of a becoming rather than a history, of a geography rather than a historiography, of a grace rather than a nature" (1994: 96).

16. Numerous critics have commented on the composition of Meursault's name as containing both references to the sea (*mer*) and to the sun (*sault* resembles *soleil*). Beginning from his very name, Camus hints at the importance of the earth for this character.

17. According to Archambault, Camus's knowledge of Ancient Greek philosophers was flawed and in great part acquired through secondary texts. He maintains that Camus's general conception of the Greek universe was laden with the ambiguities, contradictions, and confusions that were those of Greek civilization itself. He also affirms that "a reconstitution of Camus's opinions on the Presocratics is about as challenging as the reconstitution of Presocratic thought itself, for in both cases the texts are fragmentary" (1972: 39).

18. "C'est au nom de cet ordre latin que, dans l'affaire d'Ethiopie, vingt-quatre intellectuels d'Occident signèrent un manifeste dégradant qui exaltait l'oeuvre civilisatrice de l'Italie dans l'Ethiopie barbare" (1965: 1324). [It was in the name of this Latin order on the occasion of the war against Ethiopia that twenty-four Western intellectuals signed a degrading manifesto celebrating the "civilizing mission of Italy in barbarous Ethiopia."]

19. Camus adapted Aeschylus' *Prometheus Bound.* He found Aeschylus' theater "illustrative of those rare epochs of history when love of life and metaphysical despair coexist" (Archambault 1972: 21). He was also influenced by Aeschylus's conception of man in revolt. Here we might also assume that Camus read creativity and dynamism in his work, whereas Euripides stood rather for rationality and stasis. In his DEA thesis Camus writes that Euripides "tips the scales of tragedy in favor of the individual and of psychology and proclaims an individualistic drama" (qtd. in Archambault 1972: 32).

20. The distinction between the two, in this case particularly, seems in some sense fallacious, as all autobiography reveals an element of fiction. According to Serge Dubrovsky, autofiction distinguishes itself from autobiography in that in the former the writer presents a *conscious* and *willed* fictionalization of self. The similarities between author and protagonist are too numerous to enumerate for *Le premier homme,* and it has been unanimously established among Camus scholars that the work is indeed autobiographical.

21. He died with a copy of Nietzsche's *Gay Science* in the car. In this work more than any others Nietzsche makes use of an extraordinary number of metaphors of the sea.

22. Both the words *nature* and *nation* come from the Latin *nasci* "to be born." Geophilosophy takes the role of the earth as a fundamental constituent of social practices.

23. "Mais les plus grands jours étaient les jours de vent . . . Jacques sentait le vent venu des extrémités du pays descendre le long de la palme et de ses bras pour le remplir d'une force et d'une exultation qui le faisaient pousser sans discontinuer de longs cris . . . Et le soir, couché . . . il écoutait encore hurler en lui le tumulte et la fureur du vent qu'il devait aimer toute sa vie" (264–65).[But the grandest days were those of the wind . . . Jacques could feel the wind from the farthest ends of the country coursing down the length of the branch and down his arms to fill him with such power and an exultation that he cried out endlessly . . . And that night lying in bed . . . he could still hear the howling and the tumult of the wind that he would love for all his life.]

24. One even finds numerous studies on taste or gastronomy in literature and philosophy.

25. This shift from first to third person occurs from time to time in *Le premier homme* and underscores the autobiographical-autofictional dimension of the work.

26. In an interview with Clarisse Zimra, Assia Djebar states, "I had stared in awe and wonder at my own region, the region described by Camus in *Noces*. But whereas I claimed all of it, including the hinterland, Camus only hugged the shore" (1992: 177).

27. This debate surrounding Camus's work and life is the object of many works of criticism. For those who read Camus as suffering from colonial superiority see Edward Hughes, "Building the Colonial Archive: The Case of Camus's *Le premier homme*" and David Carroll, "Camus's Algeria: Birthrights, Colonial Injustice and the Fiction of a French-Algerian People."

28. I am following Camus's dichotomies here. The other writers present in this book should serve to nuance and critique these.

29. See Emile Témime. *Le rêve méditerranéen* and Thierry Fabre. *La France et la Méditerranée.*

TWO

Of Chronological Others and Alternative Histories

Amin Maalouf and Fawzi Mellah

Upon receiving the Nobel Prize for literature in 1957, Camus affirmed "le rôle de l'écrivain, du même coup, ne se sépare pas de devoirs difficiles. Par définition, il ne peut se mettre aujourd'hui au service de ceux qui font l'histoire: il est au service de ceux qui la subissent" (1958: 15). [The writer's function is not without its arduous duties. By definition, he cannot serve today those who make history; he must serve those who are subject to it.] If Camus set the stage for the elaboration of a discourse on Mediterranean humanism that was predominantly grounded in a metaphysical affinity for the earth and a critique of the misuse of reason, he was unable to express the formidable potential of those "subjects" of history he evokes in the "Discours de Stockholm" to rethink and rewrite alternate narratives of the Mediterranean. The turn to reason that led to the hubris so abhorred by Camus in the political personae of figures like Stalin or Franco might be understood differently if examined in another light, through the works of other thinkers. The appeal for rationality and knowledge prevalent in the novels, several decades later, of Amin Maalouf and Fawzi Mellah, underscores the necessity of unconventional and timely renderings of "known events." This chapter suggests that Maalouf and Mellah fashion what the historian Beverley Southgate calls "chronological others," a term he uses to describe the resurrection of historical models of the past as a way of understanding the world in the present.[1] Within these alternate narratives, and consonant with a Braudelian *histoire événementielle*, both authors privilege a deep interest in the individual, and both are careful observers of the human condition and of the way

people define themselves vis-à-vis their geographic and cultural positionings. Their protagonists question, accept, then reject and struggle with
fixed notions of time and space. How these authors conceive of selfhood
in the numerous contexts that they present and how, more importantly,
the individual fits into a larger historical paradigm points to a Mediterranean where cultural belonging transcends spatio-temporal boundaries
and metonymically reflects a global concern for the "progress" and future of history and humanity.

FROM THE LEVANT TO THE MAGHREB

This chapter primarily investigates Maalouf's works but also includes a
short discussion of Mellah's novels as evidence that Maalouf's concerns
are not unique to him. As the majority of Maalouf's seven novels reveal,
the course of Arab and Western history, Enlightenment ideals, and self-
conscious subjectivity are of primary importance, and define a vital Mediterranean ethos. His writing owes a great deal to his journalistic sensitivity to a twentieth-century world order and to his own life experiences;[2]
born into a culturally composite family—his mother was Egyptian of
Turkish origin, his father a Greek Catholic—in 1949 in Lebanon, he was,
from a very early age, exposed to multiple religions, languages, and cultural codes. Arabophone, Christian, and educated in a French Jesuit
school in Beirut, his historical and cultural points of reference are as
wide-ranging as they are revealing of the complexity of compound identities. Outside the family nucleus, Maalouf was confronted by the even
greater heterogeneity of Lebanon, his home until the beginning of the
civil war in 1975. The numerous waves of occupation and settlement
(Crusaders, Arabs, Mameluks, French) that have shaped Lebanon into a
pluralistic and often embattled nation have also been the cause of one of
the worst Middle Eastern civil wars.

The multiplicity of cultural and political influences in Lebanon—Phe-
nician, Egyptian, Mesopotamian, Greek, Roman, Arab, Muslim, Frankish,
Turkish, Armenian, and French—have come to bear on the way Maalouf
conceives of his identity. Moreover, he affirms that his experience of
identity formation is emblematic of how other Mediterranean popula-
tions conceive of theirs, given the centuries of cultural mixing. In several
interviews he explicitly speaks of a Mediterranean belonging and his
belief that it is "salutaire et même exemplaire" (Ancelovici 1997: 172)
[salutary and even exemplary]. Maalouf's assertion that there in fact exists something called a *Mediterranean* identity urges the question of what
it is that the Mediterranean exemplifies and for whom it is salutary. The
following observation is indeed symptomatic of the very vagueness of
the notion:

Je suis attaché au souvenir stimulant de l'Andalousie qui fut jadis le lieu de rencontre privilégié entre l'islam, le christianisme et le judaïsme. C'est d'ailleurs là, à Grenade, qu'est né Léon l'Africain, le héros de mon premier roman, et ce n'est évidemment pas un pur hasard . . . Toutes ces villes méditerrnaéennes . . . font partie de mon univers . . . Que des gens du Nord industrialisé comme du Sud, des gens d'Orient et d'Occident se reconnaissent une appartenance commune est une chose fort rare et fort précieuse dans le monde d'aujourd'hui. (Ancelovici 1997: 172)

[I am fond of the stimulating memory of Andalusia, the once privileged site where Islam, Christianity and Judaism came together. It is, in fact there, in Granada, that Leo Africanus, the hero of my first book, was born. And obviously not by chance. . . . All these Mediterranean cities . . . are part of my universe. . . . That people from the industrialized North, and from the South, people from East and the West recognize a common belonging is rare and extremely valuable in today's world.]

Beyond a sense of common belonging, what does the Mediterranean, ever-present in innumerable literary texts and which includes geopolitical, cultural, and historical notions of identity formation, enable? Rather than distinguishing a univocal Mediterranean, Maalouf admits that it is perhaps better to consider it in terms of a common *dimension*.[3] Yet the Mediterranean, much like the European Union, is an entity, affirms Maalouf, which has yet to be constructed.[4] This construction can only begin with the development of what he calls a "conscience méditerranéenne" (Vidal-Beneyto 2000: 55).

Amin Maalouf's oeuvre, as a whole, is both highly crafted in the most classic of novelistic fashions and at the same time carefully centered on real moments in history, or around individuals and places that once united peoples rather than divided them: *Léon l'Africain* (1986) begins in fifteenth-century Andalusia where Islam, Judaism, and Christianity had (for the most part) coexisted peacefully; *Le Jardin des lumières* (1991) highlights the religious syncretism preached by the prophet Mani in third-century Mesopotamia; *Le premier siècle après Béatrice* (1992) is a reflection on the future of humanity through the eyes of a humanist-scientist; *Le Rocher de Tanios* (1996) takes place in nineteenth-century Lebanon which at the time was of interest to the Ottoman Empire, Britain, and Egypt; and *Le Périple de Baldassare* (2000) is set in the Mediterranean in 1665 and 1666 when the Ottoman Empire was in danger of falling and the world was threatened with the fear of the Apocalypse. Although this is not an exhaustive list of Maalouf's texts, it indicates the constancy of historical settings as well as the prevalence and recurrence of the space of the Mediterranean.

CHAINS OF TRANSLATION

Maalouf repeatedly problematizes a tension between self and belonging, whether to a nation, to an ethnic community, or to a religion. He states:

> There is an extremely perverse vision of the notion of belonging. I think that for a very long time, and right up to today, it was thought that man had to belong to a culture, to a civilization, to a nation. And for me, it is the reverse: it is man who is the centre, and it is cultures which have to belong, and it is beliefs which have to belong, and man has the right, and the responsibility to be the meeting place of several cultures, of several religions . . . I support the fact that man is the centre, must be the meeting place, must be the only thing that counts. It is not man who must be at the service of ideology, it is ideology which must be at man's service. (Doray 1993: 72)

His rather uncharacteristic rigidity in this interview reveals a staunch commitment—and responsibility—to the notion of man as locus of several cultures and thus of plurality. He advocates a universal responsibility in everyone not to fall prey to seductive identitarian politics and thus to *choose*, judiciously, how one lives and practices one's religion, one's nation and one's affiliations. For man to be "the centre," as he states it, requires an ethic of perpetual openness and mobility, for cultures, ideologies, and nations are not stable, causing the centre (man) to shift and to redefine him/herself. An examination of Maalouf's conception of the self seems to be of primary importance, then; as he remarks, "La personne est plus importante que cette chose informe et potentiellement monstrueuse qu'on appelle collectivité et au nom de laquelle il y a eu bien des dérapages au cours de ce siècle" (Ancelovici 1997: 174). [The person is more important than this shapeless and potentially monstrous thing that we call community, in the name of which there have been quite a few mistakes during this century.] Maalouf endows his fictive protagonists with the agency necessary to resist herd mentalities and dangerous group dynamics.

Although each of Maalouf's novels privileges individual subjectivities over collective identifications, his 1986 novel *Léon l'Africain* most strikingly calls for a hermeneutics of selfhood. The following anecdote is based on a supposedly true story on which the novel is based: after navigating throughout the Mediterranean basin and across Africa for nearly forty years, Leo Africanus (Hassan Ibn Muhammed al-Wazzan ez-Zayyati), a sixteenth-century explorer, resolved to pause and to put into writing his observations of what he had found along the way; the work was entitled *Della Descrizione dell'Africa*.[5] Thought to have been written in Arabic around 1525 and then translated by Leo Africanus himself into imperfect Italian, the manuscript was, from its very inception, marked by multiple languages. It appears that in 1550, Giovanni Battista Ramusio, a Venetian publisher, translated and modified Leo Africanus's text substantially. Because the whereabouts and exact nature of the original manuscript remained a mystery, it was subsequently impossible to ascertain the degree to which Ramusio "improved" upon Leo Africanus's narrative. Presumed by many scholars to have been lost in a fire in 1557 or thrown into the Mediterranean Sea by pirates, the original manuscript appeared in 1931 at the Vatican library in Rome.[6]

The 1550 Ramusio edition, not the original (missing) manuscript by Leo Africanus himself, was translated into several languages, although it was not until after the middle of the twentieth century that scholars consulted Leo Africanus's manuscript and new translations were published. Access to the original manuscript was difficult for many years, and to this day disagreements over its content abound. What we can gather from this story, then, is that regardless of the version we choose to read, the original narrative written by Leo Africanus is, in part, unknown to us. The text that for almost half a millennium served as the original was already a translation. Thus, we are introduced to the processes of transformation, conversion, (in)fidelity, and reinvention explored in Amin Maalouf's 1986 novel *Léon l'Africain*. When, more than four hundred years later, this Lebanese writer of French expression undertook the writing of yet another version of the life of Leo Africanus, the question of translation was at the forefront of his endeavour.

Léon l'Africain is by no means a literal translation of any of the manuscripts mentioned above; rather, it is a fictional invention of the travels of Leo Africanus. At the center of this "imaginary autobiography,"[7] as Maalouf calls it, is the perpetual renegotiation of self; known first as Hassan Ibn Mohammed al-Wazzan, then as Jean-Léon de Medicis, Yohannes Léon, Yuhanna al-Asad, and finally Léon l'Africain, the protagonist is exiled from Granada during the Spanish *Reconquista* and spends forty years in transit between Fes, Timbuktu, Cairo, and Rome. The novel is structured along a historically and temporally specific double axis. Each chapter is set within a time frame marked by both the lunar and solar calendars beginning in 1488 (894h) and ending in 1527 (933h); East and West are brought together in time and stand side-by-side on a parallel course. In keeping within this chronological specificity Maalouf also remains faithful to both Eastern and Western geography, place names and historical figures such as Boabdil, the last Moorish ruler of Andalusia, and Pope Leo X, among the many others who populate the narrative. Because this text is grounded in historical events—running from the fall of Granada (1492) to the Sack of Rome (1527)—we become acutely aware of the tension between real and imaginary, and history and fiction. Through the juxtaposition of an imaginary autobiography with historically accurate events, *Léon l'Africain* announces the subjective construction both of personal narratives and of the writing of history itself.

TRANSLATING THE SELF

The question of translation is ubiquitous in *Léon l'Africain*: the protagonist Hassan (later Léon) continually transcends his own individual self through the various mediating positions he occupies. He fulfills the roles of ambassador, interpreter, mediator and diplomat, repeatedly acting as an agent of transmission and as the bearer of someone else's words. In these respective functions he is presumed to be a mere conduit of information, much like an "ideal" translator: that is, virtually invisible. Assigned the role of ambassador by a corsair, Hassan is instructed to present a poem to Sultan Salim in Constantinople in an attempt to flatter the monarch. Dressed appropriately in order to blend in, he begins his recitation and remarks, "Je n'étais plus qu'un automate, mais un automate qui fonctionnait, par des gestes précis que le sultan impassible semblait me dicter . . . La discussion pouvait commencer, dans une autre salle, avec les conseillers. J'y participais à peine. Mon rôle était de représenter, nullement de négocier . . ." (Maalouf 1986: 257). [I was no more than an automaton, but an automaton which was functioning with precise movements which seemed to be dictated by the impassive sultan. The discussion could now take place, in another room, with the counselors. I hardly took part. My role was to represent, not to negotiate . . .]. By representing someone other than himself, Hassan/Léon moves outside himself and promises to be "faithful" to his duties. This happens repeatedly: on four different occasions he is referred to as a mediator, four more times as (linguistic) translator or interpreter, and towards the end of his travels, as a diplomat. Exiled from Granada, he begins his journey as "fils de la route . . . et ma vie la plus inattendue des traversées" (1986: 11) [son of the road . . . and of the most unexpected of voyages], initially towards Fes but ultimately wherever chance takes him.

With this novel Maalouf mobilizes the concept of a necessary translation of self or what I prefer to call *transipseity*. By this I mean the ability to move beyond and across (*trans*) one's personal uniqueness and singularity (*ipseity*). If, as Paul Ricoeur maintains, our identities are indeed split into what he calls *ipse*-identity and *idem*-identity, both subtend transipseity. According to Ricoeur's analysis, *idem* refers to constant sameness, such as a proper name, or one's character, whereas *ipse* reflects the way in which we change over time. Narrative identity, he continues, bridges the two, both of which are constantly challenged, I suggest, through transipseity.[8] It is the absence of transipseity, Maalouf seems to announce, which explains, in part, devastating identitarian conflicts in and around the Mediterranean. In his essay "Les identités meurtrières" he writes:

> Si nos contemporains ne sont pas encouragés à assumer leurs appartenances multiples, s'ils ne peuvent concilier leur besoin d'identité avec une ouverture franche et décomplexée aux cultures différentes, s'ils se

sentent contraints de choisir entre la négation de soi-même et la négation de l'autre, nous serons en train de former des légions de fous
sanguinaires, des légions d'égarés. (1998: 44)

[If our contemporaries are not encouraged to accept their multiple affiliations and allegiances; if they cannot reconcile their need for identity
with an open and unprejudiced tolerance of other cultures; if they feel
they have to choose between denial of the self and denial of the other —
then we shall be bringing into being legions of the lost and hordes of
bloodthirsty madmen.]

Maalouf's somewhat self-evident exhortation of openness and alterity
translates into an ethics of transipseity in his novel. Translation, which
assumes the mediation of two or more dissimilar entities, must find its
place between the folds of the *ipse* and the *idem* through a constant consciousness of its necessity. In *Léon l'Africain* this continuous conversion
follows the contours of the geographical map of the Mediterranean,
through which the protagonist moves through, onto a mental map, it too
incessantly redrawn and rethought.

Hassan's first mission as translator comes when, at the age of seven-
teen, he is thrown off course on his way to Timbuktu. Happening upon
the city of Ouarzazate, he acts on behalf of his uncle, who is himself an
ambassador for the Sultan of Fes. Upon hearing that the latter is in the
environs, an unknown landowner requests a meeting with him. "Pour
bien montrer en quelle estime il tenait ce seigneur—dont il m'avoua plus
tard qu'il n'avait jamais entendu parler auparavant—il enverrait son ne-
veu lui baiser la main. Je me voyais donc subitement investi d'une am-
bassade" (1986: 162). [To show in what esteem he held this lord—of
whom as he told me later, he had never heard spoken before—he would
send his nephew to kiss his hand. Hence I suddenly found myself en-
trusted with an embassy.] The mission is so successful that the landowner bequeaths him a slave girl with whom he instantly falls in love. An
ambassador once-removed, Hassan carries out a mission in which he has
no vested interest, yet from which his personal growth benefits significantly. He is propelled into translation, commissioned to be "a copy" of
his uncle, to represent him, and thus pushed outside of himself, but unexpectedly perceptive of a potentiality within himself.

In conjunction with going beyond himself in the sense of representing
or translating *for* someone else, Hassan also goes through transversal
changes, moving *across* himself. I take "across" to mean going from one
position to another, in this case within oneself. This movement can go
back and forth and is meant to be understood as a dynamic changing of
positions. In the most salient example, Hassan is captured by Sicilian
pirates on his way to Tunis and finds himself imprisoned in Rome. He is
offered as a slave to Pope Leo X, who, impressed with Hassan's erudition, treats him with great respect, frees him and eventually baptizes him

as a Christian. During the baptism, Pope Leo X also bestows his own name upon the new convert—Jean-Léon de Médicis—a gesture meant to symbolize his full integration into the Christian world. Hassan, now Léon—or rather now called Léon l'Africain in order to distinguish him from Pope Leo—accepts his new religion as a sign of his loyalty to the Pope. Léon l'Africain lives his Christianity, fully debating the merits and weaknesses of the doctrine through lengthy conversations with Hans, a Lutheran and fellow traveler. Yet, despite his conversion to Christianity, Léon never ceases to be a Muslim. "J'avais trouvé dans la Rome chrétienne le calife à l'ombre duquel j'aurais tant voulu vivre à Baghdad ou à Cordoue. Mon esprit se complaisait dans ce paradoxe" (1986: 307). [I had found in Christian Rome the caliph under whose shadow I would so much have liked to live in Baghdad or Cordova. My mind delighted in this paradox.] As contradictory as this may seem, Maalouf points to a non-dogmatic form of religious belief where one must be open to multiple forms of believing and multiple translations of self. In his essay *Les identités meurtrières*, it is precisely exclusionary belief and strict doctrine that he cautions against. In fact, when Christianity becomes dogmatic in Rome (under Pope Adrian), Léon remarks, "J'avais appris à me méfier des évidences. Lorsque tout le monde s'agglutine autour d'une même opinion, je m'enfuis: la vérité est sûrement ailleurs" (1986: 337). [I had come to be distrustful of appearances. When everyone persists in the same opinion, I turn away from it; the truth is surely elsewhere.] His "fuite" then suggests a desire to live his transipseity to its fullest.

BECOMING-OTHER

Pushed by his insatiable desire for knowledge, the "ailleurs" referred to above, Léon moves between perpetual deterritorialization and reterritorialization as he goes from city to city.[9] "Entre l'Andalousie que j'ai quittée et le Paradis qui m'est promis, la vie n'est qu'une traversée. Je ne vais nulle part, je ne convoite rien, je ne m'accroche à rien, je fais confiance à ma passion de vivre" (1986: 258). [Between the Andalus which I left and the Paradise which is promised to me life is only a crossing. I go nowhere, I desire nothing, I cling to nothing, I have faith in my passion for living.] With each new encounter and awareness of a previously undiscovered part of himself, he becomes a combination of different assemblages—for example, "un Maghrébin, habillé à l'égyptienne, marié à une Circassienne, veuve d'un émir ottoman, et qui ornait sa maison à la manière d'un chrétien!" (1986: 261) [a Maghribi, dressed in the Egyptian style, married to a Circassian woman, the widow of an Ottoman amir, and who decorated his house like a Christian!]—and lives in a state of perpetual *becoming*. The concept of *becoming* implies coming into contact with otherness—not necessarily human—in the construction of self and is defined by a number of conditions that challenge, and require reconsideration of, regularized spaces of identification. *Becoming*-something is to combine heterogeneous elements; it implies "two simultaneous movements, one by which a term (the subject) is withdrawn from the majority, and another by which a term (the medium or agent) rises up from the minority" (Deleuze and Guattari 1988: 291). It is to be transformed with each new assemblage; it is both going beyond and across the self, where the self is to be understood as a mobile construct and not as a fixed entity. In order to become anything one must first become minoritarian by placing oneself outside of the majority through the constant discovery of a part of oneself that one was not previously aware of and through the creative expression of that discovery. Minoritarian implies that there is no standard or norm for the object or person in question.[10]

Maalouf constantly places Léon in positions of divergence where the latter subverts majoritarian models, that is to say, established dominant paradigms of cultural and political identification, the *status quo*. In this sense, even the experience of exile becomes not (only) a damaging experience but a constructive one.[11] Léon's exile is initially imposed when his family, like all Muslims, is expelled from Granada but is subsequently, with each new move (*déplacement*), driven by choice. As Deleuze and Guattari observe, "You don't deviate from the majority unless there is a little detail that starts to swell and carries you off" (1988: 292). Léon is carried off by details as small as a noise—"les bruits du lointain m'appellait, il était écrit que je ne resterai pas sourd à leurs tentations" (1986: 271) [noises from afar were calling me, and it was written that I should not remain deaf to their temptations]—and as considerable as religious conversion or, as is Léon's case, loyalty to both Islam and Christianity.

Becoming-minoritarian also means moving outside of the linear narrative that one tells oneself in order to make sense of one's identity. This narrative prevents one from confronting one's own potentialities and becomings, which reach beyond any religious, national, or ethnic belonging; they are moments and events that reveal to us something about ourselves. Thus, for Léon (who is Muslim), becoming-Christian does not manifest itself as a form of imitation, nor is it necessarily an identification with the Church, but rather a lived moment that brings him to an awareness of his self as contingent and itinerant—he is a "fils de la route" [son of the road], his "patrie est caravane" [his country a caravan], and his life "la plus inattendue des traversées" [the most unexpected of voyages]. Although Léon is Muslim and remains so throughout the text, he discovers that this is simply one aspect of his identity and that it, too, is subject to change. Deleuze and Guattari's philosophy of *becoming* culminates in what they call becoming-imperceptible; the moment when the subject becomes imperceptible because it has fused with (an)other(s), with the cosmos, to form something that was previously unrecognizable. At this stage the dialectical opposition between self and other or man and woman, for example, is effaced. Our stereotypical paradigms of what it means to be Muslim or Christian are undone and our expectations of certain norms destabilized.[12] As Léon continues his travels, acquiring knowledge as he goes, he recognizes that places change over time, that the *longue durée* is not static either: "De ma longue retraite paysanne, pourtant émaillée de contemplations et de promenades silencieuses, j'ai émergé sans certitudes. Périssables toutes les cités; carnassiers, tous les empires; insondable, la Providence. Seules me réconfortaient la crue du Nil, la ronde des astres et les naissances saisonnières des bufflons" (1986: 271). [I emerged with no certainties from my long rural retreat, studded with contemplations and silent walks. All cities were perishable; all empires devouring, Providence unfathomable. The only things which comforted me were the Nile flood, the movement of the stars, and the seasonal births of the buffaloes.] The notion of becoming is ultimately a notion of freedom, for what is privileged is no longer a fixed hierarchical structuring of one's identity but rather an earthly relation to the world where we know that we are more than simply that of which we are aware.[13]

Indeed Léon's ability to attempt to "translate" himself is due largely to his aptitude in recognizing that there is more to him than he will ever know; he is impassive without being insensitive or indifferent. Through this sense of the existence of a hidden self, which is not contingent upon anything other than the constancy of one's character, he is able to take risks and travel an uncharted path. Thus, through the choices he makes (converting, for example) and the uncontingent events that occur, Léon ends his "autobiography" with the following words which he imparts to his son: "Une fois de plus je suis porté par cette mer, témoin de tous mes errements . . . n'hésite jamais à t'éloigner, au-delà de toutes les mers, au-delà de toutes les frontières, de toutes les patries, de toutes les croyances" (1986: 348). [Once more I am borne along by the sea, the witness of all my wanderings . . . never hesitate to go far away, beyond all seas, all frontiers, all countries, all beliefs.] Regardless of the many communities to which he has belonged throughout his forty-year peregrination, these identifications are not enough to entirely define who he is. He wore the clothes of a Fassi in Fes, changed into those of an Egyptian in Egypt—when in Rome he did as the Romans—but, he says, "Le sort est plus changeant que la peau d'un caméléon, comme disait un poète de Denia" (1986: 65). [Destiny is more changeable than the skin of a chameleon.] Despite the "clothes we wear," the allegiances we ostensibly form, there is an unknown "I" which, Maalouf seems to imply through his text, one must strive to understand in order to "know-oneself." This can only happen through self-translation, Hassan/Léon's perpetual journey.

The temporal organization of the narrative further reflects the aporias that haunt a self-translating identity. The chapters are divided into forty linear segments entitled "l'année de Fortune, l'année de la chute, etc. . . ."

If this construction gives us a long and theoretically linear view of time, it is contrasted with the temporal disposition of Léon's introspective narration, which consists of flashbacks and discontinued time. Maalouf chooses to present Léon's identity *not* as linear but as composed of disjointed events and moments demonstrating that despite the linear temporal narratives one creates to explain oneself (I was born in Granada, was a rebellious teenager, and am now a father of four), they are inadequate. This may appear contradictory given the linearity of the novel, which moves from Léon's childhood to his maturity, but it in fact points to Maalouf's singular conception of how we attempt to make sense of our identities. One can go beyond and across oneself, and one *must* take risks in order to attain knowledge of self, suggests Maalouf, but this at times remains impossible, especially if one confuses one's singularity with (national, ethnic, sexual, etc.) belonging. It is only through the understanding that he is not simply from Granada, or not simply Muslim nor even a combination of all his belongings, that Léon l'Africain is able to negotiate the identitarian detours through which his travels take him.

Transipseity, like translation, is an infinite process—that is, if we understand (linguistic) translation in a Derridean sense as being an open system of the infinite deferment of signifiers. Translation of self comprises a constant recognition of otherness, whether it is the other within oneself, or another individual, but it is first and foremost through language that one enters into such a dialectic. In Maalouf's novel, Léon is commissioned to write a multilingual dictionary (including Latin, Arabic, Hebrew, Greek, and others). We might imagine Léon's response to be similar to the Saxon printer, also involved in its creation: "Je suis prêt néanmoins à lui consacrer mon existence et mon argent. Faire en sorte que tous les hommes du monde puissent un jour se comprendre, n'est-ce pas le plus noble des idéaux? A ce rêve grandiose, à cette merveilleuse *folie*, l'imprimeur saxon avait donné un nom: *l'Anti-Babel*" (1986: 321; my emphasis). [Nevertheless I am ready to devote my life and my money to it. To strive so that all men may one day be able to understand each other, is that not the noblest of ideals? To this grandiose dream, this marvellous folly, the Saxon printer had given the name *Anti-Babel*.] Understanding between human beings is equated to a "mad dream" and yet, Maalouf implies, we must not stop trying to translate ourselves in order to better connect to others. If Babel represents the site of one pure monolithic (mythical) language, *l'anti-Babel* points to the multiplicity and infinite translation to which we are destined. The necessary impossibility of dialogue, reminding us once again of Derrida's notion of translation in "Des Tours de Babel" as being both necessary and impossible, brings us back to the question of the *worldliness* of Maalouf's texts, its context.

Why has Amin Maalouf, a much translated and widely read contemporary author, chosen to set his text in the Mediterranean of the fifteenth and sixteenth centuries and to speak through Léon l'Africain? By beginning his novel in the fifteenth century during the Golden Age of Andalusia, he may have been pointing to that crucial moment in history that changed the way people saw themselves not only individually but collectively. In *Community of Citizens*, Dominique Schnapper writes:

> The national idea was progressively born in England and France as a result of the Hundred Year War which pitted them against one another and in Spain with the Catholic *Reconquista* of the Iberian peninsula at the end of the 15th century of which the expulsion of Jews and Muslims in 1492 was at the same time the instrument as well as the symbol. (1986: 132)

This *Léon l'Africain* must be read at the crossroads of two main ideas; on the one hand it is not representative nor imitative of "the world as it was" but rather, drawing on Deleuze's conception of literature as the manifestation and creation of what is not yet, what is virtual: "Writing is a question of becoming, always incomplete, always in the midst of being formed, and goes beyond the matter of any livable or lived experience" (1997: 1). On the other hand, given the concrete historical framework and the issues of ideological and identitarian conflicts it raises, *Léon l'Africain* is clearly driven by contemporary urgent ethical and political concerns. One might say that it is wishfully prophetic as well as historically revisionary. We should thus keep in mind what Edward Saïd would call the *worldliness* of the text; it interacts with the world through its cultural and social history, its political and economic being, its connections to other texts and because it is driven by both political and aesthetic concerns.[14] It also, like most autobiographies, imaginary and not, directly interpellates the reader, the "you" summoned by the "I" of the narrator. Such a strategy underscores the affective dimension of the text in favor of a (hi)story driven less by events and heroes than by affects and percepts. It highlights the at times very slippery interface between history and fiction.

By fictionalizing the story of Leo Africanus, Maalouf is clearly aiming for something beyond a "faithful" representation of life in the Mediterranean basin during the Renaissance.[15] What conclusions can be drawn? As noted previously, Maalouf strongly urges questioning the meaning of belonging, whether to a nation, a territory, a community, a family, or a group of people but, more importantly, he lays bare how such affiliations have a resounding impact on selfhood. He seems to issue a warning against the repetition of nefarious histories. Yet his aim does not appear to be prescriptive or pedagogical, for despite its sixteenth-century setting, his novel is a showcase of both what individuals in history are capable of and possibilities of a world yet-to-come. At a time when East-West, North-South relations are ever more polarized, Maalouf creates a character who awakens in his readers an ethical responsibility to reject dogmatic thinking and to understand that we are more than the sum of our belongings or most obvious, inherited identities. Given the current socioeconomic disparity in and around the Mediterranean, Maalouf's novel for now might only be seen as a prophecy not-yet-realized and as an appeal to a twenty-first-century Renaissance.[16] Southgate maintains:

> Whatever past we choose for resurrection, and for whatever motives, history's particularly important function now, in relation to our personal and public selves, derives from its ability to provide that "other," without which self-definition seems not possible. As we lose those *geographical* and racial "others" of whom we previously made use (those alien "foreigners" across the Channel or the ocean, those slaves and primitive "colonials," by whom we measured our own superiority), we may need now to seek *chronological* "others"—others in the past, other past people and values, in contrast with whom and with which we can continue to define ourselves. And in that case, we need history to provide us with models, not so much to emulate as to repudiate—models in *contrast* with which we can see what we are and should be. That is one way history can still enable humanity to know itself and make itself. (2005: 120, emphasis in original)[17]

Southgate's emphasis on "chronological others" as an instrument of modern-day self-definition brings out a fundamental aspect of *Léon l'Africain*; that is, that history does not necessarily reveal the *roots* of identity but exposes its discontinuous potentialities.

Like Braudel's pioneering work on the Mediterranean, Maalouf's novels display a sharp awareness of the polyrhythmic and non-linear nature of history; most of his texts are set in Mediterranean landscapes (the sea, port cities) that appear timeless and unchanging (that Braudel would characterize as history of the *longue durée*), many of his principal characters are travelers and merchants (*conjoncture*), and crucial events in history (*histoire événementielle*) frame almost all of his novels. Along with other historians who belonged to the school known as *Les Annales*, Braudel saw history "comme plus que l'assise d'une science des progrès de l'humanité" (Bourdé 1983; 173) [as more than the foundation of a science of the progress of humanity]. History is not necessarily progress, according to the *Annalistes*, and it must take into account elements that affect its course and that are not always predictable. In *The Mediterreanean and the Mediterranean World in the Age of Philip II*, Braudel proposes a history that is divided into various planes of historical, social and geographical time, an approach that he affirms goes along with dividing men "into a multitude of selves" (1972: 21). It is this meeting of multiple selves, and a complex understanding of history, that is so skillfully portrayed in Maalouf's works. History, according to Maalouf, is not on a straight path toward its accomplishment, and yet it is commonly perceived as just that, constituted by a beginning source, a middle and an end: "On s'obstine à regarder l'Histoire comme un fleuve qui coule en paysage plat, s'affole en terrain accidenté, connaît quelques cascades. Et si son lit n'était pas creusé à l'avance? Et si, incapable d'atteindre la mer, il se perdait dans le désert, égaré en un puzzle de marécages stagnants?" (1992: 270) [People insist on regarding History as a river flowing peaceably through flat countryside, racing wildly in hilly terrain, and here and there tumbling over a waterfall. And what if its bed is not hollowed out in advance?] The author asks rhetorically what might happen if like a river gone off course, failing to reach the sea, history never reached its "charted" destination? For history to "lose itself," as Maalouf writes, is tantamount to it going off course or becoming fossilized.

The course of history is the focal point of *Le périple de Baldassare*. Written in 1999 and published in 2000, this work poses a crucial question: what happens if we reach the end of history? Although the question is not posed in a specifically political or economic context, it echoes and contests a post–Cold War mentality driven by theories such as those propounded by Francis Fukuyama in *The End of History and the Last Man*. For Fukuyama, liberal democracy is the last stage in the history of the Western world. Ideological struggles have ended in the best of possible ways for the ideology of "West" has prevailed over the "East." Fascism and Communism are of the past, and world peace is on the horizon. Following Hegel and Kojève, Fukuyama's teleological view of history suggested not so much that history would come to an abrupt halt, or that there would be no more "grand events," but that there would no longer be a problem as to how to interpret those events, since the best possible system had been reached. In short, doubt would dissipate and complacent certainty would prevail. The "last man," as he writes, would be the epitome of all men, his intrinsic desire for recognition will level off in this new world (what, one wonders, does Fukuyama mean by *intrinsic* desire for recognition?). For the "last man" "has been jaded by the experience of history, and disabused of the possibility of direct experience of values" (1992: 306). Amin Maalouf's "last man," the protagonist of *Le périple de Baldassare*, leads us to an alternative understanding of the "end of history."

The novel takes place in 1665, the eve of the year of the beast (1666), which had been announced as the supposed end of the world. Christians, Jews, and Muslims alike have found in their holy texts signs of imminent catastrophe.[18] Baldassare Embriaco, the protagonist of the novel and "last man" in a world coming to an end, spends the year traveling throughout the Mediterranean in search of a rare—if it indeed exists—book. For it is this object alone that will supposedly protect whoever finds it from calamity and halt the impending apocalypse.[19] The book, Abou-Maher al-Mazandarani's *Centième nom*, apparently contains Allah's hundredth name and, with it, the antidote to disaster.[20] Baldassare, a shop-owner and merchant from Gibelet (present day Byblos/Jbeil), like "les négociants les plus sérieux, ainsi que les lettrés" (2000: 17) [serious merchants and scholars], is uncertain whether this book exists, as no one has ever claimed to have read it, and he remains doubly unconvinced of its supernatural powers. The few times he thinks he has come into possession of "ce livre étrange qui apparaît, puis disparaît" (2000: 11) [that strange book, appearing then disappearing], he is suddenly unable to read it, either because his vision becomes blurry or because it is confiscated. Throughout the entire year of his quest, he is riddled with doubt and hesitation, torn between reason and superstition, between believing that the world will come to an end and judging that it probably will not: "Dans le combat qui oppose en moi la raison à la déraison, cette dernière a marqué des points. La raison proteste, ricane, s'entête, résiste . . . [mais] la déraison me gagne" (2000: 20). [In the struggle that goes on inside me between reason and unreason, the latter has won some points. Reason protests, mocks, insists, resists . . . but unreason is gaining ground on me.] Baldassare struggles against his lack of rationality or judiciousness, as well as against his highly superstitious nephew Boumeh, with whom he is traveling, and who "chaque jour découvre dans une nouvelle source, latine, grecque ou arabe, confirmation de ses prévisions" (2000: 22). [Every day he finds some new confirmation of his predictions in Latin, Greek or Arabic sources.] From Aleppo to Constantinople, Smyrna, Chios, Genoa, Tangier, and further, Baldassare becomes a metonymy for the Mediterranean, which is in a state of mass hysteria, and increasingly divided between those who believe the end to be near and those who do not.

AN AGE OF REASON?

Despite his proclaimed Christianity, Baldassare is not driven by a religious belief in the Apocalypse[21]; "Je pose aujourd'hui sur tout ce qui prie et s'agenouille et se prosterne le même regard que mon père, désabusé, distant, ni respectueux ni méprisant, quelquefois intrigué, mais libre de toute certitude. Et j'aime à croire que le Créateur préfère, de toutes ses créatures, justement celles qui ont su devenir libres" (2000: 178). [I now take the same view as my father of all praying and kneeling and prostration—a view that's skeptical, distant, neither respectful nor contemptuous, sometimes intrigued, but always free of any certainty. And I like to think that out of all his creatures the ones the Creator likes best are those who have managed to be free.] He is a son of the Enlightenment *avant la lettre*, for it is through his reason, he wants to believe, that the world can be understood and controlled. His fear of the end of the world comes not from a belief that such a prediction is written in the Bible but from the necessity to question and not to blindly accept what to many appears a certainty. Baldassare attempts to free himself from the panic and hysteria that surround him through a dialectical process, by discussing—by *reasoning*—the possibility of the end of the world with his many interlocutors around the Mediterranean. In Smyrna he compares his ideas with those of a Jewish skeptic; soon after he meets a Russian pilgrim, a Dutch pastor, and a Muslim cleric, all of whom have a theory about the end of the world. Freedom and salvation from calamity do not appear to rest on religious faith; they must be attained through reason. In Maarra, Baldassare comes across a book that he refers to as "le moins déraisonnable de mes compagnons" (2000: 63) [the least unreasonable of my travelling companions]. In it he reads a poem by the Syrian poet Abu-l-Ala[22]:

> Les gens voudraient qu'un imam se lève
> Et prenne la parole devant une foule muette
> Illusion trompeuse; il n'y a pas d'autre imam que la raison
> Elle seule nous guide de jour comme de nuit. (Maalouf 2000; 100)

> [The people want an Imam to arise
> And speak to a silent crowd
> An illusion; there is no imam but reason
> It alone guides us day and night.]

Citing this poem, which draws an unequivocal (and simplistic) opposition between religion and reason, Maalouf reasserts the importance of affirming one's voice. Through this poem he underscores the image of the "crowd," or the common person, as misguided and in need of guidance. It is reason, not the Imam, which will serve as that guide, the poem concludes.

Yet reason, as we saw through the works of Albert Camus in chapter 1, if pushed to its limits, can potentially turn into dogmatism, underscoring the slippery line between it and *un*reason. Baldassare is in no way doctrinaire about his beliefs, regardless of how *reasonable* he tries to be. On the contrary, in his fear and trepidation, the very sentiments that fuel his quest for Mazandarani's book and thus his yearlong journey, he is afflicted with doubt. Fear of the end of the world inevitably evokes a fear of one's own mortality and, consequently, a *mise en question* of existence itself. For Baldassare to doubt that the end of the world is truly at hand, then, suggests an affirmation of existence, for a passive acceptance and certainty of fate might indicate a state of existential paralysis. To doubt is also to be certain of one's being. For Descartes, who wrote his *Meditations* not long before the period of time in which *Le périple de Baldassare* takes place, doubt was a fundamental step towards ontological certainty and knowledge.

However, if for Descartes doubting denoted thinking and thinking denoted existing, doubt in itself could not be its own subject; doubt could not be doubted, for to doubt one's doubt means to doubt one's existence. This, however, is impossible because the fact that one doubts proves that one exists.[23] Baldassare's pervasive doubt, then, as he says things like "moi qui doute de tout, comment pourrais-je ne pas douter également de mes doutes?" (2000: 37) [How can I, who doubt everything, not doubt my own doubts?] points only in part to a Cartesian modus operandi. His dialectical reasoning all throughout the text teaches him to always make of himself a man who questions. Questioning the end of the world, in Baldassare's case, translates into a reflection on the tenuousness of history itself and on the excesses that have, in fact, marked and determined the world. "On ne comprend rien à la marche du monde si l'on s'imagine que les hommes agissent toujours avec sagesse. La déraison est le principe mâle de l'Histoire" (2000: 214). [If you think men always act sensibly it shows you have no idea how the world wags. Irrationality is the creative principle of History.] Maalouf, who wrote the novel in 1999, draws an implicit parallel between the seventeenth-century fear of the end of the world and a twenty-first-century worldwide instability, where doubt appears to be a common characteristic. The sociologist Anthony Giddens maintains that "doubt . . . permeates into everyday life as well as philosophical consciousness, and forms a general existential dimension of the contemporary social world" (1992: 3). The existential malaise that is pervasive in the latter half of the twenty-first century can be read as the symptom of an accelerated push to access various spheres of power. Through Baldassare, Maalouf urges a reconsideration of modern rationalism, stressing the tension between acquiring "sagesse," or knowledge, and misusing the power that comes with it.

In *An 1000, an 2000: Sur les traces de nos peurs*, the *Annales* historian Georges Duby sets up an analogy between the two millennia, reminding us that whereas history was once understood as the making of God, oriented in a certain direction and controlled, today it is, in large part, driven by economics and politics rather than religion.[24] After the Apocalypse, the Book of Revelation reads "evil" will descend upon the earth. Maalouf's *Périple de Baldassare* presents us with an altered history, one not fashioned strictly by God but where religion still dictates the storyline, and where unreason *has* unleashed "evil" on the world; in 1665 it is incarnated in a false Messiah, Sabbatai Zevi, who had a large following and who attempted to overthrow the Ottoman Empire. In 2000, when the book was published, this mirrors the myriad forms of hegemony and inequality in and around the Mediterranean. Yet a critique of religious fundamentalism specifically remains central to Maalouf's conception of history and identity. Numerous characters in his novels (Mani, Léon, Omar, for instance) practice singular forms of religious belief and ask themselves whether history can be solely determined by God. Maalouf places the Mediterranean at the forefront of his work, and in its own uncertain status of having yet to be constructed, symbolizes the ambiguity that surrounds the writing and interpretation of history.

Such ambiguity, as many modern historians have shown, arises from the subjective interpretations inherent in any narration of events. Maalouf creates a protagonist who records the events he witnesses in a dated journal, the most subjective and personal written form: "Je ne sais pas encore de quelle manière je vais rendre compte des événements qui se

sont produits, ni de ceux qui déjà s'annoncent. Un simple récit des faits?
Un journal intime? Un carnet de route? Un testament?" (2000: 12) [I don't
know yet how I'll record the things that have happened, or those that
already loom ahead. Just a simple account of the facts? A journal? A log?
A will?] Baldassare's journal, and thus Maalouf's text, which contains a
number of references to historical events such as the Portuguese renunci-
ation of the city of Tangier or the great fire of London, points to the
possibility of different versions of what we tend to think of as one linear
(hi)story. In "Les identités meurtrières," he writes "Aujourd'hui on sait
que l'Histoire ne suit jamais le chemin qu'on lui trace . . . l'Histoire
avance à chaque instant sur une infinité de chemins" (2000: 113). [Nowa-
days we know that History never follows the path that we trace for it . . .
History moves forward, at every moment, along an infinite number of
paths.] The novel suggests that many versions of what happened in 1665
have not been told, and that the representation of "events" may be selective, invented, or ambiguous.

Maalouf draws our attention to the chiasmic notion that history may
be an invention and that historians may resemble novelists but, more
importantly for us here, novelists may also be historians. This, of course,
is not a new idea, as the postmodernist theorist Hayden White writes:

> It is sometimes said that the aim of the historian is to explain the past
> by finding, identifying or uncovering the stories that lie buried in
> chronicles; and that the difference between history and fiction resides
> in the fact that the historian finds his stories, whereas the fiction writer
> invents his. This conception of the historian's task, however, obscures
> the extent to which invention also plays a part in the historian's opera-
> tions. The same event can serve as a different kind of element of many
> different historical stories, depending on the role it is assigned in a
> specific motific characterization of the set to which it belongs. (1973: 6)

The deliberate integration of fact and fiction, which Linda Hutcheon has
called historiographic metafiction, undoes conventional notions of causa-
tion and allows us to imagine alternative histories. We are presented with
what could have happened, and thus, as Southgate maintains, with
counterfactual images which "bring together all the *possibilities* of the past
and so 'represent' all the *opportunities* of the future; for knowing what
was *not* we shall know what *demands to be*. After all, it's precisely because
we are not aware of such alternative possibilities that 'history repeats
itself'" (2005: 115; emphasis in original).[25] Maalouf's choices (of what
period of history to set his novels in, what figures to include) are inevitably driven by ideological imperatives and so, as readers, we are required
to be alert to their significance. This is not to say that only works of
historical fiction provoke such awareness, but such texts do prioritize
such an imperative. Not only can such fictions play a fundamental role in
the reconsideration of histories, they also provide the possibility of pow-

erful personal transformation; as Hutcheon puts it, "to change the way one reads or perceives may be the first step to changing the way one thinks and acts" (1998: 36). Re-reading history is, thus, a way out of personal and historical catalepsy, as the possibilities for change expand and unfold.

MAALOUF'S TRANSCULTURAL HEROES

Through his journeys and journals, Baldassare brings us to reflect on itinerant subjects and itinerant histories, ones that, if read through the lens of a contemporary Mediterranean, can be characterized as transcultural. Itinerant subjects in pursuit of (self)-knowledge constitute the core of Maalouf's oeuvre; as witnesses of war, of nature's wrath, of shipwrecks, and of the most trying circumstances, these "heroes" are constantly driven to relocate, remaining perpetually in motion. Baldassare and Hassan/Léon cross multiple borders and territories, each time redefining themselves as well as the places and people they encounter. Although it may appear anachronistic to speak of national borders in relation to novels that are set in the sixteenth and seventeenth centuries, Maalouf, in the year 2000, emphasizes and problematizes those same elements that are habitually considered constitutive of national and cultural identity; namely, language, religion, and geography.

From Renan to Gellner to Schnapper and others, it has repeatedly been suggested that language plays a predominant role in the unification of a nation; a nation is, in theory, composed of people who share a common language. In Baldassare's world language is unstable[26]; it is not stable in the religious texts that he encounters, nor is it a stable communicative vector between human beings. During one of his encounters with a Persian prince he discusses the possibility of multiple interpretations of the Koran. "D'après 'le prince,' l'argument de Mazandarani pourrait se résumer comme suit: si le verset en question a pu être compris de deux manières différentes, c'est que Dieu—qui est, pour les musulmans, l'auteur même du Coran—a voulu cette ambiguïté" (2000: 356). [According to "the prince," Mazandarani's argument, in brief, was that if it has been possible for the verse in question to be understood in two different ways, that is because God—who for Muslims is the author of the Koran—intended the ambiguity.] The instability and ambiguity that surrounds such interpretation is not, according to Baldassare, necessarily detrimental, but potentially constructive and creative. In fact, he creates a singular idiom of his own: "L'officier écouta mes explications, d'autant plus alambiquées que je les exprimais dans un mélange de mauvais grec et de mauvais turc, avec ça et là quelques mots d'italien et d'arabe" (2000: 279). [The officer listened to my explanations, which were all the more convoluted for being expressed in a mixture of bad Greek and bad Turkish, with a few words of Italian and Arabic thrown in.] This is not simply a mixture of different languages but a deliberate ethical stance that implies a necessary process of translation, both conceptual and linguistic. Towards the end of the novel he reflects on his journal, "j'écris dans ma langue, mais en lettres arabes, et avec le code qui m'est propre, ce qui fait bien des transactions avant que chaque mot ne soit consigné" (2000: 415) [I write in my own language, Italian, but in Arabic characters and in my own special code, and that means going through several stages before setting down every word.] Baldassare's mixing of linguistic codes reveals an awareness of the insufficiency of *one* language, of one "pure" idiom that is meant to represent him. Instead, he very much insists on the fact that he is a "Genois d'Orient,"[27] a Genoese Levantine, and thus defined by multiple languages and mixed heritages. About one of his ancestors he exclaims: "Genois, il voulait bien l'être, il l'était, *par la langue*, l'habit, les coutumes; mais Genois d'Orient!" (2000: 47; my emphasis) [He might be a Genoese—he *was* one, in his speech, his dress, his way of life—but he was only a Genoese from the East!] Maalouf's insistence on the "oriental" *and* Genoese components of Baldassare's identity—in particular language, dress and custom—reveals that cultural practices then, and now, transcend the borders of individual nations.[28]

Cultural practices transcend, transpose and translate, bearing what has been theorized by Mikhail Epstein and Ellen Berry as transculturalism: a mode of being and an approach that holds all culture to be incomplete and insufficient and thus in need of radical openness and interaction with other cultures.[29] The notion of transculturalism, beginning with culture alone, becomes a way to subvert, challenge or criticize imposed and radical modes of being. Berry and Epstein write that "transcultural models offer strategies for the invention of positive alternatives to the legacies of cultural antagonism and domination that have pervaded both Western and second world cultures" (1999: 3) and, of course, "third world" cultures.[30]

Indeed, Maalouf offers a "positive alternative" to a conception of cultural antagonism, as propounded a few years before the millennium, by Samuel Huntington in his now (in)famous book *The Clash of Civilizations and the Remaking of World Order*. Here Huntington assumes a number of criteria in the definition of culture, civilization, and history that polarize and perpetuate divisiveness in the Mediterranean world and beyond. Huntington's main thesis is that a new world order is upon us, and it consists of confrontations between cultures and civilizations rather than between nations or ideologies (as was the case before and during the Cold War). He neatly divides the world into seven civilizations and affirms that the biggest confrontation will be between the "West" and the "Rest," in particular between the "West" and the Confucian or Islamic civilizations, or both.[31] Without the slightest nuance, or conjecturing that there may be differences (of ethos, for example) within these civilizations,

Huntington implicitly excludes the possibility of other formations, among which is a Mediterranean "civilization." Such an oversight is surprising given that Huntington clearly read Braudel and even goes so far as citing him. In considering the absence of a Mediterranean space in his description of the world, numerous problems arise in his thesis: to be sure, there are greater bonds between North Africa and Sicily than there are between Sicily and Belgium. Yet North Africa has nothing to do with Europe, in Huntington's system, if not to enable missions of terror against it. While Huntington cautiously points out that the word *civilization* should not be taken at face value, for that would be to neglect the imperialistic connotation that came to be attached to it since European conquests of Africa, India and further, he makes use of it indiscriminately, often confusing it with the word *culture*.

Both Huntington and Fukuyama's theories posit a completeness and a finality that can only be fictional. Cultural identities (and civilizational ones, although other than civilizations being defined as "cultures writ large" it is not clear what Huntington intends) are inevitably incomplete, yet the "last man" living in the victorious West will be satisfied and "complete." He will have a flat affect, Fukuyama suggests, but he will want or need nothing more. This portrait stands in radical opposition to Maalouf's Baldassare. His incessant travel, even when the object of his quest is clearly no longer important to him, points to what Berry and Epstein understand as transcultural practice: "[it]is not a diminishment of, or confrontation with, our cultural selves but rather a way of expanding the limits of our ethnic, professional, linguistic, and other identities to new levels of indeterminacy and 'virtuality'" (1999: 24). In their crossings of cultures, Maalouf's characters are continuously in the process of discovering what is within them, their virtuality. Baldassare remarks "J'avais entrepris ce voyage pour les raisons les plus nobles, préoccupé par la survie de l'univers, par la reaction de mes semblables aux drames que l'on prédit . . . Le cheikh Abdel-Bassit avait raison. A quoi bon parcourir le monde si c'est pour y voir ce qui est déjà en moi?" (2000: 62) [I undertook this journey for the noblest of reasons, concerned about the survival of the universe and the reactions of my fellow-mortals to the dramatic events now being foretold . . . Sheikh Abdel-Bassit was right. What is the good of travelling all over the world just to see what is inside me already?] Discovering the difference within oneself is a necessary condition for discovering the difference in others, and in this sense transculture joins the notion of transipseity:

> Although transculture depends on the efforts of separate individuals to overcome their identification with specific cultures, on another level it is a process of interaction between cultures themselves in which more and more individuals find themselves "outside" of any particular culture, "outside" of its national, racial, sexual, ideological, and other limitations . . . located beyond any particular mode of existence, or, in this

case, finding one's place on the border of existing cultures. This realm *beyond* all cultures is located *inside* transculture. (Berry and Epstein 1999: 25)

Whereas culture, according to Berry and Epstein's model, is imprisoning, insofar as it forms static habits, transculture, they maintain, is liberating. In such a system, however, relations of power are not given consideration. Maalouf's novels are striking in their overall dismissal of questions of power. How might this relate to his wider apprehension of a Mediterranean belonging and what, then, is a *conscience méditerranéenne*? To return to one of the questions posed earlier, what does it enable?

To begin with, it is evident that Maalouf's concern with history is paramount and that the emplotment of certain figures, times and places in *his stories* is not only carefully crafted and researched but more importantly translates a clear ethical and political positioning. This positioning champions "chronological others" not as models to emulate or repudiate, but as signs that imply that we may be able to avoid catastrophe—"a clash of civilizations"—by telling "another (or *the* other) side of the story,"[32] by avoiding Manichean divisions, by always translating ourselves, by using our reason and by maintaining family ties. Southgate remarks that "our autonomy as individuals depends on our ability to continue self-consciously making those adaptations and those revisions to the story of the past that underpins us. That's what makes us free" (2005: 119). Maalouf's *conscience méditerranéenne* is defined, then, by an ethos of freedom, in particular by a freedom from the burden of narrow identitarian categorizations and subjection to the powers of dogmatism. His is a freedom, through reason, to be above the fray. This seems to be what lies at the heart of Epstein and Berry's theory of transculturalism.

If, in the sixteenth century, Leo Africanus wrote one of the most important works of history, Maalouf's texts may achieve comparable importance in the literary sphere. Of Leo Africanus's text Zhiri writes: "Historiquement, cette œuvre est une des dernières grandes contributions de la culture arabe et musulmane au savoir européen" (2001: 27). [Historically speaking, this work is one of the last great contributions of Arab and Muslim culture to European thought.] Similarly, Maalouf's non-Eurocentric perspective on identity—and on a Mediterranean identity—reverses and disturbs the trend of the North writing about the South, when for example nineteenth-century novelists such as Fromentin and Maupassant wrote about their travels to Africa. Critic Anne Roche writes, "Le temps est peut-être venu d'un autre regard: une partie de la nouvelle génération des écrivains du Maghreb regarde la France, l'Europe, l'Occident, non pas d'égal à égal—ce qui serait faire bon marché des pesanteurs historiques, amnésie qui d'une certaine façon ne nous conviendrait que trop—mais dans une sorte de retournement dialectique" (1992: 120). [Perhaps the time has come for another perspective: some of the writers of this new generation from the Maghreb view France, Europe, the West not as equals—which would overlook the weight of history and reflect an amnesia that, in some ways, would suit us all too well—but in a dialectical return.] Maalouf's dialectical return takes the form of numerous veiled references to French writers such as Montesquieu, Pierre Loti and Isabelle Eberhardt, who made "the Orient" the subject of their texts and speaks to a Mediterranean long dominated by a one-way discourse.[33]

It becomes clear that Maalouf's belief in an exemplary "Mediterranean" belonging is a way of thinking laterally and outside national identities even though this by no means resolves tensions of identitarian conflicts or the perpetuation of neo-colonial ideologies.[34] His texts suggest, in fact, that we can never completely understand the world, ourselves, or the figures we believe in. But a transcultural world allows us to invent new possibilities and continually locate new meaning, for it is "a continuous space in which unrealized, potential elements are no less meaningful than 'real' ones" (Epstein 1999: 299). This does not undermine the importance of reason, rather, it should signal that not everything is explicable or understandable. Indeed, can one explain the coincidence on page 437 of *Le périple de Baldassare* where the protagonist remarks, "Je ne voudrais pas gloser encore sur le mot 'signe.' Mais comment ne pas s'effrayer d'une telle concordance? Tout au long de cette maudite journée du 11 septembre—le premier du mois selon le calendrier des Anglais—je n'avais cessé de songer à cette prophétie de malheur" (2000: 336; my emphasis). [I don't want to speculate any more about "signs." But how can one fail to be terrified by such a coincidence? All day long on that accursed 11th of September—the 1st of September according to the English calendar—I mulled over that wretched prophecy.]

FRAMING FICTION AND HISTORY

To give historical events a human face, fictional though it may be, is to expand the horizon of possibilities and to allow for those figures such as cultural mediators and translators to emerge from the shadows of a history that is often accepted as common knowledge and thus taken for granted. The representations of historical events and rewriting of key moments in the history of the Mediterranean are not exclusive to Maalouf. His works stand to elucidate an approach, taken by others as well, that posits the Mediterranean as shifting and mutable.[35] One of the foundational moments in the history of the Mediterranean—the founding of Carthage—has been written and re-written in history as in fiction. Fawzi Mellah, born in Tunis in 1946, takes up this foundational myth to invest it with a singular narrative in his novel *Elissa, la reine vagabonde* (1988). Mellah, a novelist, playwright, essayist and journalist makes the history

of Tunisia and the Mediterranean a central problematic of his larger corpus; in his earliest works, two plays, *Néron ou les oiseaux de passage* (1973)
and *Le palais du non-retour* (1975), that have been largely under-studied
but that have been characterized by Charles Bonn as "des petits brûlots
provocateurs" [small provocative blistering attacks], he stages the life of
petty colonialists in Tunisia and the anthropophagic nature of French
colonialism. His first novel, *La conclave des pleureuses* (1987) which, according to the author, "serait plutôt question de signes, d'images,
d'ombres et de mouvements futiles" (1987: 190) [is rather about signs,
images, shadows and futile movements], is an allegory for a modern
Tunisia that is caught between the abstract concepts of tradition and
modernity. The history of a community is recounted from multiple points
of view, here too, subtended by a dialectical tension between history and
fiction; one of the main figures is criticized for wanting to be a historian
when he is a "mere storyteller" — "Mais il se voulait historien; et il n'était
que conteur" (1987: 173) [He wanted to pass as a historian but he was but
a mere storyteller]. Mellah sets up an ambiguous distinction between
journalistic reportage, history and storytelling in *La conclave*, a positioning that is clearly revealed if one adopts a holistic approach to his work
and his persona. In his reportage from 2000, *Clandestin en Méditerranée*, he
joins a group of clandestine emigrants on a boat from North Africa to
Italy. As a fiction writer, essayist and reporter, Mellah's sensitivity to the
demands and difficulties of the different genres and epochs is evident. *Le
transfert des cendres* (2009) takes place in and around Europe and the
Mediterranean in the nineteenth century and tells of the search for the
Codex Sinaïticus, a lost manuscript of the Old Testament. Not unlike
Maalouf's works discussed earlier and Mellah's other two novels, the
pursuit of evanescent and continually disappearing texts constitute the
driving impetus for human action.

WRITING CARTHAGE

The contrast between history and fiction comes to light in the very opening pages of *Elissa ou la reine vagabonde* where, quoting a saying in Italian
"se non è vero, è bello" (1988: 13) [even if it is not true it is beautiful],
Mellah sets up a distinction between "truth" and "beauty" in his work.
Rather than simply present a "different version of what happened" by
way of a Rashomon effect, he brings the reader, from the very beginning,
to a foregone conclusion: given the impossibility of objective truth, the
narrator's story is an avowed invention, based on a series of steles found
in Tunis in his grandfather's backyard in 1874. According to his story,
these steles contain Dido's letters to her brother Pygmalion reconstruct-
ing the founding of Carthage. Because the narrator is not in possession of
all the steles, his knowledge and access to the story is partial. Placing

himself alongside other chroniclers of the same legend, Dante and Virgil, Mellah—through his fictitious narrator who suspiciously signs his initials FM at the end of the introduction—advances, from the outset, that the fate of all "oeuvre humaine" is arbitrary. The narrator claims to have classified the sections and paragraphs according to his temperament and his imagination on a particular day or night and "arbitraire pour arbitraire, cet ordre purement imaginaire en vaut bien un autre . . . lisez ce manuscrit dans l'ordre que je me suis permis d'imaginer; sinon feuilletez-le comme il vous plaira" (1988: 15). [Given the arbitrary nature of the decision, this purely imaginary order is as good as any . . . read this manuscript in the order I have taken the liberty of imagining; if not, leaf through it as you wish.] Encouraging a rhizomatic reading of the text from the outset, Mellah points to a non-teleological rendering of events and to an abolition of rules so that the reader may be led to believe that it is not the overarching temporality of the narrative that is significant but each discrete experience, each of which is able to stand alone, independent from the larger framework. This is not, therefore, a simple re-writing of a historical event from another point of view, but an invitation to consider questions of origins, errancy, and democracy not only during the founding of Carthage but in present-day articulations of the Mediterranean as well.

AN ERRANT NATION

Fleeing from Tyre to escape her brother Pygmalion who, following their father's death, becomes tyrannical and despotic, Elissa sets off with an army of one hundred men. The escape itself, from the outset, is an end unto itself: "La fuite en soi me semblait une destinée; je décidai de m'abandonner à ses hasards. Je ne souhaitais pas la corrompre par l'humaine aspiration à fixer un but au voyage" (1988: 29). [Flight seemed like a destiny in itself, and I decided passively to accept whatever it would bring. I had no wish to dilute it with the human desire to fix a goal for every journey.] Stopping first in Cyprus, then in Sabratha (current day Libya), Elissa, baptized the vagabond queen by Mellah, and her subjects trace a nomadic map driven by chance and impulse. As often happens, the subjectivity of the individual in a position of power becomes inextricably linked with that of her subjects. If we commonly understand the nation to be a stable entity tied to a land, and even if we know it to be a construct, here we are forced to shift our understanding in order to conceive of a nation on the move where the state is "une nécessité de pure contingence" (1988: 45) [a purely contingent necessity]. Such a paradigm shift leads us to apprehend a Mediterranean space emblematically, where nations come into contact, merge, and conflict for reasons as much political as they are idiosynchratic and are driven by affect or the "la dimension charnelle des êtres" (1988: 41) [the corporeal dimension of human beings], as the protagonist puts it.

Arriving upon the "perfumed hill"—Carthage—Elissa and her errant nation request a piece of land, which is granted to them by king Hiarbas. Allowing them only as much as a small piece of oxhide will cover, he falls under Elissa's ruse when she ingeniously cuts the hide into strips and encircles the hill that then becomes *Qart Hadash*, or Carthage. At the origin of a kingdom, she claims, lies not only trickery and deception but illusion. This illusion is clearly represented in the reality of her subjects who believe they have no choice but to obey the destiny traced for them. They ignore that in Elissa's errant nation language is more powerful than reality, that "ce sont souvent les mots que nous changeons, non la réalité des choses . . . nous maîtrisons mieux le vocabulaire que le cours du temps" (1988: 58). [It is often the words that we change, not the reality of things . . . we are able to control vocabulary better than the progress of time.] Mellah underscores the manipulative power of language, and through his own ruse set out in the introduction, draws attention to the contingency and verifiability of interpretation. When the founding of Carthage is underway, Elissa's constituents must agree on a representation of their newfound territory. In an animated debate about religion and the problems inherent in all texts, Elissa concludes that the only thing worth scrutiny is art. Where writing is opaque and obscures, art exposes: "L'écriture camoufle bien ce qu'elle fait mine d'exposer, le dessin expose bien ce qu'il fait mine de camoufler" (1988: 141). [Writing conceals what it appears to be exhibiting; visual art exhibits what it appears to be concealing.] Admiring the representative image that Hiarbas creates for Carthage, the feminine figure Tanit, Elissa remarks upon how this emblem speaks to the senses with its harmonious lines and curves, and does not signify one specific God or tradition but rather stands in as a symbol for a *chosen* geneaology. Elissa's concern lies not in where she and her people come from but what they come from. Hers is a call to return to nature, to a prelapsarian world, not unlike Camus's. Alongside, and related to a return to nature, Elissa insists on the power of dreams and the strength of imagination.

Elissa la reine vagabonde is framed by a dialectical tension between history and fiction, between "truth" and "beauty." Affirming "cet instinct de la beauté qui habite tous les peuples" (1988: 44) [the instinct for beauty which all nations share], Elissa underscores the importance of art in nation-building. In deciding how to rule the newly founded Carthage she considers the importance of a constitution, ultimately referring to it as driven by "la force d'une fiction" (1988: 149) [the strength of imagination]. Her suggestion is thus that the order of any piece of writing is nothing but the performativity of language, an order of words rather than of meanings, of signifiers rather than of signifieds. Mellah clearly believes in the categorical validity of history as his novel is annotated with footnotes that refer the reader to several historical sources. In so doing, he draws the reader's attention even more directly, to an awareness of the different genres present in the novel. Returning to White's elucidation of the way in which fact and fiction are woven together, Mellah's novel draws attention to the imperatives of narrative, particularly when dealing with histories of conquest and coercion.

Mellah's example, following my discussion of Maalouf's works, serves to demonstrate that the rewriting of histories is not unique to the latter. Tracing Mediterranean cartographies that extend beyond the Maghreb to the eastern Mediterranean, Maalouf and Mellah insist on the circulation of texts; in the cases of the novels examined here, all focus on the premise of a lost manuscript or of circulating, elusive words. Because each character is continually in a position of having to re-invent him/herself in the face of political and historical demands, a predictable narrative becomes impossible; put differently, "Identity is formed at the unstable point where the 'unspeakable' stories of subjectivity meet the narratives of history, of a culture" (Hall 1996: 115). In parallel with the stories of individual subjectivities, these novels urge us to reflect on the internal contradictions of a single Mediterranean identity; while the fabric of this construction continues to be woven, its very making must be understood precisely as built upon the convergence of multiple histories and shifting subjectivities.

ENDNOTES

1. "The postcolonial theme of rewriting and re-presenting the past to reconfigure the present is threatening to become a fashionable orthodoxy, yet in revealing the disquieting stubbornness of a yesterday that refuses to disappear into the stillness of the ordered archive, it remains imperative" (Chambers 2008: 58).

2. Maalouf was a journalist for many years; he was editor in chief of *Jeune Afrique* and the director of *An-Nahār*, the largest Lebanese daily, before devoting himself predominantly to essayistic writing and novels.

3. The etymology of "dimension" *dimeteri* (lat.) means "to measure." This inevitably recalls Camus's eternal quest for measure in his conception of Mediterraneity even though, as we shall come to see, it is distinctly different from Maalouf's.

4. The mention of the European Union is simply an example and should not be understood to be congruent with the Mediterranean situation. It also inevitably refers to economic aspects of the question that are not the primary focus of this work.

5. This translates as *The Description of Africa*. According to Oumelbanine Zhiri, Leo Africanus left the work untitled, and it was only with the first translation by Ramusio that it acquired its title.

6. See Oumelbanine Zhiri, "Leo Africanus, Translated and Betrayed" in *The Politics of Translation in the Middle Ages* and Houria Daoud-Bricki, "Présence et absence de la *Description de l'Afrique* de Léon l'Africain dans ses traductions."

7. The novel begins with the words "Moi, Hassan . . ." [I, Hassan].

8. Ricoeur writes: "The polarity I am going to examine suggests an intervention of narrative identity in the conceptual constitution of personal identity in the manner of a specific mediator between the pole of character, where idem and ipse tend to coin-

icide, and the pole of self-maintenance, where selfhood frees itself from sameness" (1992: 119).

9. These terms come from Deleuze and Guattari's *A Thousand Plateaus* and can be generally understood to mean the process of leaving familiar territory, acquiring new practices and repeatedly forming new assemblages.

10. This is key in understanding how Deleuze and Guattari conceive of the term; it is not to be confused with minority but should be understood as singular ways of writing not practiced by "the majority." They take the example of Kafka, who "wrote without a standard notion of the people."

11. Maalouf is not the only one to see exile as more than just trauma. Albert Memmi in "Le nomade immobile" has a chapter entitled *Les fécondités de l'exil* [The Fecundities of Exile].

12. The notion of becoming-imperceptible is in fact much more complex and encourages a non-human perspective, not insensitivity but a shifting of viewpoint so that the human being's perception is not the origin of perceptions but one among many.

13. For Deleuze and Guattari becoming-animal is yet another fundamental notion of the self-as-becoming. Interestingly, Hassan's name becomes Léon and his friend Haroun is always referred to as Haroun le furet: "Curieuse habitude qu'ont les hommes de se donner ainsi les noms des fauves qui les terrorisent, rarement ceux des animaux qui leur sont dévoués" (1986: 290). [It is a curious habit which men have, thus to give themselves the names of the wild beasts that terrify them, rarely those of the animals which are devoted to them.]

14. That is to say, political concerns that inevitably tie into those questions of power that led Saïd to write *Orientalism*.

15. This is not meant to discredit Maalouf's extraordinary erudition in historical matters. Nearly all his works testify to his vast knowledge of history.

16. Oumelbanine Zhiri writes that he (Leo) "occupe une place éminemment symbolique des relations entre l'Europe et l'Islam arabe à une époque où l'une et l'autre connaissent des mutations profondes dont les prolongements se font encore sentir de nos jours" (2001: 27). [occupies an eminently symbolic place in the relationship between Europe and Islam, particularly at a time when both are seeing profound changes which are still being felt today.]

17. Southgate seems to ignore that Britain is highly populated by "geographical and racial others".

18. The number 666 is commonly referred to as "demonic" and, written in Roman numerals, the date 1666 (MDCLXVI) contains every numeral in descending order so that no more years can be added. "Les nombres sont à présent au complet. Les années sont au complet. Plus rien ne s'y ajoutera" (2000: 104). [Now the numbers are complete. And the years are complete. Nothing more will be added.] This is seen as a sign of the world coming to an end.

19. Maalouf's character is clearly based on Guglielmo Embriaco, a Genoese crusader born around 1070, and his descendants. Embriaco played a large role in conquering Jerusalem during the first crusade.

20. Allah is said to have ninety-nine names, thus the search for the hundredth seems like an impossibility from its very inception.

21. In the Bible, the Apocalypse comes in Revelation: "Then He said to me . . . I am the Alpha and the Omega, the beginning and the end" (Revelation 21: 6a).

22. This reference traces yet another Mediterranean genealogy: Abu-l-Ala was a tenth to eleventh century atheist Syrian poet whose most famous work, *Risālat al-Ghufrān*, is said to have inspired Dante's *Divina Commedia*. Maalouf includes another of his poems, which sets up an opposition between "brains" and "religion" in *The Crusades Through Arab Eyes* (1983: 37).

23. This is yet a different perspective from the one I explore in chapter 1 through Camus's and Merleau-Ponty's ideas of *being* as being formed through the senses rather than through the mind.

24. This seems to be increasingly debatable as religion seems to occupy as large a place as economics and politics.

25. Here he writes in reference to Carlos Fuentes's allegorical novel about Mexico, *Terra Nostra* (1975).

26. There are thirteen languages mentioned in the novel: Greek, Coptic, Hebrew, Syriac, Cyrillic, Arabic, Latin, Italian, Turkish, Persian, French, Armenian, English.

27. Gibelet was one of the Levantine crusader states that subsequently became part of the Ottoman Empire. Along with Genoa it was a crucial city in the flourishing of maritime commerce in the Mediterranean between c. 1100–1800.

28. Throughout the course of the novel Baldassare goes from Gibelet to Genoa where he claims to feel much more at home, as it is the land of his ancestors. He frequently refers to his "sang genois" [Genoese blood] and to his forebears (2000: 14, 341, 363, 462).

29. Transculturalism "responds to limitations inherent in some of the contemporary models circulating on the global stage. It is to be distinguished from the understanding of the global system as a collection of "discrete worlds" or "clashing civilizations" (as in Samuel Huntington's model). It also diverges from the older American "melting pot" metaphor in which cultural differences are assimilated to a national norm as well as a model of the contemporary global system as a totalized "universal cultural ecumene." Finally, it departs from the U.S. multicultural model that posits aggregates of discrete subcultures (based on racial, ethnic, sexual, or other differences), each of which seeks to constitute and maintain its cultural specificity in the face of a homogenizing dominant culture" (1999: 29).

30. The term "third world" is problematic, and it is precisely against these hierarchical divisions that I wish to work, but given the use of "first" and "second" world in the quote I use it, also in scare quotes, for consistency.

31. Huntington's civilizations are divided into the Sinic, Japanese, Hindu, Islamic, Orthodox (Slavic), Western, Latin American, and perhaps one day African.

32. *The Crusades Seen Through Arab Eyes* (1983) is the best illustration of this.

33. Léon has a Circassian lover reminiscent of Loti's Aziyadé, and many of the references to the way political regimes function recall Montesquieu's *De l'esprit des lois*.

34. Albert Memmi, in *Le Nomade immobile* (2000), espouses a similar allegiance to the Mediterranean.

35. Anouar Benmalek, Assia Djebar and Salim Bachi might be read through the same lens.

II

Beyond the Binary

THREE

Nina Bouraoui: On Gender

Systems of binary thought—and consequently alternative theories specifically formed in dialogue with them—have been pervasive throughout postcolonial and cultural studies of the last half century. In response to cultural models articulated around notions of black and white, self and other, east and west, man and woman, to name only a few, notions of creolization, hybridity, contact zones, and borderlands have emerged. With the advent of poststructuralism, deconstruction and then postcolonial studies came an acute consciousness of the extent to which the world appears overrun by discourses of Western domination, where terms attendant to white, self, and man are privileged. Rather than espousing Manichean thinking or strictly non-Western positions—privileging the typically obscured "negative" of the pair, east, other, woman for example—writers and theorists of the postcolonial Mediterranean in this book present a critique of static subject positions. The following two chapters aim to demonstrate that Nina Bouraoui and Tahar Ben Jelloun redefine what it means to be woman and southern in the Mediterranean by writing forms of gender and geography that elude the abovementioned polarized frameworks. Both authors bring the importance of fiction to the fore yet remain grounded in current sociopolitical realities.

Bouraoui and Ben Jelloun call into question binary divisions of gender in two of their earliest novels, both of which were largely responsible for launching their respective literary successes: *La voyeuse interdite* (1991) and *L'enfant de sable* (1985). In *La voyeuse interdite* the main character does violence on her body to hide her femininity and to resemble a man, whereas in *L'enfant de sable* the protagonist Ahmed/Zahra is born a girl but is raised as a boy. Despite bringing a girl into the world, the patriarch decides his child will be a son, and consequently Ahmed/Zahra lives according to male rules in male spaces. Just as there is a refusal of ac-

cepted notions of stable and unchanging genders in Bouraoui's and Ben
Jelloun's works, there is an equally discernible unease with tidy geographical distinctions between the North and South of the Mediterranean, in particular with regard to the silenced histories of French colonization of Algeria and Morocco, the countries of origin of the two authors.

For centuries the Mediterranean has been represented as a bustling
and powerful "affaire d'hommes," or man's world; historical accounts
and sociological studies have, for the most part, been written by men and
most have shown that a large majority of the societies bordering this sea
have—traditionally—been patriarchal.[1] Prevailing assumptions invari-
ably associate the Mediterranean with the structure of a nuclear, traditional family typically characterized as being composed of a *mater* and
pater familias.[2] Same-sex relationships or alternate affective formations
have, until recently, been generally overlooked or treated as anomalous.[3]
Yet, in literary studies, the trope of the Mediterranean—in analyses of
work from Sappho to Thomas Mann to Jean Genet and André Gide—has
come to signify a locus of sexual expression and discovery. In such cases,
sexual desire tends to be expressed as exoticism and escapism and is
often figured as deviant or perverse. This literature also tends to be written predominantly by men, about men and boys, the classic trope being
sexual encounters between "Northern" men and "Southern" boys. Isabelle Eberhardt's work (1877–1904), written in Algeria, provides an important exception and is significant due to her conscious manipulation of
a gendered persona in her work and life.

While it would be problematic to assume cross-cultural coherence
among gender roles or relationships across the Mediterranean, a number
of connections can be drawn among certain countries of this area. In
addition, while the parallel between sociocultural "realities" and literary
texts may appear to suggest that the latter function as mirrors of very
concrete situations, the texts in question in this chapter should be seen as
productions as well as representations of gendered and sexual realities.
In other words, they are grounded in sociocultural concerns as well as
being stylistically innovative and thus productive of a new literary "language" that is combative and confrontational. Within the realm of postcolonial Francophone Maghrebi literature, it was only thirty years ago that
Kateb Yacine, in reference to Algeria, affirmed, "A l'heure actuelle, dans
notre pays, une femme qui écrit vaut son pesant de poudre."[4] [At
present, in our country, a woman who writes is worth her weight in
gold.] Although some women have benefited from greater enfranchise-
ment in these thirty years, a long history of silencing is still patently
present in much of the Maghrebi literature written by women.[5] Literary
criticism pertaining to women, feminism, sex and gender have taken myriad and diverse forms, and much ink has been spilled on the subordination of women in patriarchal societies, to the point where many critics,
according to Winifred Woodhull, have tended to homogenize women's

experiences, creating an indiscriminate category called the "Third World woman" (1993: 3). She suggests that Algerian women, in particular, are all but a homogeneous collective.

The promise of social equality which accompanied Algeria's independence from France in 1962 was, in part, Woodhull suggests, thwarted by a "realignment with tradition." Women who rejected Muslim gender codes were generally perceived as traitors to their country and were considered as abettors of colonial intervention. Adherents to those gender codes were, however, seen as obstructing a move toward modernity. Woodhull reads the tension between these two positions as reflecting the contradictory aims of the Algerian revolution which sought to modernize the nation and to restore a culture stifled, but by no means destroyed, by French colonialism. Women, she suggests, are identified "less with tradition as such than with Algeria's 'betweenness,' its traversal by irreconcilable modern and traditional currents" (1993: 10). Posited this way, Woodhull avoids the tradition-modernity dichotomy and reads women as being emblematic of Algeria's status between this binary. Drawing on this position, this chapter questions the foundations upon which gender categories and their consequent expressions, in the France-Maghreb nexus of the Mediterranean, are constructed. Assia Djebar and Malika Mokkedem, among others such as Maïssa Bey and Leïla Sebbar, have paved the way for such a discussion, explicitly situating female subjectivities—both their own and those of their fictitious protagonists—in the Mediterranean, literally at sea (Mokkedem), on its shores (Sebbar), and around its ancient history (Djebar).[6]

"UNMANNING" THE MEDITERRANEAN: NINA BOURAOUI BETWEEN FRANCE AND ALGERIA

The Franco-Algerian writer Nina Bouraoui, born in 1967 and raised on both shores of the Mediterranean, brings to the question of a Mediterranean ethos a recasting of the androcentricism and heteronormativity of such a space. Bouraoui's novels do not solely mobilize a critique of patriarchy; they also insist on the need to understand and rethink gender roles and the construction of women in societies where tradition still holds a crucial place (like Algeria) as well as in those that have supposedly moved away from tradition (such as France). For this purpose, a—chronological—cultural critique and trajectory will be traced, beginning with representations of women as cloistered and subjected to patriarchal norms in her first novel *La voyeuse interdite* (1991) through to *Mes mauvaises pensées* (2005), in which she forces identity categories into crisis in an attempt to produce new subject positions.

Significantly, a blurring of generic categories between autobiography and fiction underlies Bouraoui's work as a whole. With the important exception of *La voyeuse interdite,* her texts do not, for example, carry the often found word *roman* under the title, and even when they do, they present us with spaces and times that correspond to the author's life. Her narrator is almost always a first-person narrator, and in a number of her novels the homodiegetic narrator is simply referred to as "je." In *Garçon manqué* (2000), for example, the protagonist and author share the same personal history and are both named Yasmina (Nina in the diminutive). Such blurring points to a willed ambiguity both between fact and fiction and more broadly between framing devices and labels.

As Bouraoui has repeatedly stated in interviews, "Je ne suis pas Beur comme les journalistes le disent, c'est à dire les enfants des Algériens nés en France mais qui n'ont jamais connu l'Algérie. Ce n'est pas mon cas . . . je suis assez ferme là dessus car je déteste les etiquettes."[7] [I am not Beur—that is to say a child of Algerian parents born in France who has never been to Algeria—as the journalists say. That is not my situation . . . I am rather strict about this as I detest labels.] Her position might be seen as somewhat atypical in that, having been born in France but raised in Algeria until the age of fourteen, she does not fall neatly into the category of either "Beur" or "Maghrebi" writers, remaining—as she herself says— "inclassable" [unclassifiable]. Like many writers before her, Bouraoui affirms, "l'écriture est mon pays"[8] [writing is my country]. The wish to remain unclassifiable, or to shed the burden of labels, is not uncommon to Maghrebi writers whom critics and the public have too easily relegated to restrictive national and identitarian categorizations. Discourse that stresses nation-building, or that foregrounds the construction of "the nation," is perhaps inevitably based on politics of exclusion and homogenization even when it may not be deliberate. This is particularly important in Bouraoui's case, for not only is she France's national "other" because of her Algerian origins and Algeria's national "other" in view of her French origins, she is also othered from both mainstream identity categories in both contexts due to her declared homosexuality, a subject that has grown central to her work: *Garçon manqué* (2000), *La vie heureuse* (2002), *Poupée bella* (2004) and *Mes mauvaises pensées* (2005) directly address same-sex desire.

REMEMBERING TIPASA: LANDSCAPES OF SOLITUDE

My inquiry into Bouraoui's works begins with locating subjectivities in a pre-discursive Mediterranean. To this end, let us turn back to chapter 1, to Albert Camus. At first glance, these two writers might not appear to have much in common: Camus died almost a decade before Bouraoui was born; while he was an "intellectuel engage" she is politically more private; sexual identity is not of fundamental interest to Camus, but Bouraoui writes of it often. Yet both were raised in Algeria, on the fringes of an indigenous Algerian society, and both express a rapport with nature and the cosmos as well as a form of social rebellion.[9] Although often dismissed as ancillary biographical traits, their relationships to Algeria irrefutably account for ways in which they both construe subjectivity and selfhood. This is nowhere more apparent than in Camus's early collection *Noces* and in Bouraoui's *Garçon manqué*, where she writes, "La mer me porte. Elle prend tout. Elle m'obsède. Elle est avant le rêve de la France. Elle est avant le voyage. Elle est avant la peur . . . je deviens un corps sans type, sans langue, sans nationalité" (2000: 8–9). [The sea sustains me. It engulfs everything and obsesses me. The sea comes before the dream of France, before the journey. It was there before I felt fear . . . I become a non-descript body, a body without a language, without nationality.] As the repetition of the preposition "avant" [before] suggests, her Algeria is a pre-linguistic locus where the body takes precedence over the mind and over language: "L'Algérie n'est pas dans ma langue. Elle est dans mon corps" (2000: 167). [Algeria does not flourish on my tongue; it takes root in my body.] Bouraoui writes Algeria in a language that is grounded in experience. Juxtaposing Camus's and Bouraoui's semantic choices, thus paying close attention to a number of passages, illuminates their shared apprehension of the Mediterranean.

Garçon manqué begins with a first-person narrator on the shores of the sea: "Je cours sur la plage du Chenoua . . . je cours avec la mer qui monte et descend sous les ruines romaines" (2000: 7). [I'm running on Chenoua beach . . . I'm running with the sea that rises and falls beneath the Roman ruins.][10] Situated in exactly the same geographic place, Camus's first-person narrator in "Noces à Tipasa" [Nuptials at Tipasa] thinks: "A regarder l'échine solide du Chenoua, mon coeur se calmait d'une étrange certitude. J'apprenais à respirer, je m'intégrais, et je m'accomplissais" (1959: 14). [But watching the solid backbone of the Chenoua, my heart would grow calm with a strange certainty. I was learning to breathe, I was fitting into things and fulfilling myself.] Where Nina, the protagonist of Bouraoui's novel, runs "*avec* la mer" [*with* the sea], Camus merges with the land, also becoming one with it. Camus's "nuptials" with the world are clearly echoed in Bouraoui's works, where she evokes another sort of nuptial with the verb "épouser" [to marry] "ma terre devient fragile et mouvementée. J'épouse ses variations. J'entre dans le bruit" (2000: 9). [My land becomes fragile and turbulent. I embrace its variations. I enter into the noise.] Echoing Camus's (in)famous belief in the quiet indifference of the world, especially palpable in *L'étranger*, Bouraoui writes that "le bleu du ciel algérien me fait pleurer. Sa pureté. Sa beauté sans fond. Sa grandeur si tranquille. *Son indifférence*" (2000: 46; my emphasis). [The blue Algerian sky makes me cry: its purity, its bottomless beauty, its grandeur so tranquil, its indifference.] Becoming one with the universe, embodied in the world, "seule en Algérie, fondue à ma terre . . . Ma terre est mon corps" (2000: 81) [alone in Algeria, fused with my land . . . My land is my body], Bouraoui's prediscursive subjectivity is one of solitude. Although it appears as a predominantly spiritual condition, it also becomes physical and, thus at times, all-encompassing. The overpowering Mediterranean landscapes only accentuate her marginalization: "la plage est immense. Souvent déserte. Elle amplifie la solitude" (2000: 26). [The beach is immense. Frequently deserted, it magnifies solitude.] Similarly Camus's acute solitude in *Noces* as well as in *Le premier homme* is overwhelming, for it appears ontological rather than merely physical.[11]

Solitude, for Camus, is a characteristic that pertains to every individual and is not endowed with a necessarily negative valence. To a certain degree, Bouraoui seems to adhere to this philosophy: "Je reste entre deux identités. Mon équilibre est dans la solitude, une unité. J'invente un autre monde. Sans voix. Sans jugement" (2000: 26). [I remain between two identities. My equilibrium lies in my solitude, a unifying force. I invent another world, without a voice, without judgment.] Recognizing solitude as inherent in the human condition rather than ascribing it to being an outsider in two countries, Bouraoui here echoes the quasi stoic acceptance free of moral judgment discussed in chapter 1. This entirely non-political self, construed through the senses, pre-exists a socially constructed subjectivity, the latter a condition that both Camus's and Bouraoui's works continually negotiate.

Yet, despite her "stoic" acceptance of solitude, Bouraoui's perception takes on a second aspect that contrasts starkly with Camus's and that deals specifically with women. If in Camus's works women are, for the most part, notoriously not endowed with their own subjectivity, and often appear as objects of male desire, Bouraoui's mobilize an acerbic and liberating conception of women in the Mediterranean. In Camus's *Le premier homme*, Cormery's mother appears virtually aphasic, illiterate and without agency; in *L'étranger*, Meursault's Marie never expresses a point of view; in *La peste* women remain merely background figures; and in *La chute*, a nameless woman drowns herself. In contrast, Bouraoui's women, who are usually marginal, solitary figures, have the power to resist the dictates of the societies that exclude them, to imagine but also to speak, act and perform.

Her first novel, *La voyeuse interdite*, written on the eve of the 1991 Algerian civil war, presents us with a female protagonist who observes the male space of a street in Algiers, from behind a window. Bouraoui writes about solitude as an ontological state *and* as a social effect, one that has its roots in gender inequality and consequent repercussions on the lives of women. The social and sexual segregation that she bitterly describes in *La voyeuse interdite* inaugurates her concern with an understanding of sexual identity and its constructedness. In this novel, which has received the most critical attention of all her works,[12] she draws a violent portrait of cloistered women in Algeria, of their subjection to male power and of the extreme solitude of the main protagonist, Fikria: "Nous

étions parmi des hommes fous séparés à jamais des femmes par la religion musulmane . . . Dès la puberté, les femelles de la maison durent vivre
cachées derrière les fenêtres d'un gynécée silencieux où le temps avait
perdu sa raison d'être" (1991: 21–22). [We were among lunatics forever
separated from women by the Moslem religion . . . Starting at puberty the
females of the house had to live hidden behind the windows of a silent
gynaeceum where time had lost its raison d'être.] As a young girl in a
"monde d'hommes" [man's world] (which we understand to be Algeria),
she suffers severe restrictions on her physical and verbal freedom as well
as corporeal abuse by her father. She and other Algerian women are
described as "fantômes de la rue, animaux cloîtrés, femmes infantiles,
muses inassouvies" (1991: 12). [Phantoms of the street, cloistered animals, infantile women! Ungratified muses!] Forced to stay indoors, she
and her two sisters masochistically deny their femininity by bandaging
their breasts and starving themselves, their biggest sin being that they
were not born male. We understand, here, how culture acts on sexual/
biological difference, and the possible troubles that can arise when one is
forced to negate, or when one chooses not to follow, culturally coded
roles ascribed to biological sex.[13] The novel traces Fikria's passage from
one form of solitude to another, from puberty to an (en)forced, loveless
marriage. Setting the premise for her subsequent works, *La voyeuse interdite* takes women as a primary category of investigation, soliciting an
initial recognition of subordinated subjects in solitary confinement.

MÉDI-TERRA-NÉE, BORN IN THE MIDDLE GROUND

Despite the distinctions between men and women, and oppressor and
oppressed, that Bouraoui sets up in this first novel, sexual identities are
presented as hybrid. Fikria paints the following portrait of her father, a
violent patriarch and extreme misogynist: "Doigts effilés, ongles soignés,
muscles imberbes et nez à peine busqué, le mâle-femelle se tenait sur le
pas de la porte" (1991: 93). [Tapering fingers, manicured nails, hairless
muscles and slightly aquiline nose, the male-female stood at the doorstep
of the forbidden door.] Juxtaposing his liminal physical position ("le pas
de la porte") [the doorstep] with a liminal sexual identity ("male-femelle"), thus placing patriarchal authority on a double threshold, Bouraoui encourages us to question our assumptions. Even the most ostensibly rigid and extremist figures—here, the pitiless patriarch—are subject
to ambivalence. Her mother is characterized as a "génitrice déguisée en
eunuque" (1991: 65) [a female disguised as a eunuch] who is nonetheless
"encombrée par ses seins, ses hanches, son bassin, son ventre" (1991: 42)
[weighted down by her breasts, her thighs, her pelvis, her abdomen]. To
further complicate this issue, Fikria continues, "ma mère désirait un pénis pour elle toute seule, un pénis qu'elle garderait toute sa vie, et là,

enfin, on la respecterait" (1991: 42). [My mother desired a penis all for herself, a penis that she would keep all her life, and with that, finally, she would be respected.] The use of "male-femelle" rather than homme-femme, the figure of the eunuch and her mother's desire for a penis point first and foremost to biological markers that are presumably unchangeable. Yet Fikria's urge is to combat this idea, to rebel against it, as she seeks to discover her father's "corps de femme" (1991: 94) [women's body] under his women's garb. Juxtaposing his feminine *body* with feminine *dress*, Bouraoui returns to possibilities, desires and instabilities of both the categories of sex and gender. The figure of the arch-patriarch is suddenly destabilized, vulnerable to identification with the second sex. The body, Bouraoui suggests, is neither static nor self-identical but rather depends on experience and cultural context. One is reminded of Simone de Beauvoir's pioneering phrase "on ne naît pas femme, on le devient" [one is not born a woman, one becomes one]. Building on Beauvoir's work (along with Foucault's), Judith Butler takes "woman" as a term-in-process and affirms that there is no necessary relationship between body and gender. Gender is discursively constructed both by and despite the subject.[14] It follows, then, that culture and cultural difference have a significant, if not capital, impact on the construction of gender.

By deploying such a critique of a segment of Algerian society, Bouraoui enacts a resistance to it and to patriarchal domination but also suggests alternative readings of gendered and sexual identities. A great deal of criticism on Bouraoui's works has focused on her position of the in-betweeness ("entre-deux") related to national affiliations. While these readings are important they ignore a disarticulation of this very notion as well as a displacement of her concern with national identity. Algeria and France are omnipresent—as will be noted further on—but to these national markers Bouraoui has added ones that pertain to gendered identity: "J'ai quatre problèmes. Française? Algerienne? Fille? Garçon?" (2000: 163) [I have four problems. Am I French or Algerian? Am I a girl or a boy?] In fact the very titles of her novels draw one's attention to gender first and foremost; *La voyeuse interdite* is a female subject who is also suggestive of sexual voyeurism since she is "forbidden." Similarly, there is a sense of taboo in her title *Garçon manqué*, which indicates a person of ambiguous gender behavior or traits, whereas *Poupée bella* conjures up images of dolls that can be "dressed up," made to look "bella" or pretty. It also suggests the imitation of a child or a young person who might be all body and no mind.

In *La voyeuse interdite* Fikria is held prisoner in what she names a "huis clos infernal" (1991: 26) [a hellish scene behind closed doors]. Bouraoui here seems to echo the metaphor of hell in Sartre's renowned play *Huis Clos* and its protagonists Garcin, Ines and Estelle.[15] Garcin desires Estelle who is also the object of Ines's desires, and the latter constantly impedes a relationship between the first two. In this infernal love triangle, the characters, as in *La voyeuse interdite,* are stuck in one room and defined by their respective gazes. As Siobhan McIlvanney states, Bouraoui's text "has strong echoes of the Sartrean notion of visual domination, entailing the obligatory objectification of the Other to an *en-soi* ("in-itself") with little room for reciprocity" (2004: 109). For Sartre, there always exists a degree of objectification of the "other," starting with the simple awareness of the "other's" presence. In *La voyeuse interdite,* objectification is rigidly fixed in a hierarchy predicated on sexual relations of power. Juxtaposing the names of Sartre's characters—garc**ines**telle[16]—we might infer that Ines, the lesbian, is always caught between the two presumably heterosexual characters. Ines is part Garcin and part Estelle, she is entre-deux *and* les deux. Building on the premise that women have been objects of a male gaze and that lesbians have traditionally been caught between parameters of normative heterosexuality, Bouraoui, beginning with her very first novel, seeks a way out through writing. *La voyeuse interdite* posits a female seeing subject, rather than taking women strictly as the object of a masculine gaze.

A distinct sense of inhabiting a middle ground takes shape in *Garçon manqué.* Nina, the main protagonist born to an Algerian father and a French mother, lives her adolescence (the same stage of life of the protagonist in *La voyeuse interdite*) between Algeria and France. As an age of transition from girlhood to womanhood, adolescence is commonly associated with self-discovery and with the consciousness of self-invention. However, it is also a period when people come under pressure to affirm their gender and sexuality. Nina's Algeria in this work is, as mentioned earlier, sensory, she is a fully embodied subject, and she fashions and refashions herself. "Ma vie algérienne bat hors de la ville. Elle est à la mer, au désert, sous les montagnes de l'Atlas. Là je m'efface enfin. Je deviens un corps sans type, sans langue, sans nationalité" (2000: 9). [My Algerian heart beats outside of the city. It belongs to the sea and the desert at the foot of the Atlas Mountains. Here, my body is erased and becomes unrecognizable. I become a non-descript body, a body without language, without nationality.] Much as they did for Jacques Cormery in Camus's *Le premier homme,* the sea and its shore act as a blank space, a space of inscription and, as such, is potentially liberating. Once in concordance with nature, Nina is not obliged to account for her skin color, the language she speaks or her nationality. Far from the constraints of the city of Algiers, a male space *par excellence,* she is free to invent herself: "Je prends un autre prénom, Ahmed. Je jette mes robes. Je coupe mes cheveux. Je me fais disparaître. J'intègre le pays des hommes . . . Amine m'aime comme un garçon" (2000: 15). [I take on another name: Ahmed. I throw away my dresses. I cut my hair. I make myself disappear and assimilate into the world of men . . . Amine likes me as a boy.] Along with the evident semantic similarity she creates between the names Yasmina and Amine (the protagonist refers to Amine, her childhood friend, as her double), both are Algerian *and* French, and both, we are led to believe, are drawn to their own gender.

When Amine's mother sees Nina looking masculine with her short hair and her boyish clothes, she declares, "Je ne veux pas que mon fils devienne homosexuel. Elle dit le mot en premier. Elle dit mon mot. A force de trainer avec cette fille. Cette fausse fille" (2000: 60). [I don't want my son to become a homosexual. She says the word first. She says my word. Under this girl's influence, this fake girl.] If the more conventional fear is one where the presence of an effeminate boy may excite homosexual tendencies in other boys, Bouraoui plays with such stereotypes by placing a girl in the lead position. By changing her name from Nina to Ahmed, shedding her feminine clothes and cutting her hair, *thus* becoming a "garçon" to her friend Amine, the female protagonist reminds us that gender is inextricably tied to that mutable and changing place that is appearance. From Ahmed, she changes her name to Steve (after the actor Steve McQueen), once again signaling the element of performance, of acting, and of the invention of one's self. Such an interpretation should not be mistaken for felicitous "play," for her name-switching is identified by the protagonist as an "infanticide" and a "suicide," signaling the hardships, along with the possibilities, of self-(re)invention. When she imagines her Breton grandmother telling her she is a "garçon manqué" because of the way she dresses and acts, she responds "non. Mes spectateurs sont fiers de moi. Je suis" (2000: 64). [No. My audience is proud of me. I exist.] By using the words *fausse* and *manqué* (and the title *Garçon manqué*), Bouraoui embraces what might be seen as a failed performance. With a photo of the author looking out at us on the cover, the book defies the reader to imply that there is anything absent, *qui manque*. She is presence. "Je suis" [I exist] *tout court* sheds the burden of the nouns and adjectives that characterize belonging.

Nina's sense of national belonging is described as a wound that is both open in the present and connected to the past. As the daughter of a French woman and an Algerian man who met and married during the Algerian war of independence, she is the symbolic offspring of a violent colonial encounter, as well as the result of a transgressive relationship: "Longtemps je croyais porter une faute. Je viens de la guerre . . . la violence ne me quitte plus. Elle m'habite" (2000: 32). [For a long time I believe I am an anomaly, the result of a wrongdoing. I am forged by the war . . . Violence no longer leaves me. It inhabits me.] As an "enfant de la guerre" [child of the war], she reflects on her genealogy. Her mother, also a symbol of rebellion for having married her father, is affectionately written into a semantic association with the Mediterranean. Observing that her given nickname is Méré, Nina remarks, "Je n'ai jamais su pourquoi. Méré. *Mare. Mare Nostrum.* Notre mer. Ma mère, en Méditerranée" (2000: 105). [I have never known why. Méré. *Mare. Mare Nostrum.* Our Mother Sea. My mother, there in the Mediterranean waters.] However, her mother is also a reminder of those years when Algeria was legally but illegitimately part of France: "L'Algérie est un pays d'Afrique. Algérie, department français. La Méditerranée borde Alger comme la Seine traverse Paris" (2000: 116). [Algeria is an African country. Algeria is a French overseas department. Algiers is hemmed in by the Mediterranean Sea like the Seine River winding through Paris.] Bouraoui calls attention to a complex Algeria, first stating that it is an African country and then returning to its status as part of France. She compares the Mediterranean, which separates France from Algeria, to the Seine, which divides the city of Paris. Reading Paris as a metonym of France, Bouraoui evokes a country whose other half is Algeria. This symbolically tragic Mediterranean evokes imperial conquests and colonial rhetoric, a period when it was seen as being no different from the Lac Léman that separates France from Switzerland. Bouraoui traces a clear connection between French/colonial Algeria, the Algerian civil war and immigration in contemporary France. "Parce que la guerre d'Algérie ne s'est jamais arrêtée. Elle s'est transformée. Elle s'est déplacée. Et elle continue" (2000: 101). [The war in Algeria has never stopped; it has hardly changed. The war simply has moved to another place and continues its course.] Implying that the Algerian War has been transposed to, and perpetuated on, French ground, her France is marked by the conflict of two nations linked by an embattled past.

Indeed, according to the historian Benjamin Stora, the Algerian war of independence is a major factor in determining the relationship of French society to the question of immigration. It is also, he says, "fondatrice de la culture française contemporaine" (Moussaoui 2006: 1) [a foundation stone of contemporary French political culture]. Critically making use of a noun now infamously associated with Nicolas Sarkozy—"racaille"—to describe the sons and daughters of immigrants, Nina imagines someone, one day on the streets of Rennes, muttering to her "ça court, ça court la racaille" (2000: 131). [Look at them run, those loitering rascals.] Bouraoui insists on the imbrication of France and Algeria first by referring to Algeria as a French department and then by thematizing an Algerian presence, through immigration, in France.

If, as Bouraoui's protagonist in *Garçon manqué* states, she is neither "fille" nor "garçon," neither "française" nor "algérienne," we can infer that she identifies with no one nation and no single gender. In *Queer Nations: Marginal Sexualities in the Maghreb*, Jarrod Hayes points out that "any attempt to narrate an Algerian identity separate from the neighboring nations, even the colonizer, will find that the course of that identity also flows into the Mediterranean, into a common identity shared by the Maghreb, southern Europe, and eastern Mediterranean countries" (2000: 154). For Bouraoui, this common identity is neither harmonious nor conciliatory: on the contrary, it is fragmented and scarred by the vestiges of colonialism.

Although caught between what at first appear to be the two very distinct cultural worlds of Algiers and Rennes, the protagonist attempts a dismantling of these binary allegiances through *other* cultural referents. *Garçon manqué* is divided into four chapters of varying lengths, which are entitled "Alger," "Rennes," "Tivoli" and "Amine." By supplementing Alger and Rennes, her parents' cities, with Tivoli and Amine, Bouraoui invites a move beyond the national binary and the "entre-deux." Through the juxtaposition of chapter headings, Amine (and by inference her gender identity) and her national attachments are afforded equal importance. "Tivoli," the penultimate chapter which is only four pages long, comes as a surprise after the repetitive intensity of her *déchirement* between Algeria and France. Moreover, the chapter begins *in medias res*: "C'est arrivé à Tivoli" (2000: 183). [It took place in Tivoli.] Free from being an outsider in both Algeria and France, Tivoli and Rome allow her to rethink the constraints of her national identity. She stands, "au milieu du Forum" [in the middle of the Forum], outside her two countries, "dans ces ruines romaines. Mais ce n'était plus Tipaza. Et ce n'était plus le Chenoua" (2000: 185). [In the midst of the Roman ruins. But it was no longer Tipaza, and it was not Chenoua either.] Tivoli, most renowned for the Emperor Hadrian's villa, lies in the foothills of Rome, on the outskirts of the city. The Emperor Hadrian (76–138 AD), like his successor Marcus Aurelius, followed the philosophy of the Stoics and was influenced by Greek values. But he is predominantly remembered for his cosmopolitanism, his extensive travel throughout the Mediterranean, and his relationship with a young Greek boy, Antinous. The symbolism of Tivoli indicates that the choice of setting for Nina's transformation is not arbitrary. We discover that the "c'est" [it] (in "c'est arrivé à Tivoli" [it took place in Tivoli]) refers, paradoxically, both to her self-fulfillment and to her ability to name desire. Desire "is an interrogative mode of being, a corporeal questioning of identity and place" (Butler 1987: 9) as well as desire for recognition and self-consciousness. Rome marks a turning point, an encounter with her otherness within; "rien ne serait plus jamais comme avant" (2000: 185). [Nothing would ever be the same again.]

Upon returning to Algiers, Nina discovers that something has changed. "Tu as changé" [you have changed], she writes, in what appears to be a farewell letter to Amine, her childhood friend, first love, and "double." However, we understand that it is Nina who has changed, and that she has projected her transformation onto Amine. Her farewell gesture to a part of herself, rather than to Amine, suggests a separation from her past and from the constraining obligations on her choices of gender expressivity.

COMING OUT AND MOVING UP

In fact, in the progression of Bouraoui's novels, *Garçon manqué* marks a major break; from this work on, the author freely writes about and promblematizes lesbianism, even though she prefers not to conceive it as such. In the context of Maghrebi Francophone literature, this subject remains taboo and uncommon. Whereas male homosexuality has received a certain degree of attention through the novels of Rachid Boudjedra, Tahar Ben Jelloun, Rachid O., and most recently Abdellah Taïa, lesbianism has not seen the same degree of textualisation.[17] In this sense, Bouraoui's works are pioneering as well as important challenges to the constraints of Maghrebi Francophone literature written by women. Bouraoui's works are stylistically and thematically combative and point to a struggle against an understanding of a Mediterranean that is still mired in convention.[18] Hayes writes that the notion of combat literature elaborated by Frantz Fanon in *The Wretched of the Earth* and by Jean Déjeux in *Littérature maghrébine de langue française* has often been limited to works that deal with independence struggles. By contrast, Hayes sees combat as potential within all Maghrebi literature, not just within works that stem from and portray anti-colonial revolution. In these other potential spheres he includes texts that challenge sexual normativity, among which Bouraoui's undoubtedly find their place. Her texts tread a thin line between overt combat and vulnerability; in evoking the pain of a ravaged Algeria, she also clearly rebels against a system that ostracizes and marginalizes women and that reinforces heterosexual norms. Insisting on the necessity to continually be capable of changing, Nina writes that "l'important c'est cette volonté de cacher. De dissimuler. De se transformer. De se fuir. D'être hors la loi. Et hors de soi" (2000: 180). [The problem lies in the desire to hide, dissimulate, and transform oneself. The problem lies in the desire to escape from the self like an outlaw, disconnected from one's being.] Locating herself "outside the law," she defies norms of gender and sexuality as well as national hegemonic discourse.

We may consider that the element of combat springs, in part, from the colonial wound, trace or mark, which Bouraoui carries with her. As a fervid objector to the violence of the Algerian wars, to the violence that men have inflicted upon women, as well as to racism in contemporary France, Bouraoui—*via* her autofictive protagonists—may be seen as a modern-day Antigone. If Camus brought us to Aeschylus and his conception of man in revolt (see chapter 1), Bouraoui brings us to Sophocles.[19] Just as Antigone is not allowed to declare, and do justice to, her love for her brother, Nina never properly "buries" the dead of the Algerian war. "Le sang reviendra" (2000: 67, 81) [the blood will return], her mother repeats. In conjunction with this stands a critique of national discourse, which in Algeria officially denies same-sex unions. Lofty as it might have seemed, Antigone's sacrifice was revolutionary in that it announced the possibility for the individual to oppose the state, and for a young woman to defy the orders of a man. As the Franco-Lebanese poet and essayist Salah Stétié puts it: "Antigone a fait, au nom de tous les Méditerranéens, *de toutes les Méditerranéennes*, une découverte capitale et qui va, pour le siècle des siècles, temps et éternité confondus, bouleverser toutes les données de la civilisation . . . c'est qu'il y a plus haut que la raison, que toutes les raisons, la toute-puissance de l'amour" (Stétié 1994: 52; my emphasis). [Antigone made a fundamental discovery, in the name of all Mediterranean people, of all Mediterranean women, that turned civilization upside down forever . . . that is, that the all-powerful force of love trumps reason, all reasons.] Counterbalancing the "order" of a dictatorial regime, Antigone brings together the Apollonian and the Dionysian, order and chaos.

Subtly presented in *La voyeuse interdite* through the interstitial positions of the protagonists' parents (i.e., "homme-femelle"), this duality reappears in *Poupée bella* where the protagonist presents herself on the first page in the following way: "Je suis une femme, je suis un homme, je suis tout, je ne suis rien" (2004: 7). [I am a woman, I am a man, I am everything, I am nothing.] Constructing herself around the oppositions of man and woman, all and nothing, pleasure and pain, brings us back to the notions of measure that were so central to Greek thought. Yet if Antigone's gesture can be also read as extreme and final, for literally sacrificing her life, Bouraoui's rejection of authoritarian rules takes the form of recurrent combat. The opening line of *Poupée bella* reads "je veux une arme pour me défendre" (2004: 1). [I want a weapon to be able to defend myself.]

Towards the end of *Garçon manqué*, Bouraoui's protagonist reflects on her name—Yasmina—or Nina for short: "Mon prénom arabe. Un si joli prénom. Celui que je donnerai plus tard, aux autres qui demandent, à ces filles qui veulent savoir, dans le bruit, dans la nuit, ce prénom que je dois toujours répéter, ce prénom qui fera de moi une étrangère à Paris" (2000: 138). [My Arabic first name, such a pretty name. It is the name I will use later, when girls I meet in the din of the night ask me, wanting to know. It is the name I must constantly and carefully pronounce, the one that makes me a foreigner in Paris.] The abbreviation of her name functions as a symbolic mutilation as, conscious of her fragmented self, she leaves Algiers for Paris. Setting the stage for *Poupée bella*, Bouraoui hints at the incommensurability and difficulties of an Arabic name in a Parisian setting, meeting "filles" "dans la nuit." These encounters with young women, at night, refer to her repetitive *fréquentage* of lesbian nightclubs, or what she names le Milieu des Filles, a term that recalls (or repeats) but differs from the cloistered feminine *milieu* in *La voyeuse interdite*. Composed in the form of a journal, the most intimate of genres, Bouraoui's first-person protagonist is, she writes, "dans le temps de mon homosexualité" (2004: 14) [in the time of my homosexuality]. This "time" is suggestive of what Mireille Rosello has recently defined as a performative encounter.

In *France and the Maghreb: Performative Encounters* (translated into French as *Encontres méditerranéennes: littératures et cultures France-Maghreb*), Rosello proposes and theorizes new readings of encounters, between France and the Maghreb, that she calls performative. By this she means "a type of encounter that coincides with the creation of new subject-positions rather than treating preexisting (pre-imagined) identities as the reason for, and justification of, the protocol of encounter" (2005: 1). These "Mediterranean subjects" (Rosello's term), she argues, are often overdetermined by our narratives of them. In other words, by thinking of subjects as Beur or as Pied-noir, for example, and by using these monikers for them, we mechanically assign them predetermined roles. Encounters between French and Maghrebi subjects are burdened, she writes, with our pre-conceived notions of petrified historical narratives that impose stereotypical subject positions. Rosello maintains that the violence of certain historical contexts—the colonization of Algeria by France being the most prominent example—have exerted such pressures that their subjects are trapped in a pre-written discourse.

Moreover, often read through the metaphor of a dysfunctional marriage (France the husband, Algeria the wife), the relationship between the two nations is characterized as heterosexual. The analogy, of course, is that France is dominant, male, active, and endowed with reason, whereas Algeria is submissive, female, passive, and devoid of it. In the tradition of Orientalist writing, the "oriental woman" often stands as a metonymy for the Orient itself, as a mysterious, veiled, closed space, and one that is suggestive of transgressive pleasures. In *Orientalism*, Edward Saïd notes how artists and writers, Flaubert for one, equated Egypt with sexual escapism and Oriental women. Writers such as Assia Djebar and Leila Sebbar have directly engaged with such depictions, dispelling and rewriting archaic *idées reçues* on "oriental women."[20] Bouraoui, who does not neatly fit into any such "rewriting," displaces the metaphor of a female "Orient" through a questioning of those original positionings and through her encounters with a "female" France. For her, "L'Algérie est un homme" (2000: 37). [Algeria is a man.] However, rather than a simple reversal of the gendered metaphor, Bouraoui posits, as I have suggested, the two entities as mutually constitutive and as hybrid. In a performative encounter, the body, its perceived gender, and its ethnic identity are performed and reembodied. Rosello's framework is particularly useful in that performative encounters are "less about 'ways of being' than about 'ways of being with'" (2005: 6), a position that brings us to the intersubjective dimension that is so critical to a Mediterranean ethos. Bouraoui's works provoke these very encounters—in the narration itself and between text and reader—and encourage us to conceptualize new subject-positions, by "making something happen where nothing was" (Rosello 2005: 183).

Bouraoui is, whether justified or not, most commonly associated with writers of Maghrebi origin and/or Beur writers; from a historical and cultural perspective women writing from and on the Maghreb have tended to depict their "sisters" as victims of patriarchal, *heterosexual*, societies. Bouraoui herself, in *La voyeuse interdite*, presents us with what can be read as the most familiar and conventional representation of oppressed women: cloistered, ignorant, veiled, and wholly submissive to male domination, to their fathers, brothers, and husbands. While such denunciation of women as victims has been—and remains—crucial, very few novels depicting Maghrebi women have taken on the question of same-sex desire.[21]

At first glance, these texts appear to fill a void and produce something that was missing: a text by a writer with Maghrebi origins about lesbian desire. Bouraoui has gone beyond the taboos that she had already so deftly challenged by naming taboos of sexuality and religion in *La voyeuse interdite*. As Jean Déjeux states, "Ce roman de 1991 est pour l'instant comme un sommet dans l'écriture feminine algérienne faisant voler en éclats bienséances et conventions dans la manière traditionelle de parler du corps et dans le refus d'écouter son langage" (1994: 101). [So far, it seems as if this 1991 novel is the apogee of Algerian women's writing, as it shatters propriety and convention, as well as the traditional way of talking about the body and the refusal to listen to its language.] Taken at a different level, encounters that might have previously been seen as unthinkable occur. Rosello argues that subjects who take the permanent duality, or multiplicity, of the hybrid and the hyphenated as a point of departure rather than a point of arrival are most successful in breaking out of the molds in which they are often placed.

Poupée bella revolves around a series of encounters between an unnamed narrator-protagonist, and a succession of young women, all of which take place in lesbian nightclubs. If, up until now, nightclubs have been often represented as sites of exclusion, a phenomenon treated with much candor by male writers Azouz Begag in *Béni ou le paradis privé* (1989) and Paul Smaïl (pseudonym) in *Vivre me tue* (1997) for example, they are here unexpectedly revealed to us as accessible places. It is in these previously contested and exclusive public places that the protagonist experiences her sexuality. "Tu rentres avec qui?" [Who are you going home with?] echoes throughout the anonymous "Milieu des Filles," a series of underground nightclubs where the protagonist lives her "désespoir amoureux" [despair of love] and engages in encounters with women identified only by the first letter of their names. The women appear interchangeable, yet they enter into intense individual encounters with the protagonist: "Quand je retrouve S. j'ai le coeur qui se serre" (2004: 45). [When I meet up with S. I feel heavy-hearted.] What may on the surface appear somewhat contradictory is in fact the very basis of Bouraoui's perspective. Instead of reconciling the oppositions that pervade her text she assumes them, creating a new rhythm and language, juxtaposing and playing on them. Thus phrases like "je regarde les femmes ensemble et j'ai envie de pleurer; il y a une vraie tristesse. Il y a une vraie beauté" (2004: 52) [I watch the women together and I feel like crying; there is real sadness. There is real beauty] form the basis of her oeuvre.[22] Such affirmation, however, is always in a slippery present-tense of finite duration: "Je suis toujours à fond dans le lieu que je traverse. Je suis dans cette instant, là. Cette permanence" (2004: 99). [I am always fully in the place that I am passing through. I am in that very moment. That permanence.] The oxymoronic "permanence of an instant" translates an ethos of experience and of attention to the "here and now" which, to a certain degree, stands in contrast to becoming, a notion otherwise so pervasive in Bouraoui's works. However, the two positions need not be seen as mutually exclusive in that the "here and now" in Bouraoui's fragmented work is perpetually renewed.

Early on, the nameless protagonist of *Poupée bella* asks "Combien de temps faudra-t-il pour trouver? Pour devenir ce que je suis?" (2004: 9) [How long will it take to find [her]? To become what I am?], referring to the search for the woman of her life in the first question and following it up with the question that haunts all the writers in this project: how to become what one is. Here we are brought to believe that sexual desire is always in process, subject to change and that there can be no *one* woman for her. Part of the answer to her question is found in the passage she makes, from affirming she is living her homosexuality in the beginning of the text where she refers to being "en devenir homosexuel," to the end where she writes, "Il n'y a aucune homosexualité. Cela n'existe pas" (2004: 128). [There is no homosexuality. That doesn't exist.] In fact, throughout her *fréquentage* of the Milieu des Filles, she is in an ambiguous liaison with her male friend, Julien, in which it is not clear whether she desires him sexually or not: "J'ai plusieurs vies. J'ai plusieurs corps sous mon corps" (2004: 17). [I have several lives. I have several bodies under my body.] This multiplicity of lives and stratification of bodies brings us back to the condition of possibility that is important to Rosello's "performative encounters," namely that multiplicity is a point of departure, not of arrival.

It is precisely this multiplicity that has been negated in national discourse, most blatantly in the case of Algeria, and until recently has been relentlessly manipulated in the interest of military-backed governments and religious fundamentalism. Subsequent to the 1991 civil war, dissidents and activists, among them women like Khalida Messaoudi, have been threatened or assassinated as part of an indirect attempt to create, or hypothetically maintain, the homogeneity of the nation.[23] The 1993 assassination of the writer Tahar Djaout testified to the climate of intolerance so prevalent in the 1990s and that still persists today. Jarrod Hayes advances the theory that Djaout's *Le chercheur d'os* and *L'invention du désert* bring "skeletons out of the Nation's closet" by writing about national liberation fighters and homosexuality (2000: 97). In *L'invention du désert*, Djaout evokes the repression of homosexuality during the Almoravid dynasty (a dynasty that ruled what is now Morocco and part of Algeria from the mid-1000s to the mid-1100s). Juxtaposing this with the "skeletons," or literally the bones, of the freedom-fighter protagonist in *Le chercheur d'os*, Hayes reveals how Djaout exposes not only the political but the sexual "secrets of the nation" (2000: 75). What is important in the context of an analysis of Bouraoui's works is that Hayes brings the issue of sexuality to the ideal of the Maghrebi nation. He convincingly links sexual and national identities positing that nation-building discourse can only work when what he calls non-normative sexualities are repressed, marginalized, and silenced. However, Hayes reminds us that postcolonial Maghrebi writing has exposed sexual dissidence and marginalized groups:

> When Maghrebian authors formulate representations of homosexuality, sodomy, homoeroticism, lesbianism, cross-dressing, the joys of emasculation, women's resistance, public unveiling, and feminist guerrilla warfare, they do not merely challenge sexual taboos, sexual normativity, and patriarchy (which they do); they also reveal the queerness of the Nation. (2000: 16)

Hayes uses the term "queer," characterizing it as different from the labels gay, lesbian, or feminist, which, according to Judith Butler, assume the existence of a stable subject (for example, the lesbian subject). Following Butler, queer theory attempts to deconstruct these categories and affirms the indeterminacy and instability of all sexed and gendered identities. "Queer" is in fact more appropriate for Bouraoui's later works (*Poupée bella, La vie heureuse* and *Mes mauvaises pensées*) as she privileges the indeterminacy and instability of gendered identities

In *La vie heureuse*, which takes place away from the Mediterranean, in Switzerland and Brittany, Bouraoui fully reveals a conception of same-sex desire. Interestingly, the word *heureuse* appears in *Garçon manqué* only when the protagonist becomes acutely aware of desire in Rome: "Je suis devenue heureuse à Rome. J'ai attaché mes cheveux et on a découvert une nuque très fine. Et encore plus. Des attaches sensibles . . . Des mains et des gestes d'une femme. Une voix plus grave et contrôlée. Je suis devenue heureuse à Rome" (2000: 185). [I became happy in Rome. I tied my hair back. We discovered a thin nape. Sensitive ties . . . Female hands and gestures. A deeper and controlled voice. I became happy in Rome.] As if only able to attempt an explanation of what it means to "be happy" and to love happily another woman by distancing herself from Algeria, Bouraoui's texts about lesbian love take place elsewhere. Written as two parallel first-person stories told by the sixteen-year-old protagonist, Marie, *La vie heureuse* juxtaposes the story of her aunt slowly losing her battle with cancer with a narrative of her own sexual discovery. The latter revolves around a turbulent love story with Diane, a bisexual classmate with whom she falls in love. In a dance club one night, Marie remarks, "Je ne voulais pas qu'on nous prenne pour des lesbiennes. Ça ne me plaisait pas" (2002: 151). [I didn't want people to think we were lesbians. I didn't like the thought of that.] Her conception of same-sex love is not predicated on a uniformity of experience or on a similarity of the sexes. Rather, she understands it as an inimitable encounter, different each time it is performed. Describing her relationship with her partner, Marie reflects on "l'histoire des filles," the story and the "non-history" of same-sex relationships between women:

> Diane *ne* remplace pas ma mère. Ce *n'est* pas ça l'histoire des filles. C'est autre chose. Ce *n'est* pas le souvenir de l'enfance, l'odeur de la peau et du lait, la petite voix qui endort, les mains qui soignent. Ce *n'est* pas cela aimer une fille. Ça *ne* remplace rien. Ce *n'est* pas nostalgique. Ce *n'est* pas détester les hommes *non plus*. C'est plus dangereux une fille. C'est plus risqué. Et ce *n'est* pas s'aimer. On *n'est* plus une fille avec une fille. On *ne* se retrouve pas en elle. On *ne* comble pas et on *ne* manque pas. C'est plus que cela. Ça *n'a* pas d'histoire. C'est *sans* passé. C'est d'une grande virginité. Il n'y a *aucun* malheur à aimer une fille. Ça donne beaucoup de force. Ça rend intelligent, à force de mentir. Ce *n'est* plus une fille alors. C'est un sujet qui surgit. (2002: 85; my emphasis)

> [Diane does not replace my mother. That is not what the story of girls is. It's something else. It is not the memory of childhood, the scent of skin and milk, the soft voice that puts one to sleep, the hands that heal. That is not what loving a girl is. It doesn't replace something. It is not nostalgic. It isn't hating men either. Girls are more dangerous. It's more risky. And it's not loving each other. One is no longer a girl with a girl. One doesn't find oneself in her. One doesn't fill a void or miss anything. It's more than that. It has no history. It's without a past. It's of the utmost virginity. There is nothing wrong with loving a girl. It is very strengthening. As a consequence of lying and lying it makes one smarter. One isn't merely a girl then. One becomes a subject.]

For Bouraoui, the way to tell women's stories, those of lesbians in particular, is through a fragmented, broken sequence of what these stories are *not*. "Antigone's no" returns to denounce the misconceptions and "negativity" imposed upon female subjects. Like Simone de Beauvoir, who was criticized for defining women in opposition to men, and therefore as privative, Bouraoui appears to define "l'histoire des filles" *en creux*, through negation. However, she ends her description by affirming that a *fille* "c'est un sujet qui surgit" [an emergent subject], that does not simply appear but also irrupts. As the force of her prose in *La voyeuse interdite* reveals, Bouraoui suggests that at the core of lesbian subjectivity is a form of epistemic violence, given that the patriarchal norms that have justified silencing of and violence towards women become even more insistent when those women escape heterosexual norms. Lesbians, Bouraoui suggests, have been reduced to a label and to imaginary objects defined as lesbian and nothing else, or worse yet, by the way they make love: "Ce n'est rien, l'homosexualité. C'est un mot inventé. C'est dans la nature de chacun. C'est une affaire de peau et de rencontre. C'est comme dire: Bonjour madame, debout ou couché? Sous ou sur votre mari?" (2002: 321) [Homosexuality is nothing. It is an invented word. It's in everyone's nature. It's all about intuition and chance encounters. It's like saying: Hello ma'am, standing up or lying down? Under or on top of your husband?][24] Continually othered by heterosexual societal norms, the lesbian subject must irrupt differently, must come into being on her own terms.

WOMEN, WAR AND WORDS

As the repetitive, disjointed prose indicates, "l'histoire des filles" is by no means a linear, smooth narrative. Bouraoui's short, lapidary prose translates fragmented and truncated experiences of self to a fragmented Algeria, to a segregated France and to an embattled coming to terms with same-sex desire. Her writing takes the form of transcribed, rather than described experiences. From her first novel, it is clear that narrative is of primary importance and, in reading her texts, we find ourselves on the fine line between the real and the fictive. Fikria, the cloistered protagonist, is rescued from her abject circumstances thanks to her ability to imagine alternate wor(l)ds:

> L'important est l'histoire. Se faire une histoire avant de regarder le vrai. *Réelle, irréelle*, qu'importe! Le récit entoure la chose d'un nouvel éclat, le temps y dépose un de ses attributs privilégiés, *mémoire, souvenir ou reminiscence*, le hasard peaufine l'oeuvre et la chose prend forme. Enfin, là, on a une aventure. Que peut-on raconter sinon une histoire? (1991: 10; my emphasis)

> [What matters is the story. To make a story for oneself before looking around at what's true. Real, unreal, what's the big deal! The tale surrounds the thing with a sudden glow, time deposits there one of its privileged attributes, memory, recall, or reminiscence, chance polishes the work and the thing takes form. And there at long last you have it, an adventure. What's there to tell if not a story?]

Imagination provides access to alternate worlds which she necessarily must see as more important than "the real" since "the real" is intolerable. However, Bouraoui's texts also point to the impossibility of escaping conditions of "reality" that entail war, violence and oppression through memories and reminiscence. The wound that Nina, in *Garçon manqué*, has

inherited from her parents' contested marriage is the driving force behind her desire to write: "Moi [aussi] j'aurais cette force. Cette envie. De
détruire. De sauter à la gorge. De *dénoncer*. D'ouvrir les murs. Ce sera une
force vive mais rentrée. Un démon. Qui sortira avec l'écriture. Ce n'est
pas soi qui compte. On arrive toujours à se soigner . . . C'est la mémoire
de nos parents qui est importante" (2000: 129; my emphasis). [I (too) will
have this strength. This desire. To destroy. To go for the jugular. To
denounce. To open up walls. A strength that will be alive but controlled.
A demon. That will come out in writing. It is not the self that matters.
One always manages to take care of oneself . . . it is the memory of our
parents that is important.] Writing, as a form of anamnesis, and as denunciation, places Bouraoui in a critical relationship to both colonizer
and colonized.

Writing, in order to reveal the violence of the colonial encounter between France and Algeria, symbolized by her parents, destabilizes the
presumably foundational principles of the nation. According to historian
Ernest Renan, there is a necessary violence at the heart of the foundation
of any nation. In order for such violence not to hinder the "spirit" of the
people, it must, Renan affirmed, be collectively forgotten. Although his
text (originally given as a speech) *Qu'est-ce qu'une nation* is now dated, its
premises are still topical today as they are revisited and rehabilitated by
contemporary nationalist discourse. Nicolas Sarkozy cited him with great
pride in March of 2007 in an attempt to galvanize the "spirit of the people": "La France c'est une culture, un idéal, une idée. 'Une âme, un principe spirituel' disait Renan."[25] [France is a culture, an ideal, an idea. 'A
soul and a spiritual principle' Renan used to say.] That violence, in today's rhetorical French nationhood, clearly concerns the—until recently
nameless—Algerian War of independence. Not until 1999 were the eu-
phemistic designated "événements" of 1954–1962, officially called a
"guerre." Pressing issues of immigration are, undeniably, even if only
partially, related to this very condition of forgetting and remembering.

To write, in Bouraoui's case, is to testify to the stifling of voices that
might "pollute" the nation: those that recall historical moments best forgotten by nationalist ambitions. Invoking the particularly brutal nature of
the OAS (Organisation de l'Armée Secrète), a division of the French army
that fought tooth and nail against Algerian independence during the war,
she writes "C'est ainsi que je vis notre histoire algérienne. En combat . . .
C'est venger les femmes algériennes massacrées par les hommes de
l'OAS" (2000: 62). [This is how I experience our Algerian history, in combat . . . Avenge the Algerian women massacred at the hands of the OAS
men.] As much as writing and narration are tied to Franco-Algerian history for Bouraoui, they are equally implicated in her critique of gender
inequality. In explaining how to pronounce her Arabic last name to an
imaginary French person she deconstructs it letter by letter: "B-o-u-r-a-o-
u-i. Non, pas Baraoui ni Bouraqui. C'est pourtant simple! Bouraoui de

raha conter, et de *Abi* qui signifie le père. Les noms arabes sont des prisons familiales. On est toujours le fils de avec Ben ou le père de avec Bou.
Des prisons familiales et masculines" (2000: 123).[26] [B-o-u-r-a-o-u-i. No,
not Baraoui or Bouraqui. It is not that complicated! Bouraoui from *rawa*
that means to tell a story, and *Abi* that signifies father. Arabic names are
family prisons. One is always "the son of" with Ben or "the father of"
with Bou. Masculine family prisons.] Returning to a criticism of dominant male social practices, such as that of patronymic naming, Bouraoui
uses her role as *raconteur*/narrator, to protect herself: "seule l'écriture
protégera du monde" (2000: 20). [Only writing will protect me from the
world.] Only writing and narrating, as Fikria the *voyeuse* also declares,
can transmit the inexplicable.

To write, then, is to testify to the violence inherent in the effects of
dominant discourses that subject and subjugate. Although Bouraoui's
works may not be considered as conventional testimonials, they nevertheless bear witness and denounce. According to Shoshana Felman, testimony is pervasive and implicated in almost every kind of writing. It is, as
she and Dori Laub suggest in *Testimony: Crises of Witnessing in Literature,
Psychoanalysis and History*, a discursive *practice* that is also a performative
speech act. In other words, it is a form that has the capability of changing
our perceptions and assumptions. Felman explains: "In its most traditional, routine use . . . testimony is provided, and is called for, when the facts
upon which justice must pronounce its verdict are not clear, when historical accuracy is in doubt and when both the truth and its supporting
elements of evidence are called into question" (1992: 6). The accuracy of
the facts about the Algerian War, the civil war, and even immigration in
France, has been questionable, problematic, and blatantly manipulated.
The statistics on gender discrimination are, as statistics go, in all probabil-
ity partially deceptive. This is not to say that testimony can necessarily fill
the lacunae and right an unjust version of history or social ills, but it does
demonstrate a form of commitment that goes beyond the individual. In
this sense, Bouraoui's re-evocation of the "événements," her denunciation of the subordination of women in Mediterranean societies, and her
narration of "new" gendered and sexual identities present an alternative
perspective rather than fill a void. After all, her texts are intentionally
fictive. As she writes in *Poupée bella* "la main qui écrit n'est jamais inno-
cente" (2004: 178). [The hand that writes is never innocent.] As if wanting
to cure a pathological societal ill, "la main qui écrit est une main qui
guérit" (2004: 31, 84, 110) [the hand that writes is the hand that heals]
appears several times in this short work on lesbian encounters.

Bouraoui's testimony takes the form of a diary in *Poupée bella* where
each entry is dated, whereas in *Mes mauvaises pensées*, the first-person
protagonist lives out a four-hundred page psychoanalytic session. The
diary (which resembles an eyewitness account) and the "confession," as
forms of testimony, bring us back to an awareness of the sometimes

invisible fault line between fact and fiction. Unlike Camus, Mellah or Ben Jelloun, Bouraoui's rapport to the Mediterranean is tragic. Her prose is crude, lacerating, and terse, and in this case in particular, the author behind the texts cannot go unscrutinized. The recurrent first-person (sometimes nameless) protagonists, and the similarities between them and Bouraoui's biography, bring me to conclude that the wounds of an inherited war along with those caused by gender trouble cannot be laid to rest even through writing. The act of writing, for the protagonist of *Poupée bella* is, she says, "la seule façon pour moi, de devenir une personne" (2004: 33) [the only way for me to become a person]. Similarly, for Bouraoui, her writing, like her becoming, is a process of infinite deferral. For although her testimony may be unique, it also, in its element of denunciation, refers outward to multiple "wronged" communities of the Mediterranean.

In a different context, Spanish writer Jorge Semprun questions whether it is possible to tell tragedy.[27] Bouraoui's style is clear, but is her "story"? In his book about surviving internment at Buchenwald, *L'écriture ou la vie*, Semprun writes of his conviction that literature is an imperfect medium, but the only one through which to translate the inexpressible:

> Pourtant, un doute me vient sur la possiblité de raconter. Non pas que l'expérience vécue soit indicible. Elle a été invivable, ce qui est tout autre chose, on le comprendra aisément. Autre chose qui ne concerne pas la forme d'un récit possible, mais sa substance. Non pas son articulation, mais sa densité. Ne parviendront à cette substance, à cette densité transparente que ceux qui sauront faire de leur témoignage un objet artistique, un espace de création. Ou de recréation. Seul l'artifice d'un récit maîtrisé parviendra à transmettre partiellement la vérité du témoignage. Mais ceci n'a rien d'exceptionnel: il en arrive ainsi de toutes les grandes expériences historiques. (1994: 23)

> [I start to doubt the possibility of telling the story. Not that what we lived through is indescribable. It was unbearable, which is something else entirely (that won't be hard to understand), something that doesn't concern the form of a possible account, but its substance. Not its articulation, but its density. The only ones who will manage to reach this substance, this transparent density, will be those able to shape their evidence into an artistic object, a space of creation. Or of recreation. Only the artifice of a masterly narrative will prove capable of conveying some of the truth of such testimony. But there's nothing exceptional about this: it's the same with all great historical experiences.]

The Algerian War and the Holocaust present two significantly different situations, but what Semprun expresses may very well pertain to the pain that Bouraoui transmits through her prose. That is to say, a pain that comes from past and present Franco-Algerian encounters, and in no less painful a way, from the lifelong negotiation of gendered and heteronormative spaces. In Bouraoui's Mediterranean, the tragic past of the Algerian wars, of present French nationalism and of being a "garçon manqué," is still being written. "Unmanning" the Mediterranean, as Bouraoui's works testify, means queering it, "unpolicing" it and undoing the androcentrism that for so long has determined gender relationships in the area. By queering it she brings out the indeterminacy and shifting nature of gender, by unpolicing it she draws our attention to the draconian laws still in place today and displaces man as normative model.

ENDNOTES

1. Braudel, Horden and Purcell, and Georges Duby have significantly under-represented women in their studies.

2. Patriarchy in Mediterranean societies differs among nations. In Algeria and Morocco, the countries present in this chapter, the nuclear family has become increasingly widespread. Up until recently, extended families tended to form the family unit, but recent reforms in family codes in both countries have led to a diversity of configurations.

3. Studies on Classical Greece are an exception to this oversight and in fact account for much of the work done on homosexuality in the Mediterranean. See Aldrich (1993).

4. Introduction to Yamina Mechakra's *La grotte éclatée* (2000).

5. Family codes differ significantly in the countries of the Maghreb: whereas in Morocco and Tunisia laws pertaining to women became more permissive after independence, the Algerian family code is still very conservative. It should also be noted that situations differ considerably between women in urban and rural settings, as well as between those who are literate and those who are not.

6. Equally important in this discussion are the male writers Mohammed Dib and Nabile Farès who have theorized and problematized the position of women as well as broken down binary notions of sexuality.

7. Interview with Rosalia Bivona in *Nina Bouraoui: un sintomo della letteratura migrante nell'area franco-magrebina*. Doctoral Thesis, University of Palermo. http://www.limag.refer.org/Theses/Bivona.PDF.

8. In an interview "Ecrire c'est retrouver ses fantômes" by Dominique Simonnet in *L'Express*, 31 May, 2004.

9. Charles Bonn uses Barthes's term *écriture blanche*, a term often ascribed to Camus's work, to describe Bouraoui's writing (1999: 20).

10. The site of Chenoua intertextually links Bouraoui's novel to Assia Djebar's 1978 film *La nouba des femmes du Mont Chenoua* as well as to Camus's *Noces*. Djebar's film, in which women's recollections of the Algerian War are interspersed with documentary footage, is a rare rendition of a previously unrepresented feminine space of expression.

11. Bouraoui's solitude inscribes itself in a positioning also established by Yamina Mechakra in *La grotte éclatée* where the first-person protagonist is born into solitude: "Je suis née solitude" (Mechakra 2000: 2). [I was born solitude.]

12. See in particular Van Zuylen, Bivona, and McIlvanney.

13. In Ben Jelloun's *L'enfant de sable* and *La nuit sacrée* the moment of birth is the decisive moment of gender inscription; his texts recall Judith Butler's claim that it is at the moment of birth (i.e., the exclamation "it's a girl!") that our socialization into gender begins. Ahmed/Zahra's gender ambivalence throughout the novels precludes any essential sexuality, and Zahra is raised as Ahmed thanks to the discursive structures of which he/she is part.

14. In this context "discursive" should be understood as a derivative of Foucault's use of "discourse," that is to say a set of linguistic rules and structures through which

we are constructed and through which we apprehend the world. The body is also "read" and "interpreted" through discourse.

15. In an interview with Rosalia Bivona, Bouraoui acknowledges having read and been influenced by Sartre.

16. I owe this formulation to T. Jefferson Kline, who brought it to my attention in a course at Boston University.

17. Jean Déjeux compares Bouraoui to Boudjedra, affirming that "l'écriture audacieuse de Nina Bouraoui est le contraire du pudique: elle est sensuelle, pathétique, charnelle telle que Rachid Boudjedra la souhaite pour le roman algérien et telle que lui-même essaie de pratiquer" (Déjeux: 1994, 93). [Nina Bouraoui's daring writing is the opposite of modest; it is sensual, pathetic, bodily, just like Rachid Boudjedra wishes the writing in Algerian novels to be, and just as he himself tries to write.] However, her affiliations to writers and artists who have broken the silence of homosexual expression are not those that critics such as Déjeux compare her to, but rather we find references to the European artists Hervé Guibert and Klaus Nomi in her texts.

18. This is not to say, of course, that other forms of sexuality are not practiced. The anthropologist and psychoanalyst Malek Chebel goes as far as suggesting that there is such a thing as "Mediterranean sensuality" and that "l'homosexuel maghrébin existe et fleurit: toutes les marginalités sexuelles coexistent là, comme ailleurs, même si, ici, elles sont moins bien connues que là. Cette inclination naturelle de la minorité sexuelle au Maghreb est, ni plus ni moins, aussi baroque, aussi richement assortie que toutes les autres sensualités et, *a fortiori*, que la sensualité méditerranéenne" (2003: 21). [The Maghrebi homosexual exists and flourishes : all sexual marginalities coexist there, as elsewhere, even if here they are less well known than there. This natural inclination of a sexual minority in the Maghreb is, neither more nor less, as baroque and as rich as all other sensualities and *a fortiori*, as Mediterranean sensuality.]

19. Interestingly, the plays of Aeschylus, Euripides and Sophocles, the three principal Greek tragedians, often served as criticisms of family structures. Sophocles' Antigone is the daughter of Oedipus, and sister of Polyneices, who died in a struggle with his brother for the power to rule over Thebes. Wishing to do Polyneices justice and to give him a proper burial, Antigone goes against the orders of Creon, the king. She carries out her act and then commits suicide.

20. See for example Djebar's *Femmes d'Alger dans leur appartement* (1980), *L'amour la fantasia* (1985) and *Ombre Sultane* (1987) as well as Sebbar's Shérazade trilogy: *Shérazade, 17 ans brune, frisée, les yeux verts* (1982), *Les carnets de Shérazade* (1985) and *Le fou de Shérazade* (1991).

21. The reason for this may be twofold; on the one hand depicting same-sex desire in women risks reproducing Orientalist tropes. On the other, the subject is clearly still taboo in a number of traditional societies with strong repressive factions.

22. These constructions are reminiscent of Marguerite Duras's style, "tu me tues, tu me fais du bien" [you kill me, you do me good], in *Hiroshima mon amour.*

23. Messaoudi was threatened in response to her opposition to the conservative Algerian Family Code that went into effect in 1984. This law put women at a great disadvantage by instituting measures which included that women are considered minors and married women are to be under their husband's supervision. The Family Code was revised in 2005.

24. In an interview Bouraoui makes a similar statement: "L'homosexualité, ce n'est qu'un mot. Quand j'ai osé l'écrire pour la première fois, je me suis dit: 'Ah! quelle incroyable victoire!' Mais le langage nous emprisonne. 'Ah, vous êtes homosexuelle?' On imagine tout de suite comment vous faites l'amour!" (Simonnet, 1) [Homosexuality is only a word. When I dared to write if for the first time I said to myself 'Oh! What an incredible victory!' But language emprisons us. 'Oh, you're homosexual?' They right away imagine the way you make love!]

25. Discours de Nicolas Sarkozy. Caen, 9 mars, 2007, p. 1.

26. In *La venue à l'écriture* Hélène Cixous, who was also born and raised in Algeria, similarly probes the meaning of her name and links it to the act of writing. Her notion

of *Algériance,* like Derrida's *Nostalgérie,* both evoke the sense of having left Algeria physically but not spiritually. Although both the notions of *nostalgérie* and *algériance* are highly personal, Bouraoui's relationship to Algeria may stand in an interesting comparison.

27. Jorge Semprun was born in Spain but as a young boy his family was exiled to France due to the Spanish Civil War. Semprun writes primarily in French.

FOUR

Shifting Geographies

Tahar Ben Jelloun's Neapolitan Baroque

Tahar Ben Jelloun's literary career spans more than forty years, includes winning the Prix Goncourt (1987), several nominations for the Nobel Prize, and recurrent appearances on bestseller lists throughout Europe. For decades, attention to his works has tended to focus on his dual allegiance to France and Morocco and to the two cultural and linguistic worlds that he inhabits. Although his early works revolve around Arab traditions and myths and are often inflected with Arabic syntax, more recently his books betray a concern with Moroccan sociopolitical issues and with questions of metropolitan French Islam, immigration and racism. In his latest works, however, he takes the reader north of Morocco, and south of Paris, to Italy and Spain; for a writer with a very distinct sense of time and place—Fes and Tangier, for instance, are charged with symbolism in almost every one of his works, and many of his novels end with the date and place in which they were written—the choice of these two countries is not simply arbitrary. The physical proximity both to France and to North Africa may be the simplest explanation for this choice; after all both Italy and Spain share borders with France, there are a mere 14km between Tangier and Tarifa, and only 200km separate Tunisia from Sicily. But Ben Jelloun's works suggest more than this.

Just as Bouraoui's performative encounters undo petrified narratives by breaking free of ascribed gender roles, so too do a number of Tahar Ben Jelloun's works rewrite and recast a France-Maghreb dyadic relationship. Along with questions of gender and sexuality in *L'enfant de sable* and *La nuit sacrée*, two issues dealt with in detail by Valérie Orlando and Jarrod Hayes, Ben Jelloun makes use of narrative strategies that privilege multiple viewpoints, including perspectives from several geographical

93

locations. In this chapter I argue that the expression of these encounters takes the form of what can be called a baroque poetic; here, the notions of polyphony, multiple perspectives and movement are coupled with metaphors and allegories of past, present and future time. According to critic Dominique Chancé, writers who tend toward a poetic of the baroque are often those who question world order, laws and chaos and who prefer contradictory, unfinished, ephemeral figures to classification and categorization. This has been the sort of postmodern poetic that has frequently been ascribed to Ben Jelloun's works.[1] However, I suggest that this approach is also in constant dialogue and redefinition not merely because of its bicultural specificity but because it relates most productively to the larger Mediterranean. Ultimately Ben Jelloun's baroque poetic, along with the textual strategies it enacts, conveys a way of being, challenges reason, homogenous geographies and linear time. With Mourad Yelles we may say that the baroque is "l'expression endémique d'une résistance éthique et esthétique à l'hégémonie de la règle" (2001: 239) [the endemic expression of an ethical and aesthetic resistance to the hegemony of rules].[2]

In this context, the term "baroque" is not to be understood as referring to the specific historical period of the seventeenth century, nor simply to an aesthetic style, for as historian José Maravall justly argues, style cannot be isolated from its defining cultural context. Rather, it should be seen as a reflection of a mentality, built indeed upon traces of what has been understood as baroque—a seventeenth-century aesthetic concept born in reaction to rationalism and classicism that sought to appeal to the emotional senses—but which is at the same time radically unique. If, in the seventeenth century, it was a predominantly European phenomenon, a modern understanding of baroque should come to encompass artistic works regardless of their national and temporal provenance.

In 1990 Ben Jelloun was invited, by the director of the Neapolitan daily *Il Mattino*, to Naples, Calabria, and Sicily, where he was to observe the Mafia-dominated sociopolitical climate and subsequently draw from it a work of fiction.[3] In 1992 he published *L'ange aveugle* [translated as *State of Absence*], a collection of fourteen short stories based on his notes and interviews with judges, lawyers, political militants, shopkeepers, victims of the Mafia and their Neapolitan equivalent, the Camorra.[4] Given the *Italianness* of the phenomenon of the Mafia, and Ben Jelloun's longtime concern with France and Morocco, his signature on such a work at first appears out of place and unusual. Yet, in the preface to the collection, he notes that he has always been drawn to Italy "par affinité méditerranéenne" [by a Mediterranean affinity] and, more interestingly, he writes that his time in Italy "m'a permis de me ressourcer et de m'exposer à la violence d'un quotidien *étrange* et troublant" (1992: 10; my emphasis) [enabled me to get back to my roots and to expose myself to the violence of a daily existence at once strange and disturbing]. Thus, *L'ange aveugle* begins under the sign of a paradox between "affinity" and "strangeness."

Politically and economically, the Mediterranean South has long been defined in negative opposition to the North, where countries that now belong to the European Union—France, Italy, Spain in particular—are set against and above those that do not, such as the countries of the Maghreb, Turkey, or Egypt. Whereas the North benefits from economic prosperity, the South is still seen as backward and as a latecomer to modernity. However, such divisions are not as easily drawn along cultural lines; from a cultural point of view, the notion of the "South" signifies differently, and in Ben Jelloun's works is inextricably tied to questions of historical domination and oppression and is—still today—part and parcel of the effects of imperialism and colonialism.

The term "south" is not intended to reproduce empty categorical divisions based solely on geography or on a static idea of culture. Rather, it is meant to convey the existence of a set of values and a spatiotemporal dynamic that is particular to the southern shores of the Mediterranean. Positioned as such, it is a south which is geographically specific but that at the same time extends "outwards to invest the on-going becoming of the rest of the world" as Iain Chambers puts it. He sustains that "it is in this mutable space" of the Mediterranean that one can challenge "the abuse and excess of [the] unilateral management of language" that "always reflects the positivity of those in political power" (Chambers 2005: 51). It is in the Mediterranean that one is able to pose questions, "seemingly forbidden elsewhere." Why in this particular space? It is a space, he writes, that reveals "an open, creolized complexity that the narrow requirements of modern nationalism and identity are unable to contain" and where "the intricate pattern and design of language . . . extricates us from the predictable and propels us towards the unconsidered and the unknown" (2005: 55). If we follow Chambers's line that unpredictability is what cannot be "contained" within national/political discourse, we can add that the "unconsidered" and the "unknown" are those elements that turn into the marginal. It is here then, in a space that extends between and beyond France and Morocco, that Ben Jelloun's figures—who are almost always marginal—can be understood as subjects in their own right, valorized in their difference.[5]

SETTING OUT: THE FOREIGN AND THE FAMILIAR

On the one hand Ben Jelloun is a foreigner to Italy, and the "quotidien étrange" [strange daily existence] that he encounters seems in part due to his position as an outsider, as an "observateur étranger et intrigué" (1992: 10) [a curious outside observer]. On the other hand, the issues that have been the trademarks of his works—issues of oppression, violence, and injustice—appear, in this work, to haunt him. Despite the fact that in Italy he is culturally "other," the position Ben Jelloun occupies is not simply foreign, but also familiar. In fact, certain aspects and figures of Southern Italy appear so familiar that he cannot help but invest them with doubles, with their Moroccan equivalents.

In the story "Pietro le fou, Pietro le sage" [Pietro the Fool, Pietro the Sage] (Story VI in *L'ange aveugle*), Pietro patently mirrors Moha in Ben Jelloun's well-known novel *Moha le fou, Moha le sage* (1978); like Moha, Pietro is a *conteur* who makes regular appearances in public squares to denounce social injustice and to speak truth to power.[6] Moha deplores the effects of French colonialism in Morocco, whereas Pietro curses the corruption of the Italian government. Forced to break with his aspirations of being an actor because of a speech impediment ("il bégayait" [he stuttered]), Pietro sets out for several towns in Italy, and then Morocco, to tell the story of a bleeding South, of a *Mezzogiorno*[7] that he calls "une immense blessure" (1992: 106) [a huge wound]. His oratory tour begins in a run-down theater, a ruin, where he denounces the ills of the Mafia, political corruption, and religion. He is only able to speak without stuttering if he is not interrupted. The story is thus punctuated but told as if in one breath. Pietro is excessive in every way; his disproportionate height scares children into thinking he is an ogre and his loquaciousness is overwhelming. Yet he attempts to enlighten common citizens about one of their greatest ills—the lack of a responsible state and the powerful illegitimacy of the Mafia. He proclaims that the newspapers are full of stories about abuses of power and fraud, but people live their lives as if they are at the theater, as if real life is elsewhere. Out of fear they ignore the fact that churches are turned into brothels, a seaside town becomes a wasteland, and teenagers kill their lovers at random.

Pietro ends up in a large square in Marrakech, no doubt the Jemaa el Fna, and continues to speak in public but this time to entertain people. That Pietro brings speaking to an extreme—once he starts he cannot stop or else he stutters—suggests that the only way to have a voice, to speak out against oppression, is by transgressing limits and finding an idiom of one's own. The alternative, as we witness with Pietro's move from his hometown of Caltagirone, in Sicily, to Marrakech, is departure. Ben Jelloun sets up a clear parallel with post-independence Morocco, where under King Hassan II protection from the State was nominal and those who spoke out were, at best, forced to leave or were eliminated.[8]

The *conteur* takes on a denunciatory role; he crosses linguistic borders, and subverts hierarchy and points to the agonistic relationships within Moroccan and Italian societies. If, as Marc Gontard remarks, the figure of the *conteur* [in *Moha le fou*] reflects a traditional Moroccan practice (that of storytelling), for Ben Jelloun, the *conteur* cannot be reduced to being simply Moroccan. For neither Moha nor Pietro le fou are totally unique. Pietro has a "brother," who, like him, is Sicilian; "Cicciu Busacca, mon alter ego, mon frère et maître, celui qui clame la vérité en chantant" (1992: 105). [Cicciu Busacca, my alter ego, my friend and master, he who proclaims the truth in song.] Cicciu Busacca, who lived between 1926 and 1984, was a Sicilian "troubadour" and was famous for his political and comical commentaries.[9] One of the songs he was known for, "Lamentu pi la morti di Turiddu Carnivali" (Lament for the Death of Turiddu Carnivali) tells the story of a socialist politician who was gunned down by the Mafia. The song begins "Ancilu era e non avia ali" [He was an angel and had no wings]. In Ben Jelloun's title story, "L'ange aveugle" [The Blind Angel], an angel also loses its wings after getting them caught in an electric pole. Pietro and Cicciu, one fictive, the other real, one an apprentice and the other a "maître" [master], are drawn together to enrich each other's stories, in what Ben Jelloun establishes as a brotherly bond.

The ties between Pietro and Moha also suddenly become ones of filiation: Pietro remarks "on m'a dit que j'ai un frère, un sosie qui va de ville en village, de Marrakech à Asilah, de Tanger à Tlemcen. Il s'appelle Moha . . . Il m'arrive de le chercher en Sicile même . . . Il m'a même semblé le voir à la casbah de Mazara del Vallo . . ." (1992: 105) [They tell me that I've a brother, someone just like me, who goes from village to village, from Marrakech to Asilah, from Tangier to Tlemcen. He is called Moha . . . I sometimes try to find him here in Sicily . . . I seemed to caught sight of him in the casbah of Mazarro del Vallo . . . [sic]]. Reminding us that there are cities in Sicily where certain areas are still called *casbahs*, from the seventh and eighth centuries when it was ruled by Arabs, Pietro seems unconditionally linked to Moha by a fraternal and ancestral bond. Similarly, Moha in *Moha le fou* has a Jewish "brother" Moché with whom he decides to form "un groupe 'de démence infernale' pour lutter contre l'occupant" (1978: 114) [a group of 'infernal insanity' to combat the occupier]. What emerges then, is a picture of Mediterranean fraternity that is positioned against a hegemonic power, in this case that of France as Motherland. If we are to follow this old colonial metaphor, we might instead say that in place of France as hegemonic, overbearing mother, Ben Jelloun favors the Mediterranean, also often referred to as *mèr(e) Méditerranée*.[10]

In setting up mirror images of Moroccan and Italian real and fictive characters, Ben Jelloun partakes in an act of literary self-imitation. In his fictional world Moha precedes Pietro and is also a mainstay of his oeuvre, appearing in *Harrouda, La réclusion solitaire, La nuit de l'erreur* and *Partir*. Thus, Pietro the copy is, to a certain extent, already "coded." Once more, the specter of a Moroccan character—that is, of a deterritorialized Moha—in the tight-knit clan-driven society that is the Mafia, is defamiliarizing. Thanks to his name and his characteristics, Pietro recalls the legendary seventeenth-century Sicilian poet and troubadour Petru Fudduni,[11] a "poet of the people" who rallied *lo spirito popolare*—the spirit of the people—during a somber era of domination in Sicilian history. The surname by which he is known—Fudduni—is said to be a distortion of Fullone, but there are also hypotheses that it comes from the Sicilian for crazy/mad (fodde). Moha le Fou and Petru Fudduni hence share the same "surname." Ben Jelloun rewrites and resituates the typical Sicilian figures of Cicciu Busacca and Petru Fudduni, linking them by blood to Moha the Moroccan *conteur*, bridging the seventeenth century with the contemporary Mediterranean. In fact, Pietro only obtains full meaning if we know the (hi)story of Petru Fudduni *and* of Moha; this may be tantamount to saying that it is in this plural interplay that Mediterranean cultural signifiers also obtain their full meaning.

This joins Marc Gontard's investigation of the plurality of tones that traverse "la voix marocaine." Gontard writes:

> Dans un environnement aussi mouvant où l'ouverture et le métissage sont vécus, tantôt comme une chance, tantôt comme une menace, le Moi qui fait retour à lui-même se trouve confronté à sa propre opacité de sorte que l'écriture, au Maroc, ces dernières années, me semble travaillée par cette figure fondamentale d'un *Moi étrange*, ambivalent, *pluriel*, et bien souvent indéchiffrable. (1993: 8; my emphasis)

> [In such a fluid environment, where openness and *métissage* are sometimes lived as fortuitous, and sometimes as a threat, the I that returns to itself finds him/herself faced with his/her own opacity so that writing, in Morocco in these past years, seems concerned with the fundamental figure of a foreign me, that is ambivalent, plural and often incomprehensible.]

Ben Jelloun's "moi étrange" is underscored in Italy but, if we heed Gontard's words, we might say that simply by virtue of being a Moroccan writer he is already positioned and *familiar* with his "étrangeté," with his plurality and with that of other cultural signifiers. For, given Morocco's pre-colonial and colonial history, the Moroccan writer is rarely monolingual and monocultural. Living a situation that Gontard calls bilingual, but that in several cases is *pluri*lingual, writers like Ben Jelloun are keenly aware of how the subject develops a strange familiarity with the other within the self. Khatibi makes this very claim in *Maghreb Pluriel*, in which he places North Africa in relation to the larger Mediterranean and foregrounds the multiplicity of languages (Tamazight, Arabic, French, Spanish) and the traces they have left in Morocco in particular.

The mirroring of protagonists, such as Pietro and Moha, is coupled with that of parallels in time. Throughout this collection, in which Ben Jelloun declares that his task, which he sees as tantamount to that of literature in general, is to "cambrioler le réel apparent" [steal a march on the real], there is a distinct critique of the metaphysics of destiny, which goes hand in hand with an ambivalent relationship to progress. In "La relève" [Taking Over] (Story XIII) the main character remarks about San Vito lo Capo, a small town on the northwestern tip of Sicily, "Quand on était né dans cette ville, on ne pouvait pas échapper à la fatalité. Notre destin est tracé d'avance" (1992: 183). [When one is born in this town, one cannot escape a certain destiny. Our fate is settled in advance.] Firmly believing in destiny being *traced*, or one might say written, this Sicilian character echoes numerous other Ben Jellounian figures who also perceive of life as being governed by destiny, by that which is written (*maktub*). Not only is it written, but according to Moha, it is written by the sea. He taunts: "Allez, courez à votre commerce. Courez et ne vous retournez pas . . . Le temps vous échappe; il tourne en rond et moi je rigole . . . Regardez un peu plus la mer et apprenez à y lire votre destin. C'est facile. La mer écrit lisiblement. Elle change mais il suffit d'être attentif" (1978: 21). [Go ahead run to your business. Run and don't turn around . . . Time escapes you; it goes in circles and I laugh . . . Look at the sea a little harder and learn how to read your destiny in it. It's easy. The sea writes legibly. It changes but all you have to do is be attentive.] Urging a consciousness of destiny, Moha advises not to look back at the horrors of the past and derisively mocks those who move too quickly into the future. Destiny, in both the Moroccan and Italian contexts, is expressed through an incitement to resist controlling both it and time:

> Aujourd'hui nous sommes tous dépassés. Les choses ont changé. Le territoire est entre les mains de jeunes gens dynamiques et qui ont des diplômes. Ils travaillent avec les machines de la technologie moderne . . . Essayez de ne pas vider entièrement votre âme . . . Voici ce que dit encore mon vieux compagnon "Qui gravit les plus hautes cimes n'a cure des tragédies jouées ni davantage des tragédies vécues." (1992: 185).

> [Today, we are all out of date. Things have changed. The land is in the hands of young people who are energetic and have diplomas. They work now with modern technology . . . Try not to let your soul run completely dry . . . This is what my old companion says "He who climbs the highest peaks has no mind for the tragedies being played out nor the tragedies he lived through."]

In this last quote, after which Ben Jelloun cites Nietzsche, in whose *Thus Spake Zarathustra* he says "je relis tout le temps" (in Aresu 1996: 2) [I re-read all the time], we read a clear warning against the power of speed and technology in overtaking man.[12] Moha sarcastically incites to "courir au commerce" [run to your business], suggesting in fact the contrary, that commerce should *not* be a driving force, nor should we run towards it. If we consider Ben Jelloun's lexical choice of the word "commerce" instead of "affaires," for example, we might consider a veiled critique of capitalism. Moreover, if capitalism is associated, especially by thinkers like Fukuyama, with progress and the "end of history," then Ben Jelloun's position appears to be one of opposition.

Can societies that privilege violence and destruction be considered harbingers of progress? Nietzsche, as Foucault reminds us in "Nietzsche, Genealogy, History," wrote to dispel the myth of pure origins *and* the myth that progress would lead to emancipation. Read in dialogue with a Nietzschean critique, Ben Jelloun's positioning on origins and progress harks back to a colonial dichotomy that is unquestionably part of his oeuvre. The myth of pure origins was used to convince the colonized of their inferiority and difference, whereas the myth of progress served to justify colonial presence in colonized territories, for it promised to bring the superiority of European "civilization" and improvement to conquered and occupied lands. Both these notions, which are also at the heart of colonial discourse, are undermined in *L'ange aveugle* both because of the destructive, rebellious nature of the Mafia and more importantly because they are not valued or privileged, Ben Jelloun seems to say, in a Southern ethos.

The notion of progress in the context of southern Italy is slippery, for it conjures up both resistance and yearning. The title story, "L'ange aveugle," which sets the premise for the collection, reflects such ambivalence: Ben Jelloun shows that in a society ruled by disorder and random violence, there is no protection from above, neither from the state, nor from God, nor, symbolically, from angels or the heavens. The image of the angel, which Walter Benjamin analyses through Paul Klee's painting *Angelus Novus*, provides a useful insight into this very question of progress. Benjamin saw a comment on the destruction and violence that came with the ideology of progress in the figure of Klee's angel. For Benjamin

> the angel is an allegorical image that allows us to see what is not normally seen and to say what we see rather than remain silent. The power of the figure lies above all in this relation between seeing and saying . . . The angel, ambivalent in its intermediary state between genders, between humans and God, between heaven and earth, allows us to see that our world is uncertain and topologically complex rather than certain and linear. (Law and Hetherington 2006: 5)

The uncertainty and topological complexity that lies behind the figure of the angel is brought out fully in "L'ange aveugle." As Ben Jelloun states clearly in the first story, the blind angel is an allegory for devastation and catastrophe where no one is spared from the randomness of violence. Both images of the angel depict a witnessing of horror and subjugation to arbitrariness and lawlessness; both are caught in senseless wars. However, where Klee's angel is caught between seeing the devastation and saying, Ben Jelloun's angel is blind. Like the madman who has the gift of an alternative reason, the blind angel, perhaps like Homer the blind poet, has a unique power of sight. Whereas Benjamin's contextual frame is World War II, Ben Jelloun's, in this case, is the Mafia. He depicts the excessive and pathological perpetuity of violence, suggesting in fact that this *cannot* be a positive evolution in the story of mankind:

> Comme l'ange d'Alexandra Alpha, dont *l'histoire est rapportée* par José Cardoso Pires, il [l'ange] lui arrive de survoler la ville . . . a dernière fois il s'est pris les ailes dans les fils électriques de haute tension et s'est écrasé sur un rocher. Depuis, une petite fumée monte de la pointe élevée de ce rocher noir. On dit que c'est l'âme incandescente de l'ange aveugle qui se consume *à l'infini*. (1992: 14; my emphasis)

> [Like the angel of Alexandra Alpha (whose story is told by José Cardoso Pires), who from time to time flies over the city . . . The last time, he caught his wings in the high-tension wires and crashed on a rock. Ever since, day and night, a little curl of smoke can be seen rising from the topmost point of the black rock. People say it is the incandescent soul of the blind angel being everlastingly consumed.]

Framing stories within stories, Ben Jelloun points to the infinite nature of catastrophe and to the total loss of reason. He exposes a facet of southern Italy that echoes the media outlets, namely a place that appears fated to an aporetic condition of incessant violence. Behind this "réel apparent," though, lies another dimension of the south, another way of life, of being and of thinking. In the figures of Moha le fou and Pietro le fou, we discern an alternative form of reason. In Ben Jelloun's works the madman is usually he who sees the truth, he who is able to speak the unspeakable and represent the unrepresentable. This "other" ethos, which defies linearity and convention, challenges the ideology of progress and is inscribed in a poetic that privileges different layers of perception and multiple subjectivities.

A TWENTY-FIRST CENTURY BAROQUE

Those who inhabit the southern places described by Ben Jelloun are victims of an absent state, forced to make their own rules and chart their own time and space with all the unpredictability or defiance of reason that this may entail.[13] Among these places, Naples has recurrently appeared in his works.[14] As critic Pascale Lismonde writes, Naples presents us with "l'une de ces 'villes-monde' chères à l'historien Fernand Braudel: tumultueuses, polymorphes, dionysiaques, décidément inclassables, ces villes pour lesquelles on épuiserait en vain la liste des adjectifs disponibles dans le répertoire de l'excès, et dont la découverte peut bouleverser nos habitudes mentales et sensorielles" (2003: 7). [One of these world-cities, so dear to the historian Fernand Braudel: tumultuous, polymorphous, dionysiac, clearly unclassifiable. One of those cities for which one could use all the adjectives that have to do with excess in vain, and whose discovery can turn our mental and sensory habits upside-down.] The Naples presented in Ben Jelloun's novels is rife with elements that in official discourse are deemed detrimental to Italy's future and its modernity: nostalgia, decrepitude, and destruction. Iain Chambers maintains that

> Naples presents itself as both a Baroque and an abysmal city. Its innumerable seventeenth-century buildings and unsure foundations are silent witnesses to the continuing disruption of linear development as urban and architectural design dissolves into sounds, streets and bodies that do not readily bend to the structural stability sought by the modern will. (2001: 130)

One of these very buildings of unsure foundations—L'Albergo dei Poveri—is the setting and home of the numerous marginal characters of *L'auberge des pauvres*. Built in the eighteenth century by Charles III as an asylum for the poor, it was intended to keep the downtrodden out of sight and to compensate for the excessive luxury that the monarch afforded himself.[15] The novel operates along a commonplace premise inasmuch as it initially appears as a parody of the numerous exoticizing and orientalizing narratives primarily written by nineteenth-century French writers on their journeys to Italy and North Africa. Weary of his orderly, monotonous life as a professor in Marrakech, the central character, Larbi Bennya, a Moroccan who goes by the name "Bidoun" ("without" in Arabic), decides to write his own version of *Ulysses* and to voyage to Naples—slowly, he emphasizes—by sea.[16] Soon after his arrival, an anonymous caller reads him an excerpt from Stendhal's *Rome, Naples, Florence* over the phone, informing him that in 1817 the writer visited the Albergo dei Poveri. Setting his trajectory against that of a typically "classical" writer like Stendhal, Ben Jelloun underscores the familiar and the strange, drawing our attention however to the non-classical, to his baroque text and to that of his protagonist. He takes the marginality of Bennya, a Moroccan writer (reminiscent of Ben Jelloun even though his marginality, as an author, is highly debatable) and reverses the archetypal "Orientalist" gaze, where he is no longer the object of fascination but its subject.

Determined to rewrite Joyce and Stendhal, Larbi Bennya/Bidoun arrives at the Albergo dei Poveri only to find a gargantuan ruin surrounded by debris. As if swallowed into the sewers of the city, Bennya descends into the lower levels of the labyrinthine building and does not emerge for what appears to be five years, although most temporal markers are blurred. There are no windows in the basement, and time slows, the ruin a constant reminder of another time, far in the past. For Bennya, time in the Albergo is punctuated by a continual loss and recovery of his bearings. Upon arriving he remarks "J'ai eu du mal à retrouver mon chemin. Il y avait plusieurs entrées et sorties du sous-sol. Les sentiers souterrains bifurquaient dans ma tête; je tournais en rond comme une bourrique" (1999: 75). [I had a hard time finding my way. There were many different entries and exits to the cellar. In my head, the underground paths forked; I was going in circles, losing my mind.] The self-appointed guardian of the Albergo, an old woman who goes by the name of "la Vieille," holds the protagonist captive, warning him that "ici on est de l'autre côté du labyrinthe, et le labyrinthe c'est moi!" (1999: 49) [here we are on the other side of the labyrinth, and I am the labyrinth!] and forbids him to leave the premises. If she is beyond the labyrinth and at the same time the labyrinth itself, we may infer that she is beyond herself, that she exceeds herself, that she is unrestrained and baroque. In this ruin, he cannot escape being reminded of the inevitable passing of time, the impossibility of escaping from it, all of which may explain "the preoccupation with fictions, fantasies and fate" (Buci-Glucksmann 1994: 9).

His fate is in the hands of "la Vieille," and through her, in the hands of the city that ceaselessly acts on his sensory and mental perceptions: the putrid smells that emanate from the old woman and her surroundings, the shocking stories she tells and the dizzying portraits of the often downtrodden visitors to the Albergo. She points him to a pile of boxes: "chaque carton . . . contient un grand livre, un manuscrit écrit par des mains anonymes. On y raconte Naples d'il y a longtemps. Il y a le carton des voleurs, le carton de Dieu, le carton des putes, le carton des menteurs et des hypocrites" (1999: 52). [Each box contains a large book, a manuscript written by anonymous hands. It tells the story of Naples long ago. There is the box of thieves, the box of God, the box of whores, the box of liars and hypocrites]; the list continues for a full page. The piles of manuscripts, like the inordinately long sentences in the novel, evoke pieces of the history, the heterogeneity and the sounds of Naples. They are nothing like the state archives that are also housed in this building, remarks the old woman, for those are merely "des registres des naissances et des décès. D'immenses pages écrites à la main et qui n'ont aucun intérêt . . . Si au moins ces archives nous parlaient de l'âme! . . . Les archives l'ignorent (1999: 47) [rosters of births and deaths. Huge hand-written pages that are of no interest . . . If at least these archives told us about the soul! . . . Archives ignore it]. Whereas the state is concerned with numbers and material (financial) figures, the stories of foreigners, immigrants and musicians but also of liars and prostitutes, are reflective of the soul, of affects. These are the (hi)stories of how people live the city and their passions, these are stories that don't appear in the books on Italian history.

Referring to Derrida's work on the topos of the archive as an institutional cooptation of memory, Chambers glosses that "history is cited to be resited" and that

> [Here] the present is not merely haunted by the past, but is shot through with heterogeneous fragments whose redemption can only render the world unhomely, "out of joint." Contrary to the ordered

memory of the archive, to the filed away names, events and explanations, there is the persistent murmur of a world whose insistent "noise"
betrays the order it seeks to regulate and, in the end, remove it. (2005:
316)

Removing order, in Chambers's terms, is not to be perceived as objection-
able. Rather, he suggests, it is meant to allow the many facets of a city to
open up new possibilities so that "the denied and the silenced" can "bear
witness to both a past and a present that the solutions of modern
progress have systematically excluded from their historical and political
accounting of time and space" (2005: 317). The Albergo dei Poveri, a
metonymy for Naples, which in turn might be seen as a metonymy of the
Mediterranean, has centuries of stories to tell, and as the old woman says
to Bennya, like his "livre sur Naples, c'est comme les poupées russes, ça
peut s'ouvrir à l'infini" (1999: 140). [Your book on Naples is like a Russian doll, it can be opened infinitely.]

Much of the novel is driven by the allegory of *la Vieille* as *the ville* of
Naples. She explains, "Si tu poses ta tête sur mon ventre, tu entendras
Naples vivre et mourir. Le genre de bruit dépend de l'heure que tu choi-
sis pour écouter le ventre de la ville" (1999: 48). [If you place your head
on my belly, you will hear Naples living and dying. The kind of sound
depends on the day you choose to listen to the belly of the city.] Replete
with what one might imagine to be contained in a *ventre*/belly, the old
woman's stories vacillate between the grotesque and the repulsive while
also revealing the moving and human stories that constitute Ben Jelloun's
Naples.[17] The baroque pulls one in precisely because of the "appearances
and play—[that] joins up with metaphysical wretchedness on the ground
of grief or melancholy" (Buci-Glucksmann 1994: 71). Momo, a Senegalese
immigrant who frequents the auberge, is depicted as disproportionately
tall and yet as an infant who calls the old woman *maman* and sits on her
lap to hear her stories. If from the outside this appears playful, it translates the solemn interiority of someone who is rootless and suffers from
being displaced. These stories, told in the first person but punctuated by
Bennya's narration, are those of a Moroccan, a Senegalese, an old Judeo-
Muslim woman, an autochtonous Neapolitan couple, a funambulist, and
a disabled person. But appearances are deceptive and we are led into the
realm of *trompe l'oeil* and illusion; "Derrière les choses, il y a d'autres
choses" [behind things, there are other things], warns the old woman.
The sentences are at times three pages long, at times three words long.
Every so often the stories intersect and fold into each other. Bedazzled
and overwhelmed, our clarity of vision verges on blindness as the stories
begin to blur together and we are left with a fragmented understanding
of each individual and of Naples. The mise-en-abyme becomes even
more vertiginous and fragmented as we are pushed to consider multiple
subjectivities, at times unsure of whose mind we are inhabiting.[18]

In *Folie du voir*, Buci-Glucksmann investigates the role of viewpoint and the faculty of sight within baroque aesthetics: "Un voir, une forme-force, une écriture en palimpseste: trois éléments de la sensibilité baroque du dix-septième siècle. Le monde est à la fois un miroir de miroirs, un livre des livres, et un univers esthétique de formes-forces en équilibre/déséquilibre permanent" (1986: 79) [a way of seeing, a form-force, a palimpsestic writing: three elements of a seventeenth-century baroque sensitivity. The world is both a mirror of mirrors, a book of books and an esthetic universe of form-forces in permanent balance/imbalance]. Despite the fact that we repeatedly return to the central character, we are continuously led in different directions by way of myriad devices. Shifting voices with each form we come across a list that resembles an inventory, a letter, a fragment of a journal, a poem, and occasional turns of phrase that resemble a folktale. ("Ecoute mon histoire. Ecoute-la bien." [Listen to my story. Listen to it well.]). Such a multiplicity of subjectivities causes us to consider infinite connections and unexpected encounters, but most importantly it suggests that "there is no hegemonic arrangement of truth: everything is a product of perspectives" (Buci-Glucksmann 1994: 6).

The reader is left with the distinct impression that the book Bennya plans to write will not resemble Stendhal's classical observation of the art and architecture of Naples. Nor will his book resemble Zola's descriptions of the *ventre de Paris*, despite the clear association we are tempted to make between the two through the metaphor of the belly. Rather, his perceptions are informed by references to *One Thousand and One Nights*, Mohammed Khair-Eddine, Vladimir Nabokov, André Gide, and Maxim Gorki's *The Lower Depths*. Such implicit and explicit referencing resembles a parodical re-reading and countering of classic texts. Ben Jelloun's reverse gaze, however, does not accomplish what, for example, Maryse Condé's rewriting of *Wuthering Heights* (*La migration des coeurs*) or J. M. Coetzee's *Foe* does; it is not a *writing back* but rather an internal dialogue where the question of colonized/colonizer is displaced, and where different identities come together in a *writing between*. Salman Rushdie first pronounced the phrase "the empire writes back to the center" in reference to writers from Britain's colonies who (like Coetzee or Jean Rhys) strategically rewrote "master narratives" from the point of view of their marginalized characters. Rather than adopting this strategy, Ben Jelloun privileges no single point of view and gives no clear evidence of whom he is writing *to*. Inserting Italian and Arabic phrases and references in the text, the novel points to the inherent intertextuality (in the widest sense of the term) of culture in general, rather than to a dichotomous "master-slave" paradigm, where the latter writes back to the former.

Ben Jelloun allows us to consider the idea of rupture, of revisiting classical expectations, by setting this premise as the very catalyst of his novel, and of his protagonists'. By leaving Morocco, Larbi Bennya creates the conditions of possibility for a new existence for himself as well as for his wife, to whom he writes letters, imagining her with a different name and more alluring qualities. He resuscitates what is meant to be hidden, the "undesirable" elements of society, the segregated and downtrodden with which Charles III, for one, did not want to have to contend. Like the Naples of the Bourbon king, Ben Jelloun's contemporary Naples hides the "different" (the poor and the mad in the case of the former, the immigrant and the old for the latter), where controlling and surveilling institutions aim(ed) to keep them on the fringes of society. The life stories of "the wretched of the earth" evoke the melancholy nature of the baroque space of the auberge, and because they are told in a seemingly arbitrary order, create a confusing sense of temporality. The temporal markers that do exist indicate the ephemeral nature of time; the old woman grows even older and dies, and the protagonist exhausts his passion for Naples and the decaying ex-asylum through a failed love affair. *L'auberge des pauvres* closes with the protagonist's return to Morocco after five years in Naples, only now his home is no longer familiar, and there is no Penelope awaiting him. His wife has decided to remarry, and he has been *"rayé des cadres"*—stricken from the system—fired from his job as a professor. In fact, he discovers greater familiarity in the face of an Italian tourist in Marrakech than in the faces of his fellow nationals. He has discovered the other of himself. Upon seeing the Italian, he remarks, "j'étais sûr que cet homme était mon double" (1999: 188) [I was sure that this man was my double], reminding us that it is not necessarily national identities that define individuals; people from Marrakech, he comments, "sont des méditerranéens sans avoir la mer" [are Mediterranean without the sea]. Interestingly, upon his arrival at the Albergo dei Poveri, the protagonist experiences a sense of familiarity so great that he feels he had always been there. Conversely, upon returning to his purported home, Marrakech, everything is unfamiliar.

TURNING BACK TO LOOK FORWARD

Two factors are important in understanding the particular foreign/familiar dynamic that subtends Ben Jelloun's Italian works. The commonly heard dictum, "Italy ends at Rome. Naples, Calabria, Sicily, and all the rest are part of Africa,"[19] as literary critic and poet Pasquale Verdicchio reminds us, "encapsulates the whole question of what might constitute the nation (and consequently national literatures). Definitions of southern Italians as 'other' are fed by commonly stated references to Naples as 'the doorway to the Orient.'" Verdicchio suggests that Italy suffers from a form of internal colonization and that one of the failures of postcolonial discourse in unmasking the workings of imperialism rests on the "problematic designations such as white versus non-white and First versus

Third World" (1997: 191). Driven predominantly by economic disparity whereby the industrialized north holds power over the more agrarian south, this internal colonization is reflected in social and cultural practices. Drawing on Antonio Gramsci's theory of the South of Italy as intrinsically "othered" by the North, Antonio Negri, in his essay "Italy, Exile Country," describes the nature of this relationship:

> In Italy, the dialectic of the master and slave has never existed. The master has been too cruel and too strong, while the slave has been too generous and too strong. On the one hand, therefore, we have the disillusioned, ferocious, and cynical power of the master; on the other, hope and an ever-renewed capacity for rebellion. There is no dialectic; the master and the servant do not nourish each other. There is no mediation, no conciliation. (1997: 44)[20]

Reading between the lines, the master in this case might be the capitalist north and the slave the "rebellious" south. Breaking down the master/slave dialectic in this way, Negri suggests that Italy is profoundly split. After the unification of Italy (1860) and until the 1920s, a third of the population emigrated to America, to Italy's African colonies and beyond. More emigrants followed after World War II, and of the approximately ten million people who departed, most were of southern descent. This left both those "at home" and abroad with a sense of displacement, instability, and increasing dissatisfaction with the government. Consequently, those who remained "at home" may also have found themselves in a situation of unfamiliarity, this time within the bounds of their own nation.

According to Negri "both literary history and social history in Italy are continually marked by the presence of exile . . . there is not a single episode of any large-scale Italian identity that is not marked by exile" (1997: 43). He explains that this is the case because "Italy is the only country that has produced all the modern revolutions without having ever enjoyed victory in any of them" (1997: 44). According to Sandra Ponzanesi, Italy is a paradoxical country in which what Negri calls "modern revolutions" are coupled with "civil immaturity . . . organized crime . . . and government corruption." This does not, she continues, compare to British, French or German models of modernization, making Italy an exception in Europe, and thus "in a way closer to other Mediterranean realities" (2004: 128). There is an implicit suggestion here that Italy (and the Mediterranean) is backward with respect to the rest of Europe, an insinuation that reinforces a unilateral vision of its national identity, relating it to an ideal of modernization and progress that is temporal and based on an expectation of acceleration. If Italy is lagging, the implication is that it is late, slow, and behind. This perspective assumes that Britain, France and Germany are ideal models of progress while Italy is not. These need not be exemplary models. As Franco Cassano puts it: "Siamo di fronte non a una difesa della società tradizionale contro la società moderna, ma a una critica della falsa neutralità e universalità dei modelli culturali dominanti" (2011: 1). [This is not a defense of a traditional society versus a modern one, but criticism of the false neutrality and universality of dominant cultural models.] The internal and external "colonization" that Italy suffers from may be what has sharpened Ben Jelloun's "affinité méditerranéenne"; by linking Morocco to Italy, he proposes a relationality that is *not* set against dominant cultural models where shared notions of time are valorized rather than stigmatized.

Furthermore, Ben Jelloun redefines the experience of exile by treating it as a familiar and auspicious state of being that denotes openness. From the old woman exiled from the world in the Albergo dei Poveri, to the downtrodden individuals she hosts, to the protagonist himself, there is a sense of openness and common understanding. Tahar Bekri, a Tunisian author similarly convinced of the notion of a Mediterranean identity, maintains that:

> l'exil, générateur des connivences et de croisements littéraires, est cet appel à la rencontre de l'Autre et un rejet de l'espace clos, une volonté d'échapper à l'identité statique et figée . . . oui, l'exil est aussi ce lien libre entre l'ici et l'ailleurs, l'appartenance à une terre particulière et à l'univers. La vraie maison natale serait la maison ouverte aux quatre vents, capable d'écrire sur ses murs les pérégrinations des hommes et des choses, qui serait habitée par les « solennels départs », à l'écoute des retours porteurs des voix des autres, mais aussi la voix singulière et intérieure. Et afin que l'exil cesse d'être un récif de la douleur, j'ose imaginer une odyssée homérienne où heureux qui comme Ulysse a fait un beau voyage! (1994: 176)

> [Exile, which brings about complicity and literary cross-fertilizations is an invitation to encounter the Other and a rejection of closed spaces. It is the will to escape a static and set identity . . . yes, exile is also this free connection between here and there, it means belonging to a particular land and to the universe. The house where one is truly born would be a wide open house, a house able to write the peregrinations of men and things on its walls, and which would be inhabited by "solemn departures," attentive to returns carrying both the voices of others, and a singular, internal voice. And in order for exile to cease being a reef of pain, I dare to imagine a Homerian odyssey where, happy is the man who, like Ulysses, has made a fine voyage.]

Bekri's words weave a literary web through the conjuring up and conjoining of Homer's *Odyssey* and Joachim Du Bellay's *Les Regrets*. But his words are also evocative of Ben Jelloun's protagonist who solemnly departed from his domestic constraints to find other voices, and other open "homes." Exile no longer only connotes pain but promise as well. Whether Bekri and Ben Jelloun write of literal homes, of spiritual homes, or of the metaphorical home of the nation, both authors urge considering the Mediterranean as a hyphen between self and other, that other encountered at home and elsewhere.

Ben Jelloun brings to light a specifically Mediterranean postcoloniality, where limits and boundaries of national identities are challenged and relations of power are called into question. In this scenario, then, it is no longer a question of a struggle between (ex)colonizer and (ex)colonized, for in Ben Jelloun's work France is symbolically displaced as a hegemonic center of power, but rather what we perceive is a fundamental desire to connect to other places and to other people. Southern Italy and Spain, which have paradoxically been considered Europe's more retrograde members, emerge, through Ben Jelloun's texts, as being in a wider relationship with the Mediterranean, and thus in a position where identity politics must go beyond facile perceptions of backwardness. The works analyzed here challenge us to examine the contemporary subject in the space of the Mediterranean—particularly on its southern shores—as well as the notion of Francophone literature that Ben Jelloun's narratives ostensibly typify. A southern ethos is both harmonious and discordant; *L'ange aveugle* and *L'auberge des pauvres* reveal the heterogeneity and palimpsestic time of a south—in particular Naples—that resists and defies linearity.

As Cassano puts it, "Il sud non è solo un non ancora nord, una patologia infinita dalla quale bisogna guarire per diventare finalmente civili e degni del dono della parola" (2010: 1). [The South is not only a not-yet North, a never-ending pathology from which one must recover in order to finally become civilized and worthy of the gift of the word.] The southern Mediterranean, in particular the Maghreb and southern Italy, has been caught between depictions of exoticism and backwardness, which, like the "Orient" for Saïd, has often been the theater of western European fears and fantasies. Ben Jelloun's works have both reinforced and dispelled this view of the Mediterranean; as a non-European writer he does not write from a strictly "Western" point of view, but at the same time he has dangerously revisited typically "exotic" tropes, bringing upon himself accusations of self-orientalizing and of "selling out" to Parisian literary expectations.[21] The interstitial position between French and Moroccan cultural spaces that Ben Jelloun occupies can be characterized as what Homi Bhabha calls "hybrid" or "third." In *The Location of Culture* Bhabha conceptualizes "an *inter*national culture based not on the exoticism of multiculturalism or the *diversity* of cultures, but on the inscription and articulation of culture's *hybridity*" (1994: 37; emphasis in original). In this sense, all cultural systems are traversed by potentially contradictory and disparate elements. "By exploring this Third Space" he continues, "we may elude the politics of polarity and emerge as the others of ourselves" (1994: 56). The southern Mediterranean, similar to Bhabha's definition of postcolonial cultures, is also intrinsically hybrid due to the centuries of cultural mixing and colonization that it has witnessed (Arab conquests of Spain and Sicily, Spanish conquest of Italy, Roman, French and Spanish conquests of North Africa among many others).[22] The notion of hybridity, which comes to light in Ben Jelloun's *L'ange aveugle* and *L'auberge des pauvres*, is greatly disturbed through *Partir* (discussed at length in chapter 5), which exposes bitter relations of power and inequalities unacknowledged in Bhabha's early theory of hybridity.

Ben Jelloun, like other Francophone writers of his generation such as Abdelkébir Khatibi and Abdelwahab Meddeb, who were educated in French schools in the Maghreb, is *already* in a situation of what Khatibi called radical bilingualism. Referring to the double linguistic registers that these writers inhabit, Khatibi urges the necessity of decolonization through writing. By adopting writing strategies that cause the monolingual French reader "to lose his/her way," such as the insertion of Arabic calligraphy into a text, or the use of direct Arabic syntactical constructions in French, Khatibi indeed effects a sense of alienation in the monolingual reader. For Meddeb, this means "l'écriture française nous 'livre' à l'autre, mais on se défendra par l'arabesque, la subversion, le dédale, le labyrinthe, le décentrage incessant de la phrase et du langage, de manière que l'autre se perde comme dans les ruelles de la casbah" (cited in Déjeux 1994: 104). [Writing in French gives us over to the "other," but we will defend ourselves through the arabesque, subversion, the maze, the labyrinth, the ceaseless decentering of sentences, of language, so that the "other" will lose his way as if in the narrow streets of the casbah.] Unlike Ben Jelloun's earlier texts, *L'enfant de sable* and *La nuit sacrée*, which effect the subervsion and estrangement mentioned by Meddeb through a complex use of language, the texts analyzed here tend more toward a thematic of "the labyrinthine." Although potentially compromising originality of style, a shift from linguistic to thematic stratification may point to the diminished sense of necessity on the part of a writer like Ben Jelloun, to "alienate" the language of the former colonizer. Occasional lexical choices and turns of phrases not consonant with French appear in most works discussed here, but overall these texts do not bear significant signs of linguistic play such as recurrent use of multiple idioms, structures calqued on other languages, or "feminized words."

Bouraoui and Ben Jelloun produce textual spaces in which the interpretive lens of an Arabic/French dichotomy or of a heterosexual/homosexual grid is rendered inoperative. By writing beyond the binaries of gender and geography, they not only draw readers into a Mediterranean that denies the monolithic, they also produce new subject positions that reflect a rejection of pure identities. For Ben Jelloun, producing new Mediterranean subject positions that are already hybrid means thinking towards a common future and back to eighth-century Arab Sicily or Bourbon Naples—these have been the examples here—in order, also, to displace the rhetoric of the so-called clash of civilizations in the Mediterra-

nean. Preferring not to conform to national or biological forms of identification, Ben Jelloun and Bouraoui's characters instead tackle and engage
the limitations of binary modes of analysis and apprehension, revealing
the tenuousness of the very foundations upon which such a praxis of
interpretation, and of reading, is built.

ENDNOTES

1. See Marc Gontard, *La violence du texte*, Abdallah Memmes, *Signifiance et intercul-
turalité*. John Erickson, *Islam and the Postcolonial Narrative*.
2. See UNESCO "Mediterranean Multaqa" project on the Maghreb and the Mediterranean led by sociologist Noureddine Abdi, with contributions by Mourad Yelles,
Beïda Chikhi and Margaret Majumdar.
3. One of the most well-known Sicilian writers, Leonardo Sciascia, remarked the
following, on the importance of writers in the south: "Sappiamo bene che c'era già una
'questione meridionale': ma sarebbe rimasta come una vaga 'leggenda nera' dello
Stato Italiano, senza l'apporto degli scrittori meridionali." [We know that a Southern
Question already existed: but without the contribution of southern writers it would
have remained a vague 'black legend' of the Italian State.] The "questione meridionale" ["Southern Question"] refers to the cultural and economic split between Northern and Southern Italy.
4. Most of these short stories were originally published in Italian, in *Il Mattino*,
with the collaboration of his then translator and friend, journalist Egi Volterrani. This
fact alone would have raised considerable controversy had Italy and Volterrani been
France and a French journalist; how "authentic" is Ben Jelloun's text and to what
degree might the text have been "colonized"? In dealing with Italy and the Italian
language, the question of colonization vis-a-vis a Moroccan writer appears misplaced.
Volterrani's participation in the drafting of the text is virtually impossible to ascertain,
but to anyone who is familiar with Ben Jelloun's works, there is no doubt that the short
stories are "authentically" his. Typically Ben Jellounian metaphors and images
abound, as do stylistic traits played upon in previous as well as subsequent novels.
5. Ben Jelloun's marginal protagonists include Ahmed/Zahra in *L'enfant de sable*,
Moha in *Moha le fou, Moha le sage*, Harrouda in *Harrouda*, among others.
6. The title is also reminiscent of Jean-Luc Godard's 1965 film *Pierrot le fou*, where
the central character leaves Paris for the Mediterranean. The name "Moha" is said to
perhaps come from a combination of Mohamed the prophet and Juha, the Arabic
"trickster" and folkloric *conteur*. Juha was transformed into Giufà in Sicily during the
Arab conquest and is still part of Sicilian cultural tradition.
7. "Mezzogiorno," literally midday, is the Italian word used to designate the south
of Italy.
8. Ben Jelloun takes this up in his denunciatory novel *Cette aveuglante absence de
lumière* (2001). Here he condemns King Hassan II's incarceration of political dissidents.
The main character, detained in the infamous Tazmamart prison, reads Camus's
L'étranger: "Avec Camus, j'étais à l'aise, et je me faisais un plaisir de rappeler certains
passages. Cela leur conférait une importance magnifique, qui allait au-delà de
l'histoire du crime. Un roman raconté dans une fosse, à côté de la mort, ne peut avoir
le même sens, les mêmes conséquences que s'il était lu à la plage ou dans une prairie"
(136). [With Camus, I felt at ease and was only too happy to recall certain passages.
This conferred on them an immense importance that went far beyond the story of the
crime. A novel related in a dungeon, in the presence of death, cannot have the same
meaning, the same consequences, as it would when read on the beach or in a mead-
ow.] By focusing on the passages that describe the sea, the sunlight, and nature to
alleviate the pain of imprisonment, Ben Jelloun acknowledges the relation of the physical to the rational that frames my analysis in chapter 1.

9. A CD entitled "Cicciu Busacca; un uomo che viene dal Sud" [Cicciu Busacca; a man from the South] was re-released in 2004. The title confirms the importance of place with respect to Busacca and thus to Ben Jelloun.

10. Numerous writers have played with the phonetic and semantic polyvalence of mer/e Méditerranée (from Camus and Audisio to Dominique Fernandez, with his novel *Mère Méditerranée*).

11. Sicilian dialect for his name in Italian, Pietro Fullone.

12. Ben Jelloun describes his affinity for Nietzsche, citing: "L'alliance de la poésie et de la philosophie. L'absence de systèmes rigides, contrairement à Kant et à Descartes. Et cette réflexion folle, et en même temps très profonde, sur la condition humaine. Cela m'a beaucoup impressionné" (qtd. in Aresu: 2) [the bond between poetry and philosophy. The absence of rigid systems, unlike Kant and Descartes. And this mad—yet very profound—reflection on the human condition. That left a strong impression].

13. Interestingly, the English translation of *L'ange aveugle* is entitled *State of Absence*, and the Italian translation is *Dove lo stato non c'è*, which translates as *Where there is no state*.

14. In *Les raisins de la galère* (1996) the protagonist moves to Italy, and *Le labyrinthe des sentiments* (2001) is set entirely in Naples.

15. It was during this era that the Illuminismo Napoletano (Neapolitan Enlightenment) took form. Based on similar premises of the French Revolution, the Neapolitan Revolution took place in 1799.

16. It is interesting to note that Ben Jelloun chooses Joyce's *Ulysses* instead of Homer's. Aside from the fact that Ben Jelloun has stated, in numerous interviews, that reading *Ulysses* was what allowed him to survive the military camp to which he was sent by the government, we might attribute this choice to the fact that Joyce's work deals with a city. Or perhaps Ben Jelloun sees possible similarities between Ireland's past and present political situation and other "divided" countries.

17. Published in *L'ange aveugle* eight years before *L'auberge des pauvres*, the short story "Napolita" appears to be its direct precursor. Once again, Napolita, a woman, "une Lolita qui a pris de l'âge" [an aged Lolita], represents Naples. "Si mon ventre est lourd, s'il est chargé de tant de secrets et d'objets insolites, ce n'est pas de ma faute" (201) [if my belly is heavy, if it is full of so many secrets and unusual objects, it's not my fault], she declares. Prefiguring the old woman's replete belly in *L'auberge des pauvres*, Napolita also appears to speak for the city itself. Her double, Tangea, speaks for Tangier.

18. It is this very notion of fragmentation, according to Buci-Glucksmann's reading of Walter Benjamin, that characterizes the rhetorical figure of allegory. Allegory, according to Benjamin, is one of the main aesthetic expressions of modernity, but it finds its most effective and widespread articulation in seventeenth-century baroque art and literature. "Long before modern art, allegory testified to the preeminence of the fragment over the whole, of a destructive principle, of feeling, as the excavation of absence over reason as domination. Only the fragment is capable of showing that the logic of bodies, feeling, life, and death does not coincide with the logic of Power, nor with that of the Concept" (1994: 71).

19. This statement was originally uttered by one of Napoleon's men, Augustin Creuzé de Lesser in 1806, upon returning from a trip to the south of Italy.

20. Antonio Negri is most well-known as a Marxist philosopher and for his activities against the Italian state, for which he was imprisoned and exiled from Italy.

21. Notably Jacqueline Kaye and Abdelhamid Zoubir in *The Ambiguous Compromise: Language, Literature and Identity in Algeria and Morocco*.

22. Cultural expressions borne from such forms of hybridity tend, as a number of Caribbean and Latin American writers and critics have also shown (Glissant, Borges, Carpentier), to cultivate a poetic that inaugurates a "*new* Baroque". A Mediterreanean baroque signifies differently from the Caribbean context as the slave trade in particular has raised a specific set of tropes in the latter. Although, as Ben Jelloun's novel

Partir demonstrates, today's shoddy boats carrying clandestine immigrants across the Mediterranean evoke other vessels carrying people in inhumane conditions, be they slave ships or makeshift boats moving in other waters.

III

Crossing the Straits and Moving the Center

FIVE

(E)migration, Imagination, and Dissonance

Mahi Binebine and Tahar Ben Jelloun between Straits

In his 1973 novel *Le déterreur* Mohamed Khair-Eddine writes:

> Je suis né au milieu de fleurs de cactus. Les mêmes que vantent les prospectus du Club Méditerranée et les photographes officiels. Parmi des grèves de cheminots, des joutes de scorpions, des ruses périmées, des épingles de nourrice et des fibules rouillées. On ne veut pas encore se débarasser des agences de voyages qui trouvent une cible idéale dans l'ouvrier! Le noient dans le soleil, le beau soleil pouilleux des plages du Sud! Elles l'exécutent avec ses propres économies en le baladant dans des régions dites tempérées mais dont le peuple (on en célèbre encore le génie éculé et la folklorité) est tenu en laisse ou cloué au plancher croulant des préceptes que l'Occident lui-même n'admet pas sur son radeau ... ou peu s'en faut! (1973: 14)

> [I was born among cactus flowers. The same flowers that are proudly displayed in Club Med brochures and official photographs. Amongst train strikes, scorpion contests, old tricks, nappy pins and rusty brooches. We don't yet want to get rid of the travel agencies who see the worker as an ideal target. They drown him in sunshine, the beautiful lousy sunshine of the southern beaches. They kill him with his own savings, traipsing him around supposedly temperate regions whose people (their hackneyed genius and folklore are still glorified) are kept on a leash or nailed to the crumbling floor, under the rules that the West itself does not allow on its raft ... or just about!]

With the above images of cacti, scorpions, pins, brooches, and nails, Khair-Eddine, known as the "enfant terrible" of Moroccan letters, evokes the thorniness of a Mediterranean paradox articulated around Club Med

tourist propaganda and the aftermath of the damage done by colonialism. Here, Khair-Eddine unambiguously denounces the dissonance of a
divided region and the traumatic disconnect between North and South.
Central to this site of trauma and of haunting lie nodal points such as the
strait of Gibraltar, a microcosm of a history of suffering and a space
charged with the stories of men and women in transit. The historian and
sociologist Zakya Daoud characterizes the strait of Gibraltar as "un des
chemins les plus empruntés de l'univers . . . un des points les plus signifi-
ants de la planète par la charge mythique que les peuples lui ont dévolue,
par le poids de l'histoire que le hante" (2002: 13) [one of the most
travelled paths in the universe . . . one of the most significant points on
the planet, given the mythical charge that people have conferred upon it
and given the weight of the history that haunts it]. It is a place that
"condense toutes les tensions qui parcourent depuis toujours le monde
méditerranéen" (2002: 188) [condenses all the tensions that have forever
traversed the Mediterranean world]. Indeed the body of water between
Tangier and Algeciras is a conjunctural place that is highly charged with
an unfolding history marked by tragedy and loss. The same may be said,
following Daoud's suggestion, for the waters between Algiers and Mar-
seille, or Tunis and Lampedusa.[1] The shores of these nodal points are
spaces of human transaction, where bodies are subjected to heightened
surveillance and where time comes under suspension; emigrants and
immigrants, both clandestine and licit, pass through these places, leaving
behind all-too frequent stories of defeat and deferral that are carefully
glossed over, or treated as mere statistics, in the everyday practices of
nation states.

Since the 1990s, the experience of emigration—clandestine emigration
in particular—has become a recurrent literary topos, predominantly in
novels from the Maghreb and in particular from Morocco.[2] With the
transfer of power from Hassan II to his heir Mohammed VI in 1999,
restrictions on freedom of expression have been, to some extent, lifted.
With the *années de plomb*, or the Lead Years, seen as a stain of the past,
Mohammed VI's reign has led to a number of liberalizing reforms and to
greater freedoms, including freedom of artistic expression and creation.
While it is difficult to obtain reliable statistics as the topic is sensitive for
nation-building constituencies, the treatment of clandestine emigration
and immigration in the media, and more interestingly in the arts, has
burgeoned.[3] Whereas many Francophone novels by the first generations
of writers reveal the process of arrival and the hardships of assimilation
in France, the texts in this chapter fictionalize the moment and the process of emigration where France is no longer a central or focal locus, thus
undercutting the postcolonial bind where colonizer and colonized are
locked into a mutually exclusive relationship.[4] More importantly, this
chapter argues that beyond simply restating the abysmal (economic) disparity that exists between the northern and southern shores of the Medi-

terranean, a number of these works—that may best be characterized as dissonant narratives—enact practices of denunciation and deferral. These emerge clearly both in the novelistic language itself and in the subject matter of the very novels.

If the Mediterranean as a metaphor for trauma appears in a feminine or gendered fashion in the works of Bouraoui as the previous chapter reveals, it also surfaces as a traumatic male space in a body of literature that deals with clandestine emigration and immigration between the Maghreb and Europe.[5] Mahi Binebine's *Cannibales* (1999) and Tahar Ben Jelloun's *Partir* (2006), the novels that are considered in this chapter, are based on recognizable historical events, on people and places that are, in part, localizable and verifiable in books and on maps. On the other hand, they reveal an aporia of representation, or rather, the impossibility of adequately representing the event of clandestine emigration and thus they sublate and subject the real to the fictive. This chapter suggests that in so doing, they present narratives of the Mediterranean that, like the emigrants themselves, are both suspended in time but also anchored in a distinct historical moment. These narratives bring depth and perspective to the silenced subjectivities of a Mediterranean at the mercy of neo-imperialist practices and political puppetry. They bring out the challenge, cogently elucidated by Derrida in *L'autre cap*, of a Europe caught between liberal democratic ideals with its attendant laws, and the necessity for receptiveness from other "caps" [headings], the imperative of diversity and difference—not simply in paying lip service to these concepts—in regard to those who wish to partake in a new Europe.

DISSONANT NARRATIVES

In literary critic Dorrit Cohn's view, a dissonant narrative features a narrator who does not have the same vantage point as the protagonists; while this is the case for both novels in question, it is in theme more interestingly than in style that they strike a dissonant chord in the national narratives of Morocco, France, Italy, and Spain. For postcolonial critic Iain Chambers, dissonant narratives from the "empire" (Europe) about the colonies actually query their own "cultural formation." Binebine and Ben Jelloun's novels, which do not fit neatly into narratives from the "empire" or from the former colonies, query unorthodox practices in Morocco, practices that lead to the disaffection and despair seen through the eyes of the clandestine emigrant. With both authors we witness an approach that is similar to what Chambers detects in postcolonial English literature, "the insistence on a historical problematic and cultural constellation that seeks to indicate both the resonance and the dissonance between language and land, nation and narration, both today and yesterday . . ." (2008: 30). It is clear through the two novels that the contemporary problem of clandestine emigration draws its roots from economic disparity. Such an imbalance is in part inherited from the inequalities created under colonialism, itself part of a larger cultural constellation with a long history. The dissonance between language and land, which in this context might imply writing in French from and about Morocco, re-evokes the long-standing question of language central to Maghrebi Fran-cophone writers and explored elsewhere in this book. But as this chapter sets out to demonstrate, the cleft between nation and narration is where the dissonance of these novels is most striking. As Salman Rushdie once put it, "The nation requires anthems, flags. The poet offers discord. Rags" (2002: 59).

Cannibales and *Partir* share a parallel premise; the former is a novel recounted in flashbacks, about a heterogeneous group of individuals from different parts of Africa, on the eve of their clandestine journey across the straits of Gibraltar. On the shores in Tangier, they await a signal for departure. Similarly, Ben Jelloun's *Partir* takes place in Tangier on the eve of a new millennium and, like *Cannibales*, is written as a gal-lery of portraits of characters waiting on the shores to leave Morocco.[6] Although in both kaleidoscopic situations there is a main protagonist, the structures of the novels suggest that both authors stress the necessary bond between the individual and the collective, as well as the discrepan-cy between the loss of an ideal and the apprehension of an all-too violent twenty-first-century reality. Both novels explicitly denounce modern-day Morocco and implicitly condemn the ills of globalization in the Mediter-ranean, an area itself in crisis and caught between the politics of single nations versus collective identification and unity.[7] To use Chambers's terms again, both works "exist beyond the official accounts supplied by both colonial and postcolonial power," represented most commonly in political discourse and in the media, exposing how "the continuum of history fragments under the pressure of the unassimilated, and the re-sulting remains are worked over in a poetics that punctuates and exceeds the narrow logic of an inherited political view" (2008: 59). The inherited dominant political view favors barbed wire and closed borders in the creation of a controlled nation. The clandestine emigrant-turned-immi-grant, therefore, is he/she who exceeds, or spills out from, the frame or the border, and who tarnishes the image of the regulated nation, of both the countries of departure and of arrival.

OF DREAMS AND NIGHTMARES

Although there are no specific temporal indications of when *Cannibales* takes place, the use of the word *ḥarrāga* to designate clandestine immi-grants dates the action of the novel sometime in the late 1990s, or later, when the term came into consistent use.[8] Tangier is immediately recognizable in the novel through the central role played by the café France, which is situated in the same area as the "grand boulevard du centre-ville" (215) [major boulevard in the city center]. Clearly evoking the well-known Gran Café de Paris, situated in the Place de France at the top of Boulevard Pasteur, the reader is in a distinct place and time; the spatio-temporal coordinates refer to mappable times and places. Similarly, *Partir* opens with a scene located at the Café Hafa, a café that is famous for its setting on a cliff that overlooks the Mediterranean and from which one can see Spain. Here, Ben Jelloun has not modified the name, his readers know exactly where they are from the opening line of the novel: "A Tanger, l'hiver, le Café Hafa se transforme en un observatoire des rêves et de leurs conséquences" (2006: 11). [In Tangier, in the winter, the Café Hafa becomes an observatory for dreams and their aftermath.] The dream of Spain, as seen through the tired eyes of numerous hopeful cafe-goers, is the first image that is imparted to the reader, and irrupts into the realism of the familiar setting. "Comme dans un rêve absurde et persist-ant" (2006: 13) [as if in an absurd and persistent dream], the protagonist dreams "d'enfourcher un cheval peint en vert et d'enjamber la mer du détroit" (2006: 14) [of mounting a green-painted horse and crossing the sea of the straits]. If on the one hand the dream is very "real" as it per-tains to a current socioeconomic phenomenon, it is also marked by a highly imaginative desire to escape those dire conditions.

Commonly associated with imagining Eldorado and fantasizing about what lies across the straits, the emigrant is in a perpetual state of dream-ing, imagining and desire. Anticipating what lies beyond the straits, he conjures up imaginary geographies reversing those Orientalist notions of the nineteenth century where the fantasy, or dream, was the Maghreb. The topos of the dream is frequently evoked in many emigration novels and appears repeatedly—in fact obsessively—in *Cannibales* and *Partir*.[9] A conversation among emigrants in *Partir*, for example, is expressed in the following terms:

> —Partir où?
> —Partir n'importe où, en face par exemple.
> —En Espagne?
> —Oui, en Espagne, França, j'y habite déjà *en rêve*. (2006: 98; my empha-sis)

> —Leave for where?
> —Anywhere, across the water, for example.
> —Spain?
> —Yes. Spain, França—I already live there in my dreams.

France and Spain are already familiar in their imaginaries as the charac-ters already "live there," yet France still seems slightly more familiar, closer to Morocco, as the speaker here Arabizes "France" to *França* but leaves "Espagne" as is rather than Arabize it as well.

The dream-as-metaphor that first appears is that of a better life on the other side of the Strait of Gibraltar, a life in a place that is less than twenty kilometers away and yet so ostensibly unattainable. It is toward this mental space that the go-between in *Cannibales*, Momo, also known as "l'Expulsé européen," fuels dreams of future success, dreams that are at their apogee at the conjunctural moment of emigration. The main character leads the reader into a simple comparison between dream and reality: "En vérité, les rêves s'étiolent à basse altitude; ils ont besoin d'espace, d'azur, d'infini . . . Les contraintes de la vie sont bien entendu les ennemies des rêves; elles n'ont de cesse de vouloir les capturer, les lester, les désailer" (1999: 93). [Because the truth is, dreams fade at low altitudes. They need space, blue sky, infinity . . . Of course life's hardships are the enemies of dreams, they never stop trying to capture them, weigh them down, clip their wings.] The flashbacks elucidate these hardships and explain how the dreams of departure are continually weighed down, fraught with apprehension and truncated by the very irruption of the real; the moments of reverie, in *Cannibales*, are punctuated by memories of the hardships of each individual. Binebine sets up a paradoxical and conflictual notion of the dream: "Nous disons ceci: chacun de nos rêves est gardé du côté droit par un ange, du côté gauche par un djinn. Deux entités en perpétuel conflit" (1999: 79). [This is what we said: each of our dreams is guarded by an angel on the right and a *djinn* on the left, two entities in perpetual conflict.] The dream is, from the outset, a space of discord and contradiction, shot through with menace. Even when the notion is evoked in passing, it is doubly trenchant; when the protagonist describes a school of nuns that took him in when he was a young boy, he qualifies the room he is assigned as "une pièce de rêve, dotée d'un confort inespéré" (1999: 99) [a dream room, more comfortable than I could ever have hoped] but then suddenly feels like he is being "avalé" [swallowed up] (1999: 100) by the bed. The distinction between dream and reality recedes, becomes blurred, further confusing and complicating the subject position of the disoriented emigrant.

REALITY DEFERRED

In recounting the dynamic between the group of emigrés and the go-between, Azzouz, the narrator, explains "nos yeux de futurs clandestins, de *conquistadores anonymes*, s'allumaient à ceux, plaisamment hautains, de l'Expulsé européen. Il ménageait une pause comme pour nous laisser le temps de bien assimiler nos rêves" (1999: 31; my emphasis). [Our own eyes—of would-be immigrants, anonymous conquistadors—would light up in turn. He'd pause significantly as if to give us time to fully digest our dreams.] While Momo has a well-defined identity marked by two names, and haughtily boasts having crossed the sea three times, the group of emigrants waiting on the shore are, despite having proper names, forced into a state of anonymity.[10] The lives they desire, suspended and dependent on a successful crossing of the straits, have yet to begin. When Azzouz and his cousin are left behind after the group of émigrés sets off to sea, they walk back to town in search of something to eat: "Le monde continuait de tourner. Nul ne se souciait de nous. C'était comme si nous n'existions pas, comme si nous n'étions jamais nés" (1999: 212).[11] [The world went on turning. No one bothered about us, it was as if we didn't exist, as if we'd never been born.] These characters summon up the characters of Camus's *Le premier homme*, men whose roots and whose faith will end up in unmarked graves or washed away at sea, men and women whose lives will have been fought against the tyranny of inequality, whose roots lie buried in the annals of a silenced history.

Exactly halfway through *Cannibales* and *Partir* both the dream-as-metaphor and the realism of the novel are shot through with fantastical occurrences, effecting a sense of magical realism that interrupts the narrative cohesion of the works. Momentarily invited to leave the shores of Tangier, the reader is drawn to understand events symbolically. In *Cannibales* Momo dreams—or rather, has a nightmare—about being literally eaten alive in Paris. In trying to identify the experience he calls it "le rêve, non cauchemar" (1999: 113, 122, 125) [the dream, no nightmare] repeatedly, underscoring the double-faceted nature of the dream. Having been deported numerous times from France for being there illegally, Momo, "l'Expulsé européen," is at the mercy of his boss's gaze: "Installé au bar, derrière la caisse, M.José mangeait Momo de son regard avide" (1999: 119). [At the bar, sitting behind the till, Mr.José devoured Momo with his greedy bloodshot eyes.] In Momo's dream, M.José grins through teeth described as pointed, shiny forks, envisions eating him and repaying each limb—commensurately—with ideal compensation for an illegal immigrant; a promotion in rank (a toe), an apartment, a salary increase (an arm) or with working papers (another arm and two legs). The devouring gaze turns to greedy consumption, until all that is left is Momo's head which is hurled into a Parisian garbage dump.[12] This cannibalistic event, whose relevance is more than merely episodic, signals the trauma of one of the clandestine immigrants who succeeds in crossing the strait, and lends its title to the novel. Momo envisions himself being consumed by a fellow immigrant as M.José is Portuguese.[13] If the realism that precedes the dream sequence focuses on the hope and desire of escape, here it is only through a dream that Binebine is able to show the extent of what happens once the strait has been crossed and the other side of the Mediterranean has been reached. The dream strikes at the uncanny, the familiar strangeness of a fellow immigrant, for example, and yet, in retrospect—and in flashbacks—it is still, despite its unseemliness, otherworldly: "Demain il fera chaud, on ira au café France, on fumera, on verra le paradis dans les rêves de Momo" (2006: 208). [It'll be hot tomorrow, we'll go to the Café France, we'll have a smoke, we'll see paradise in Momo's dreams.] *Cannibales* ends on a note that is cognitively dissonant, as it presents the return of the dream in which the infernal journey begins anew—Azzouz and his cousin will once again return to being anonymous faces in the crowd of hopeful emigrants. The power of the dream of Eldorado—irrational though it may be as it is a clear denial of reality—is stronger than the fear of failure, death or anonymity. The anonymity of "les damnés de la mer"[14]—those who perish at sea—and that of individuals like Azzouz and his cousin, further defies and defers convention—or "reality"—where individuals are expected to be identified by markers such as name, address and place of employment. Attempting to cross the straits is a matter of life or death; this duality of outcomes stands in contrast here with the multiplicity of interpretations of dreams.

DEFERRAL AND DENUNCIATION THROUGH NARRATION

In both novels multiple narrations seem the only way to explain clandestine emigration and, by metaphorical extension, the Mediterranean. Crossing the sea means the pursuit of hope, but also the threat of death, of disorientation as boats set out only to go off course, or to arrive in unfamiliar places. *Cannibales* opens like this: "Dans mon village, les vieux nous avaient maintes fois raconté la mer, et de milles façons différentes" (1999: 9). [Back in the village, the old people were always telling us about the sea, and each time in a different way.] Juxtaposing the space of the sea with the act of recounting, or narrating, Binebine creates a link between the mutable history of a space, the Mediterranean, and an interpretive tool, narration. It is not so much what is narrated but the very act of narrating that becomes important. The dream of leaving is what repeatedly fuels the stories that are told. In Ben Jelloun's *Partir* these dreams are articulated around a mythical figure named Toutia, "un mot qui ne veut rien dire" (2006: 12) [a word that means nothing] who lends her name to the title of the opening chapter of the novel, and who will presumably appear to take them across the sea to a new life or perhaps to their death. "Comme des enfants, ils croient à cette histoire qui les berne et les fait dormir le dos calé contre le mur rêche" (2006: 13). [Like children, they believe in this story that comforts them and lulls them to sleep as they lean back against the rough wall.] Toutia's mythical status as the bearer of one of two destinies underscores the nexus between the necessity of imagination and storytelling in the lives of those who will anonymously mark the writing of the Mediterranean. It is through belief in her that the reality of daily life and everyday practices is deferred.

The flashbacks that occur as the protagonists are on the shore awaiting the boat to take them across the straits of Gibraltar frequently recall regular gatherings at the Café de France where future emigrants meet to discuss conditions and procedures of departure. Yet, it becomes apparent that the dream has nothing to do with reality and reality is far from a dream; both are deferred, both are represented as illusions. Europe becomes a cannibalizing force as it metaphorically ingests those immigrant workers who make it across the straits. For all but two of the characters in the novel who never arrive in Spain because swallowed by the waters after a storm, the Mediterranean Sea becomes an engulfing and voracious executioner. The main character never actually manages to leave and in a poignant scene toward the end of the novel, he looks through a shop window only to see, on a brightly lit television, that same cannibalizing sea captured by the cameras of the nightly news as it reports—in a matter-of-fact manner—the deaths of his companions. The novel closes with his return to the café—the place where departures are negotiated with the smuggler—a circular maneuver suggesting the eternal return of the dream and its deferral. Binebine's disenfranchised characters are part of the same generation as Ben Jelloun's character Malika, who works around the clock for a Dutch multinational in Tangier.

Like *L'auberge des pauvres* before it, *Partir* is divided according to its characters' life stories. The only two chapters in *Partir* not to bear proper names (Azel, Malika, Noureddine, etc. . . .) are entitled "Le pays" and "Revenir." "Le pays," that is Morocco, and "partir/revenir" or movement—which here happens across the Mediterranean—frame these voices and suggest that the collective telling of one's stories are inextricably linked to their geographical location, as the opening line of the novel, set at the Café Hafa, suggests. The lights of Tarifa, which are frequently mentioned,[15] fuel the ubiquitous obsession to leave—*partir* (the word appears repetitively)[16]—that consumes the protagonists of the novel: "Partir, partir! Partir n'importe comment, à n'importe quel prix, se noyer, flotter sur l'eau, le ventre gonflé, le visage mangé par le sel, les yeux perdus . . . Partir!" (2006: 149) [Leaving! Leaving! Leaving any way at all, at any cost, drowning, floating on the water, belly bloated, face eaten away by the salt, eyes gone . . . Leaving!] The year is 1995, and the "campagne d'assainissement," a highly mediatised attempt to eradicate corruption led by Minister of the Interior Driss Basri, is underway. Ben Jelloun's reference to Basri is clearly ironic as he served as one of Hassan II's closest advisors during the Years of Lead. The press, remarks the protagonist, reported the successes of the campaign but, he maintains, "si un jour elle dit la vérité, ils l'interdiront" (2006: 59). [If the papers ever tell the truth one day, they'll be shut down.] The press lies, institutions lie, and young men, women and children are desperate to leave Morocco and Hassan II's corrupt and stagnant monarchy. Azel, the twenty-three-year-old main character, with his "désir fou d'aller au-devant de son destin" (2006: 16) [crazy desire to rush toward his destiny], wishes he were a crate of merchandise, a wax mannequin, or "un objet inanimé, pas un être humain qui respire" (2006: 40) [a lifeless object instead of a breathing human being] in order to board one of the boats carrying goods between Morocco and Spain. After having studied and obtained his diploma in international relations he, like many others in his situation, is unable to find a job. A third of the way into the novel, his chance to leave comes in the form of Miguel, a homosexual Spanish artist who lives out his exotic and erotic fantasies with and through Azel.

Miguel loves "la peau mate des Marocains, leur maladresse . . . leur disponibilité" (2006: 46) [the olive sheen of their [Moroccans'] skin . . . the "awkwardness" . . . their availability] and embarks on an ambiguous relationship with Azel who, in order to repay Miguel for having helped him (and eventually his sister) to Spain, enters into a sexually charged relationship with him. The bond between them, although punctuated by moments of sincerity, resembles that of a pimp and his prostitute, or master and slave. Azel, like other Moroccans he meets in Spain, falls into a life of debauchery.[17] In a game of double deception he extorts money from Miguel, who in turn humiliates him and takes advantage of him. During a party at his villa, Miguel forces Azel to dress in women's clothes and wear makeup; showing him off to his friends he proclaims jokingly "mes amis je suis heureux de vous présenter ma dernière conquête: un corps d'athlète sculpté dans le bronze, avec en supplément un chouia de féminité . . . Azel est simplement un très bel objet, un objet de toutes les tentations. Voyez donc sa peau magnifique!" (2006: 112) [My friends, I'm delighted to present my latest conquest to you: the body of an athlete sculpted in bronze, with a piquant soupçon of femininity . . . Azel is simply a most beautiful object, an object to tempt every eye. Just look at his magnificent skin!] The repetition of the word *object* to describe Azel unequivocally attempts to put him in a stultified position where he presumably lacks both agency and humanity. In an effort to please his "benefactor," Azel goes along with the charade but soon grows tired of it: "Azel se considérait comme un employé, un travailleur au service d'un patron lunatique" (2006: 113) [Azel tried hard to concentrate, telling himself over and over that he was an employee, working for a lunatic boss.] The emphasis here is placed on an economy of exchange that reflects working conditions in Spain, where the Moroccan immigrant worker is at the service of a Spanish boss. Reinforcing a master-slave dialectic, this relationship evokes Europe's need for and misuse of immigrant labor but also its need for affirmation on a global world stage. Using its foreign-born workforce allows a continued hegemonic hold and at the same time disavows the purity wished for by national economic and ideological apparatuses. In many ways, Azel's story, like others in this novel, reflects the closeness and interdependence between two disparate and presumably antagonistic entities as well as the dramatic abyss that separates Spain from Morocco.

For Azel, the abyss that is the Mediterranean is a cemetery (2006: 14, 27), a place where many have lost their lives in their quest for better futures. This, for example, is the story of his cousin Noureddine who drowned at sea, a victim of human trafficking and the defective boats used to cross the Mediterranean. The gruesome stories that are publicly discussed do not stop Malika, the youngest character in the novel, from succumbing to the same logic of desperation. "Que veux tu faire plus tard?" [What do you want to do later on?] asks Azel. "Partir" [Leave], she replies. "Partir? Mais ce n'est pas un métier!" (2006: 98) [Leave? But that's not a profession!] exclaims Azel. Instead, her *métier* is to peel shrimp in the cold and unsanitary buildings of a Dutch-owned factory in the port of Tangier. A perfect example of the ills of globalization and ensuing exploitation, the shrimp come from Thailand, via Holland, to Morocco to be peeled "jour et nuit" [day and night] by "des petites mains avec des doigts fins" (100) [small hands with slender fingers] to then be canned and preserved somewhere else to be sold on the European market. The characters of the novel blame the dictatorial regime of Hassan II for complying with such a system and for keeping educated Moroccans from realizing their potential. They appear consumed, or cannibalized, by the system. Malika metaphorically becomes an object of consumption as her fingers literally disintegrate; "Elle avait mal au dos et ses doigts ressemblaient aux crevettes qu'elle décortiquait. Ils étaient tout roses et abîmés" (2006: 101). [Her back hurt, and her fingers, all pink and battered, now resembled the shrimp she shelled all day.] Ben Jelloun clearly points out, however, that the vision of a better life in Spain is simply that: a dream. Towards the end of the novel, when Azel has been thrown out of Miguel's house and is jobless, he remarks:

> Si tu voyais comment on traite *las espaldas mojadas*, c'est comme ça qu'on nous appelle, nous qui avons réussi à passer entre les mailles du filet . . . las *espaldas mojadas*, voilà ce que nous sommes . . . nous sommes les *Moros*, les *Zarabes*, des *Zarabes* aux épaules mouillées, nous surgissons de la mer comme des monstres ou des fantômes! A présent je me tire! (2006: 153)

> [If you saw how they treat *las espaldas mojadas*, "wetbacks," that's what they call us, we who've managed to wriggle through the net . . . *las espaldas mojadas*, that's what we are . . . we're *los moros*, the wetback Arabs, we lumber out of the sea like ghosts or monsters! And now I'm off!]

Instead of leaving, as the above quote suggests, Azel becomes "un militant du non-partir" (133) [an antideparture militant] and an informant for the Spanish police. Ashamed and afflicted with self-hatred, he ends his days tragically assassinated in Barcelona by Muslim fundamentalists. Lured into a life of religious extremism where nothing is left to interpretation, Azel perishes; in order to survive, the author seems to suggest, one must remain within the multiplicity of narrations and of interpretation. However, that is not all; like the hopeful cafegoers, whose lives are constituted by stories and who are literally seated at the threshold of the nation looking out onto the lights of Tarifa, Ben Jelloun invites readers to consider the very act of narration. Unknowing of what the next chapter of the story may bring or what life events may occur, it is precisely on the threshold that one must sit.

Exactly halfway through the novel, in chapter twenty (of forty), an elderly, still mad, yet still wise, Moha appears out of the souk in Tangier.[18] The Moroccan press, he proclaims, lies. Those who want to leave are fooling themselves if they think life is better in Europe. "Je vais en Afrique, la terre de nos ancêtres, l'Afrique est immense" (2006: 147) [I'm heading for Africa, land of our ancestors, vast Africa], he exclaims. Placed at the very center of the novel, Moha marks the liminal space between the real and the imaginary; Moha is he who denounces the press in order to tell the truth and at the same time, within the economy of the novel, he is one of two characters who is not realistic in the way Azel, Miguel and the others are as he possesses magical powers and has no linear life story. For Ben Jelloun, only the outsider has clarity of vision. Moha carries the weight of truth in his cloak. He reflects: "Combien de gars ont disparu dans la nature, on ne sait même pas s'ils existent encore . . . mais moi je sais où ils se trouvent, ils sont là dans ma capuche, ils sont entassés les uns sur les autres, tapis comme des voleurs, et attendent la lumière pour sortir, c'est pas une vie" (2006: 146). [How many dissolved into thin air and we don't even know if they still exist . . . but me, I know where they are: they're here, in my jellaba hood, all piled on top of one another, lying low like thieves, waiting for the light in order to emerge, and that's not a life.] Whereas in *Moha le fou, Moha le sage* he affirms "Je passe ma vie à me battre avec des abstractions comme un Don Quichotte" (1978: 123) [I spend my life fighting abstractions like a Don Quixote], in *Partir* he ironically overcomes abstraction in order to criticize the reality of Moroccan politics. Don Quichotte is also a fleeting character who appears at the end of the novel, as an absent *sans-papiers*, held up by border patrols (2006: 264). The national giants of French and Spanish literary canons—Flaubert, Zola, and Cervantes—are rewritten here, sounding a dissonant and unanticipated note.

The very realistic portrait of immigration that Ben Jelloun paints turns into a baroque show of novelistic artifice at the end of the novel. The last chapter, "Revenir," stages a boat harbored in the port of Tarifa, awaiting all those who had emigrated from Morocco to take them back. Flaubert, a Camerounian who works for a Franco-German NGO, arrives, like a *deus-ex-machina*, to wash away the pain and suffering of the novel's characters. Although he appears only briefly in the novel, he is accorded a crucial place. At the very beginning of the novel we read the following incipit: Mon ami camerounais Flaubert dit 'j'arrive' pour partir et 'nous sommes ensemble' quand il quitte quelqu'un. Une façon de conjurer le sort" (2006: 9). [My Cameroonian friend Flaubert says 'Here I am!' when he's leaving and 'We're together!' to say goodbye. A way to ward off bad luck.] Turning what we take for granted upside-down and transforming Flaubert into a black immigrant, we are forced to reconsider our *idées reçues*. With an unmistakable *clin d'oeil* towards Gustave Flaubert's *Madame Bovary* (where "il n'y a pas de nègre" [there's no black guy], this Flaubert reminds us), Ben Jelloun suggests that "classic" texts can be recuperated or rewritten across temporal and national borders and that literature is instrumental in exposing multiple realms of possibility. Ben Jelloun's Flaubert continues: "Et si ce bateau n'était qu'une fiction, un roman flottant sur les eaux, un roman en forme de bouteille jetée à la mer par tant de mères éplorées et fatiguées d'attendre? . . . Quand j'y pense, devenir un personnage de roman, c'est ce qui pouvait m'arriver de mieux" (2006: 261). [What if this ship were just a fiction, a novel cast upon the waters, a book in the form of a bottle tossed into the sea by all those weeping mothers so sick of waiting? . . . Now that I think about it, becoming a character in a novel is the best thing that could happen to me.] Flaubert *is* a character in a novel, and here he presents us with a triple mise-en-abyme, for there are multiple Flauberts; the original author who wrote *"Madame Bovary, c'est moi"*, the Flaubert in *Partir*, and the potential Flaubert among the pages into which Ben Jelloun's character dreams of slipping.

Evoking the harmonious and the discordant we are drawn back into the realm of the baroque (see chapter 4), as this seems to be the most productive perspective to espouse: "Ce bateau a pour moi quelque chose de familier et à la fois d'étrange, ce n'est peut-être pas un bateau, juste une maquette, un trompe-l'oeil . . ." remarks Flaubert [This boat seems both familiar and strange to me: perhaps it isn't a boat, only a model, some trompe-l'oeil . . .] (2006: 257). Placed at the threshold of the foreign and familiar and recognizing the possibility of illusion the reader is drawn once again to the openness of interpretation and therefore to the rewriting of culture through literary texts.[19] As the literary critic Armando Gnisci writes, "Attraverso la riscrittura interculturale di miti e testi, la cultura ricevente si fa protagonista attiva di un processo di mondializzazione di elementi che non le appartengono sin dalle origini, ma di cui essa si appropria in un movimento di ricodificazione, di 'cannibalizzazione,' e di contaminazione con elementi e testi culturali diversi" (Gnisci 2010: 140). [Through the intercultural rewriting of myths and texts, the receiving culture becomes an active protagonist in a globalizing process. It does so also through the inclusion of elements that do not belong to it to begin with, but which it appropriates through recoding, "cannibalization," and contamination with diverse elements and cultural texts.] Ben Jelloun and Binebine write the Moroccan nation as ailing from the inside and emphasize the destruction of the globalizing processes and cannibalization extolled by the above critic. However, through recoding dominant trajectories (European incursions by aritists and politicians into Morocco of the

nineteenth and twentieth century versus clandestine Moroccan incursions into Europe of the twenty-first century), they present readers with a
provocative chiasmus by rendering the foreign familiar and the familiar
foreign. The resonance and dissonance that emerge from these novels is
not limited to their reception or to their authors but begins in the diegesis
of the narratives.

Like Ben Jelloun's own positioning in Italy explored in chapter 4,
Flaubert and Azel's positionings in Spain are marked by the sense of a
foreign and familiar space. Throughout his time in Barcelona, Azel frequently thinks back to his mother in Tangier and remembers Morocco
nostalgically. Even before arriving in Spain, he reads a letter he had written to his "pays" [country]. In it he writes, "Mais, cher pays. Je ne te
quitte pas définitivement, tu me prêtes seulement aux Espagnols, nos
voisins, nos amis. Nous les connaissons bien, longtemps ils ont été aussi
pauvres que nous" (2006: 73). [But, my dear country, I am not leaving
you forever. You are simply lending me to the Spanish people, our neigh-
bors, our friends. We know them well. For a long time they were as poor
as we were . . .] A country across the Mediterranean, this time Spain
rather than Italy again treads the line between similarity and difference.
On the one hand, Ben Jelloun points to the racism of a country that would
rather repress its history and assert its difference: "Les Spanioulis, ils
n'ont pas avalé les siècles d'or et d'argent des Arabes en Andalousie, ils
se disent, c'est pas possible, des *Moros* ont occupé le sud de notre pays, *los
Moros* et *los judìos, lyahoud,* tous dehors, sinon on les brûle . . . dès qu'ils
voient un *Moro,* ils se méfient, ils voient *una mala pata, una cosa negra*"
(2006: 157). [Those Spanioolies, they just can't get over the golden age the
Arabs had in Andalusia, sticks in their craw: the *moros* occupied the south
of our country? Impossible! *Los moros, los judìos,* Moors and Jews, every-
body out, or we burn them! . . . soon as they see a *moro,* they get their
backs up, they see *una mala pata, una cosa negra.*] If al-Andalus is typically
glorified as a time and place of harmonious *convivencia,* here Azel recognizes how it actually takes on an opposite status in present-day Spain.
Azel remarks that the Spanish too easily conflate past and present and
view Arabs and Jews as harbingers of tension and bad luck. The boundaries of the nation thus appear more rigid than ever and peaceful coexistence among Mediterranean people appears illusory, or at best marked
by ambivalence. Ben Jelloun's use of the word "spaniouli" rather than
"Les Espagnols," or even "al-issbaniyoun" serves to underscore the linguistic familiarity, beyond the hostility, between Moroccans and Span-
iards. Linguistically speaking, Moroccan Arabic uses a number of words
borrowed from Spanish, a phenomenon that dates back both to al-Andalus and the Spanish Protectorate.

On the other hand, Ben Jelloun makes a clear connection between
Spain under Franco and Morocco under Hassan II, thereby bringing attention to the similarities in cultural and political climates between these

nations. What Miguel says about Spain is exactly what the Moroccans in the novel say about Morocco: "L'Espagne était invivable. Franco ne voulait pas mourir et son système religieux et militaire sévissait partout" (2006: 51). [Spain was unlivable. Franco wouldn't die, and his religious and military regime infested everything.][20] Religion and the army are to blame, the character remarks, for infesting all realms of society; both appear to be pervasive in the respective societies. In fact they are so far-reaching that the cities began to look alike topographically; when Azel goes to Malaga, "il eut l'impression qu'il était revenu à Tanger dans les méandres du Petit Socco" (2006: 88). [He felt as though he were back in Tangier, in the labyrinth of the Petit Socco.] When Spain begins to resemble Morocco too much, Azel contemplates turning south, to the Sahara, into Africa. "Azel leva les yeux vers le ciel et rêva d'Afrique. Il se demandait pour quelles raisons les Marocains ne se sentaient pas africains et ignoraient tout de ce continent" (2006: 220). [Azel looked up at the sky and dreamed of Africa. He wondered why Moroccans did not feel African and knew nothing about their own continent.] In thinking about a postcolonial southern and Mediterranean identity, this question merits attention.

In order to bring out their singularities, national spaces—especially postcolonial ones—are often defined geographically, politically and culturally against others. As Margaret Majumdar remarks in a series of essays on the Mediterranean, "Il reste difficile de deviner qui pourrait être cet Autre non-méditerranéen dans la constitution de cette nouvelle identité méditerranéenne—à moins que ce ne soit l'Africain qui joue ce rôle. Il est vrai que jusqu'ici cette dernière hypothèse n'a pas été développée" (1998: 220). [It remains difficult to guess who this non-Mediterranean Other might be in the creation of this new Mediterranean identity—unless the African plays that role. To be sure, this last hypothesis has not been cultivated.] Majumdar's words, pronounced more than a decade ago, are provocatively prescient, as the "othering" of sub-Saharan Africans in the Maghreb has become increasing racist in character. With the growing numbers of migrants from Senegal, Ivory Coast and several other nations, some in transit, others to stay, the way Maghrebi countries conceive of their identities is undergoing significant change. More apt therefore to look north rather than south—the political Maghreb is renewing ties with the larger Mediterranean. Many writers and artists, however, continue to try to dispel such arbitrary divisions in an effort to recuperate those who are the targets of everyday racism. This may account for Moha's turn south of the Sahara, in *Partir*, and for Ben Jelloun's uncommon inclusion of a Cameroonian protagonist (Flaubert) and his cousin, a librarian from Douala, Emilzola. More interestingly, Ben Jelloun plays with canonical French literary giants in order to reinscribe them in a different history.

AUTHORS AND TEXTS

Writing about the clandestine emigrant does not simply fill the gaps in an established historical mosaic. As Chambers puts it:

> The forgotten do not complete the picture; rather, they query the frame, the pattern, the construction and advance what the previous representation failed to register. For this is not simply to propose the heroic space of the counter-narrative that offers the promised homecoming of an alternative history, identity, and autonomous sense. Here the divisions between the colonizer and the colonized, the hegemonic and the subaltern, the victors and the victims decline into a more disquieting critical complexity that frustrates all unilateral desires to complete the picture. (2008: 59)

Ben Jelloun's baroque south, with its ruins, labyrinths and makeshift boats effectively causes us to *perdre le nord,* to lose our bearings, but in the process we develop an alternative form of reason, an awareness that with progress comes subjection and with subjection, violence. The author's own subjection to French colonialism and Moroccan dictatorship has now receded into the background; he has spent most of his life writing in, from and about France, at the same time shifting toward places—Spain and southern Italy—that provide stories and voices both foreign and intuitively, or affectively, close to him. A southern ethos does not exist without this recognition of the possibility of the other within, even if it ushers in tension.[21] Writing allows such a recognition: "L'ecriture permet aux identités de se jouer et de se déjouer les unes des autres. Elle constitue des frontières poreuses, traversées par les rêves. Elle détotalise, elle institue un droit au fantasme d'être autre, d'ailleurs, par-delà, en deçà, en devenir." [Writing allows identities to play with and elude each other. It constitutes porous boundaries, themselves interspersed with dreams. It detotalizes and establishes the right to fantasize about being other, from elsewhere, beyond, below, in perpetual becoming.][22] The dream of becoming other is not limited to the protagonists of Ben Jelloun and Binebine's novels; in moving among countries and continents over the last several decades, these writers also continually operate in positions of being "other," albeit in radically different modes than those of their characters. For what also emerges conspicuously is that the moment of emigration is one of such ambivalence and gravity that it can only be recounted in flashbacks, deferred from the moment of its occurrence.[23] Illicit in reality and invisible in the texts, the journey across the sea in deplorable conditions becomes unrepresentable. Fiction, then, seems to be the way to circumvent the social constraints that do not permit the unsightliness of naked truths. These texts indeed act as a stage for what is too difficult to say directly, for the disquiet and anxiety that characterizes confronting one's own mortality when one is willing to risk it all.

Binebine and Ben Jelloun are far from being the only Maghrebi writers who underscore the double movement occurring across the sea. Khair-Eddine, Khatibi, and Meddeb, among others, all come back to the notion of a Mediterranean paradox. Discussing the presence of "Europe" in Tangier and evoking several of the tropes just discussed (the dream, images from the media), Meddeb writes:

> Comment cette terre soumise au même climat s'avère-t-elle tant différente, pourquoi est-elle perçue comme celle dont témoignent les images d'un autre monde volées à la télévision, porteuses d'un rêve que tout actif se sent capable de réaliser, pourquoi ce lieu très proche conduit-il à un monde si lointain, pourquoi faut-il pour s'y conjoindre, subir l'épreuve d'un rite initiatique où le candidat qui se propose risque sa vie, paradoxal paysage qui donne à respirer la mort et la beauté . . . (2005: 105)

> [How does this earth, subjected to the same climate, prove so different? Why is it perceived as the one that the images stolen from television represent, carrying a dream that anyone feels capable of fulfilling, why does this place, which is so close, lead to a world which is so far away, why is it necessary, to meld with it, to undergo a painful initiation rite during which the candidate risks his life, paradoxical landscape in which one breathes both death and beauty . . .]

Concomitant with the paradox of death and beauty is the tragic irony that once the other shore has been reached the desire to return, fueled by memory and nostalgia, surges forth.

Much like the trajectory of the literary word—errant, at times uncertain, mutable—the path of the clandestine emigrant is uncharted. As sociologist Smaïn Laacher reminds us in a chapter entitled "Partir. Une ligne droite qui se brise" [Leaving. A Straight Line Breaks], "Ce n'est pas la destination qui préside à l'itinéraire du clandestin mais bien, de plus en plus, l'itinéraire qui commande la destination finale" (2007: 79). [It is not the destination that directs the clandestine immigrant's itinerary, it is increasingly the itinerary that determines the final destination.] Both the act of narrating and that of emplotting a story become attempts to make sense of the mad desire that seizes entire groups of young people from the Maghreb, and elsewhere, to risk their lives for an unknown destiny. In this sense, narrative is a crucial tool, both for the *ḥarrāga* protagonists and for the creators of those very characters, for it is through the imaginary and through images that such abjection and hardship can be mediated. By telling stories the characters deflect the reality of the moment of departure, and by writing novels Ben Jelloun and Binebine issue a warning to defer the often-illusory conviction that life is better elsewhere and thus to keep at bay the desire to leave. One of Derrida's many contributions to the study of literature is precisely the idea that literature holds a secret, something that remains open and unmasterable, and thus able to counteract power: "The undecidable in literature refuses sovereignty its own ipseity, rendering the sovereign divisible and no longer sovereign" (2008: x). These narratives of emigration not only allow us to break down the power of the bittersweet seduction of that *ailleurs* that is Europe. They also point to the breaks and rifts in those very structures of power; they signal the fact that sovereignty is porous, the sovereignty of the dream is undermined by images of death, and finally they point to the incapacity of the putatively powerful Fortress Europe to keep out the undesirable.

ENDNOTES

1. One of the most troubling images of the fourteen kilometers that lie between Tunisia and Sicily is the profusion of migrants, attempting to cross the sea. On the heels of the 2011 "Arab Spring" and the devastation that has ripped through Libya (pushing hundreds into Europe via Tunisia), the numbers of migrants and bodies missing at sea has—in less than one short year—grown dramatically. According to the UNHCR (United Nations High Commissioner for Refugees), in the first six months of 2013, 8,400 migrants, most of them from North Africa, arrived in Italy and Malta. http://www.unhcr.org/51d6b8a56.html

2. For a detailed list of such works see in particular Najib Redouane, *Clandestins dans le texte maghrébin de langue française.*

3. Yto Barrada, Mahi Binebine, and Kader Attia have treated the topic of clandestine emigration in the visual arts.

4. Francophone novels of acculturation include Tahar Ben Jelloun's *Les raisins de la galère* (1996).

5. As Hakim Abderrezak has pointed out in a semantic explanation of his concept *illiterature*, narratives of emigration are for the most part male authored (hence the "il" in the prefix).

6. This appears to be a common "formula" for novels about clandestine emigration. Along with Binebine's *Cannibales* and Ben Jelloun's *Partir*, Youssouf Amine Elalamy *Les clandestins* (2001) also features the stories of thirteen émigrés.

7. On the one hand, Ben Jelloun affirms a rather naïve vision of the Mediterranean. He states, "Les Marocains sont d'authentiques méditerranéens, dans le sens où la Méditerranée est une culture, un état d'esprit, une conception du temps et de la durée, et puis une relation affective et solidaire entre les gens. Pour eux, la Méditerranée est une vision du monde basée sur l'échange et la solidarité" (2005: 1). [Moroccans are authentic Mediterraneans, in that the Mediterranean is a culture, a state of mind, a way of conceiving of time and its duration. There is an affective relationship and a sense of solidarity among its people.] On the other, his novel *Partir* bitterly announces a very different sort of exchange; as Ben Jelloun remarks, "Plus on parle de fraternité, plus on se bat." [The more we talk about fraternity the more we fight.]

8. *Ḥarrāga*, comes from the Arabic root (ha-ra-qaf), to burn, and indicates "those who burn." This refers to the actual act of burning one's documents in order to avoid repatriation, but the term is also used to designate those who metaphorically "burn" the sea, in the way that one would "burn one's bridges" and thus be unable to return to the point of departure. The word *ḥarrāga* has now become commonly used in the Maghreb and in French media.

9. Sociologist Mohammed Koudiri claims: "Au début, on pensait que c'était la misère qui les poussait à partir mais en réalité c'est surtout le rêve d'un autre mode de vie. Ici, les jeunes vivent avec beaucoup d'interdits et la destination—l'Europe et l'Occident en général—est sublimée par les chaines de télé occidentales." [At first we thought it was poverty that pushed them to leave but actually it is most of all the dream of another way of life. Here young people live with many prohibitions and the

destination—Europe, and the West more generally—is sublimated by Western television stations.] (In Nelle 2009.)

10. The trope of anonymity is common in literature that deals with emigration and immigration. Interestingly, in Akli Tadjer's *Les ANI du Tassili*, the protagonist has no papers, he is a *ḥarrāga avant la lettre*.

11. As Katarzyna Pieprzak remarks in her article *Bodies on the Beach: Youssef Elalamy and Moroccan Landscapes of the Clandestine*, "the beach itself holds disenfranchised bodies in existential parentheses as they attempt to imagine and articulate landscapes of hope elsewhere" (2007: 6). She adds that the clandestine emigrant is in a "condition of waiting to exist" (2007: 104). Although one of the protagonists makes a similar claim, positing that they are waiting to exist implies that their identities outside of that of the emigrant are negated. In fact, in *Cannibales* Binebine focuses on past histories of the protagonists, allowing for them to emerge—to exist—in all their complexity, as beings endowed with more than their dream of leaving.

12. Several times the characters in *Cannibales* evoke the idea of returning to the earth after death: "En vérité—la triste, la vieille, l'unique vérité qui soit–nous finissons inéluctablement par retourner à la terre (117). [The truth is—the sad, the old, the only truth—we all inescapably return to the earth.] In this sense Binebine calls to mind Camus's *Le premier homme* (see chapter 1).

13. Interestingly Binebine does not write M.José as a French character and thus avoids what would have been too obvious an allegory.

14. This term was used by Djamel Ould Abbès, during his tenure as Algerian *Ministre de la Solidarité nationale* [Minister of National Solidarity]. (http://www.lematindz.net/news/8-limmigration-clandestine-vers-leurope-prend-de-lampleur-des-fonc.html) and by Abdelaziz Barrouhi in an article for *Jeune Afrique*, "Les damnés de la mer," February 17, 2009.

15. For example, p.39, 52, 68, 74.

16. For example, p. 23, 25, 32, 36, 37, 39, 50, 51, 80, 98, 101, 146, 149, 153, 183.

17. See Soumaya, one of the Moroccan women he meets in Spain, turns to prostitution after her husband, a Kuwaiti businessman, abandons her in a hotel in Barcelona. This is the premise for Ben Jelloun's previous book set in Naples, *Le labyrinthe des sentiments* (1999), where two Moroccan women are abandoned in exactly the same way. Ben Jelloun returns to his parallels between Barcelona, Naples and Tangier, building links across nations as well as between his works.

18. Moha is a key character in Ben Jelloun's literary world. First appearing in 1978 in *Moha le fou, Moha le sage*, he is a court jester, mad but wise, and the one who speaks truth to power. See chapter 3 for a more in-depth discussion of Moha.

19. The Strait of Gibraltar, writes Daoud, is "traversé d'influences, nourri de conflits, il est aussi, par son exceptionnelle promiscuité, un jeu de miroir et une illusion optique" [criss-crossed by influences and subsists on conflicts. Because of its exceptional promiscuity it is also a game of mirrors, an optical illusion.] It is "la figure de la rupture en même temps que celle de l'improbable rencontre, le mythe et la realité" (2002: 12). [It is the very figure of rupture and at the same time of unlikely encounters, it is myth and reality.] The novels in question here can indeed be placed in a historical trajectory that sees this conjunctural space as a long-standing locus of contradictory and creative events and their narrations.

20. Ben Jelloun is also keen to point out that the cities of Ceuta and Melilla in Morocco are still under Spanish jurisdiction, and therefore that part of Spain is in Morocco and vice-versa. "Allez à Ceuta et vous êtes déjà en Europe, oui Ceuta et Melilla" (2006: 147). [Go to Ceuta and you're as good as in Europe, yes, Ceuta and Melilla are European towns.]

21. Ben Jelloun's works set in Spain and Italy are clearly not a matter of happenstance; in 2006, two books came out in Italian before appearing in French, in France. The first, a small book modeled on the quick sell *Le racisme expliqué à ma fille* is entitled *Non capisco il mondo arabo* (Bompiani 2006) [I don't understand the Arab world], and takes the form of a fictitious email correspondence between Ben Jelloun's daughter

and an Italian teenager. The second is a novel about the author's mother entitled *Mia madre, la mia bambina* (Einaudi 2006) which was published a year later by Gallimard in French (*Yemma*). Two works, one involving his daughter, the other his mother, point to Ben Jelloun's emphasis on family ties and cycles of life. Those family ties that appear so clearly between Pietro and Moha, and those cycles of life that allow Flaubert to return as Camerounian and Don Quichotte as Moroccan.

22. Although Régine Robin is a specialist of Québécois literature and thus may appear out of place or anachronistic here, her reflections on writing are universally pertinent.

23. This differs significantly from a text such as Fawzi Mellah's journalistic reportage *Clandestin en Méditerranée* (2000), which is written in a linear fashion.

SIX

Addio Farança: Into the Twenty-First Century with Abdelmalek Smari, Mohsen Melliti, and Amara Lakhous

Emigration from the Maghreb toward Europe is not, of course, only and always clandestine—in fact the majority of those who emigrate do so legally. During the last few decades, a growing number of young Maghrebis have chosen to emigrate to countries other than France, a country that despite its role in a fraught neocolonial relationship is familiar at least inasmuch as most young Maghrebis who emigrate typically have a working knowledge of French. What might urge a move toward countries where the very first and most significant obstacle is language? In observing the linguistic dilemma that has faced, and still faces, numerous Maghrebi writers today, it is clear that the question is still highly relevant in understanding the cultural production of literary texts. Recalling Albert Memmi's characterization of the linguistic situation of the Maghrebi writer as a "drame" shortly after independence from France, Fouad Laroui, a voice from a later generation, refers to the "malediction" of the Moroccan writer in the same terms. Laroui titles his 2011 book *Le drame linguistique marocain*, suggesting that at least in Morocco, the situation might still be characterized as dramatic. Similarly, in Tunisia and Algeria, there continue to be fervent discussions in the media and in literature about the role of French, Arabic, Tamazight, and other languages spoken in all three countries. Yet an important paradigm shift is occurring alongside this still-anxious relationship to language: a disengagement from French. Furthermore, for a number of writers who have left the Maghreb, in particular those who have opted for countries other than France, the choice, or even rejection of certain languages, both national and literary, reveals worldviews of a postcolonial Mediterranean that dismantles and contests a Francocentric discourse. In the cases that I evoke in this chapter, the dismantling of Francocentricism (which, like Eurocentrism, is a "bad epistemic habit" in the words of Ella Shohat and Robert Stam) is carried out in a European language from within a European context.[1] For, if Eurocentrism began with Europe spreading outwards, in order to conquer and control, I draw attention to a Europe that is, today, focused on itself and protective of its national identities.

This chapter is intended as a case study for literatures by Maghrebi writers in Mediterranean languages other than French and Arabic. Dealing specifically with the recent and ongoing production of literature written in Italian by Arabophone and Francophone Maghrebi writers, it examines the use of languages, both national and literary, in the works of three novelists: Mohsen Melliti, one of the first Maghrebi writers in Italian; Amara Lakhous, the author of the widely read *Scontro di civiltà per un ascensore a piazza Vittorio* (2006),[2] which unlike most Maghrebi literature was translated into English (*Clash of Civilizations over an Elevator in Piazza Vittorio*, 2008); and Abdemalek Smari, author of *Fiamme in paradiso* (2000) and *L'Occidentalista* (2008). While numerous Maghrebi Italophone writers have produced one literary work and then ceased writing, these three writers (and in Melliti's case, filmmaker) continue to partake in the Italian cultural and literary scene and to build a substantial artistic corpus. This chapter seeks to understand what determines the choice of Italian for these multilingual writers and to lay bare the effects of their writing. Is it even a matter of choice, and if so, what role do their other languages play? In exploring these questions, the chapter addresses issues that may also prove pertinent to literature written by Maghrebi writers in other Mediterranean languages.

The history of what is now commonly known as Italophone literature (after the ever problematic term Francophone literature) is well-documented by numerous European and North American scholars and includes writers whose backgrounds span the globe.[3] Over the past thirty years Italy has witnessed a radical demographic change with ever-increasing arrivals primarily from Eastern Europe, North and West Africa, and Asia. According to the International Organization for Migration, immigrants currently account for 7.4 percent of the population.[4] Unlike what drove the immigration patterns of Maghrebi citizens to France, there is no evident or overarching common denominator to the experience of emigration to Italy besides geographical proximity. Gradually moving from a country of temporary migration to one that has become a final destination for many, Italy is now more than ever in a period of transition, growth, and re-definition. On the political side of the spectrum, embracing a new heterogeneity appears increasingly challenging in a climate driven by a hostile conservatism.

NAMING AND LANGUAGE

Out of this embattled situation, a new literature has emerged; struggling to find apposite monikers for such a body of work, critics have debated the terms "Italophone literature," "Italian Literature of Migration," "Nascent Italian Literature," and numerous others. While the term Italophone echoes the better-known term Francophone—and therefore risks setting up a hierarchical distinction between literature by writers who are "authentic" Italians versus everyone else who writes in Italian, as is the case with French and Francophone—the coinage "Italian Literature of Migration" appears inadequate insofar as not all writers under this rubric have themselves migrated, nor necessarily write about the experience of migration.[5] "Nascent Italian Literature" risks infantilizing such works and treating them as yet-to-be-developed, immature products. Finally, it is also at times referred to as "Letteratura Postcoloniale."[6] Definitions are of course slippery and context-specific, however, in an Italian context "Letteratura Postcoloniale" seems most appropriate to designate literatures that have ties to the former Italian colonies of Somalia, Eritrea and Libya, and even then it may not be quite adequate. It does not seem to accurately describe the relationship between Italy and the Maghreb which, although not new, is "a contemporary bond formed of geographical proximity and cultural links . . . The issues of post-colonial criticism are background issues in relation to a very specific inter-cultural experience in the foreground" (Burns 2001: 160). As Jennifer Burns mentions, there is an attempt to depart from issues of exile, displacement, racism and alienation in Italian literature by Maghrebi writers, even though these writers have elected to live in Italy due, to some extent, to what can be considered the long-term repercussions of European imperialism, that is to say a neo-colonial distribution of power under the aegis of a unified Europe that continues to undermine the Maghreb, among other places.

In part, the problem of nomenclature comes from Italy's complicated politics beyond its borders. Italian colonization was most pervasive in Somalia, Eritrea, Ethiopia and parts of Libya. Compared to British and French colonization the Italian case differed significantly in scale of land "conquered" and in duration (approximately fifty years). Of the Italian conquests most were settler colonies, although settlement was far from massive, and as several scholars have emphasized, Italy's colonial role did not come to an end with popular revolutions but with military defeat and diplomatic "agreements."[7] Nevertheless, Italian colonialism has been buried in the nation's unconscious, and only recently have scholars begun to excavate the complex web of relations that Italy held, and continues to foster, with its (post)colonies across the Mediterranean (one thinks of Berlusconi's close ties with Libya). The fact that there are fewer Africans from the former Italian colonies living in Italy than there are Moroccans, Romanians and Albanians, helps to obfuscate Italy's colonial history.[8] Scholar Teresa Fiore calls the phenonomenon of migration to Italy an anomalous "indirect postcoloniality," as most of Italy's immigrants come from countries formerly colonized by other European powers or with no direct history of colonization at all (Fiore 2012: 73). While this chapter might address some of the compelling writers such as Cristina Ali Farah and Igiaba Scego, who have ties to the former East African Italian colonies, I prefer to remain along an "indirect" trajectory that continues to draw connections from and to the Maghreb.

INDIRECTLY DIRECT TEXTS

The question of the radical bilingualism and of the plurilingualism of Maghrebi writers has been written about extensively and convincingly by Abdelkébir Khatibi.[9] Khatibi's work on language renders apparent, through his own conjunctural works of fiction and theory, the interstitial position, again linguistically speaking, of Maghrebi writers. For Khatibi, the linguistic situation of the Maghreb creates modes of expression that escape, divert, compromise and obscure the transparency of the word and of any one language. This manifold relationship to language, he writes in *Maghreb Pluriel*, is permeated by multiple languages; here he underscores the presence of the multiplicity of idioms that are at the disposal of many Maghrebi writers (classical Arabic, dialectical Arabic, Tamazight, and French among others). Khatibi signals the presence of Italian, as well as Spanish, in the cultural and linguistic backgrounds of the Maghreb. Citing, for example, Abdelwahab Meddeb's affinity for Dante, and Dante's connection to Ibn 'Arabī, Khatibi provides a compelling genealogy—in the Foucaultian sense of the term, that is to say, a topical genealogy set against totalizing discourses and teleological histories—that underscores the interface between these disparate but common linguistic and cultural spheres.

Critics tend to date the first Italophone texts to the year 1990, a watershed year in Italian immigration policy thanks, in part, to the Martelli Law which granted undocumented immigrants legal status and state support.[10] Frequently referred to as a genre that is more sociological than literary, many of the early texts were co-authored with native speakers of Italian and tended to focus on accounts of personal journeys and the ensuing processes of adaptation to new cultural norms.[11] The relationship these writers had, in the early days, with the Italian language appears driven by a sense of insecurity, and marks a phase where the praxis of linguistic acculturation was (self-)consciously fully underway or in process. Two decades later the number of writers who have single-authored novels in Italian has grown significantly, and the issues pursued have become increasingly varied and comparatively more complex.[12]

If some of the first texts by Maghrebi writers were co-authored, it seemed to be in the spirit of dialogue between a host country, Italy, and its new immigrants. According to Saidou Moussa Ba, one of the first African writers to write in Italian:

> Negli anni Ottanta noi immigrati eravamo tutti identificati col nome di "marocchini" e la stampa ci trattava come "vù cumprà." Il desiderio di scrivere è nato perché in fondo noi eravamo sconosciuti. Come fare per farci conoscere? Se l'immigrato prende coscienza di sè può presentare se stesso in modo che l'altro, di cui l'italiano ha sentito parlare soltanto in termini generici, possa definire se stesso. Nei loro libri, gli immigrati vogliono presentare se stessi ed anche l'"altro": noi siamo così, ma anche voi siete così; ed è nata una discussione con gli italiani, una possibilità di dialogo in cui questi libri sono gli strumenti di confronto. (quoted in Di Maio 2012: 104–105)

> [In the 1980s we immigrants were all identified as "Moroccans" and the press called us "*vu' cumprà*." The desire to write was born because we were essentially unknown. What to do to make ourselves known? If the immigrant becomes aware of himself, he can represent himself so that the other, whom the Italian has heard discussed only in generic terms, can define himself. In their books, immigrants want to represent themselves and also the "other": we are like this, but you are like this too; and a discussion with Italians was born, a possibility of dialogue in which these books are the means of exchange.]

Critics such as Armando Gnisci (2003) and Alessandra Di Maio (2012) have seconded this perspective, namely that numerous writers from Africa wrote in order to gain visibility and enhance dialogue, first and foremost with their "collaborators."[13] Although this may raise skepticism about the intent of the co-authors of these works (and indeed there have been instances of authorial dishonesty and disagreement) it is clear that several writers from this first generation were committed to directly writing to and for Italians even if this meant relying on another person.[14] Regardless of whether this dialogue was then co-opted and/or misconstrued, there emerge the *desire* and the drive on the part of these early writers to express themselves in Italian and to foster interaction with their immediate surroundings and attendant communities.

For the writers in question in this chapter, departure from Tunisia and Algeria was often a matter of survival due to increasingly stringent and threatening circumstances brought about by growing intolerance and a rise in fundamentalism, a situation not directly caused by, but certainly connected to, the long aftermath of French colonization. Although their reasons for leaving the Maghreb differ, they share the experience of exile. They are, in Saïd's words, "the nay-sayers, the individuals at odds with their society and therefore outsiders and exiles in so far as privileges, power, and honors are concerned" (1994: 39). Melliti, Smari and Lakhous are French-educated, yet they appear only tangentially subjected to, or constrained by, a (sub)conscious colonial burden.

AN ACCENTED LITERATURE

Mohsen Melliti belongs to this first generation; born in Tunis, he arrived in Italy in 1989 after being politically exiled from Tunisia, and quickly established himself as a filmmaker, documentarian and writer. His first novel, *Pantanella. Canto lungo la strada*, was published in 1992. Originally written, but not published, in Arabic and translated into Italian, this début novel signals the complicated relationship to language experienced by many during their first years in Italy. Having written the novel shortly after his arrival in Italy, when he was not yet in command of Italian, Melliti uses, as he says "the only instrument at [his] disposal," Arabic.[15] His relationship to French, he maintains, is functional and does not appear to be in any way consonant with his literary sensibilities. As one of his characters notes, "la partenza è l'unica medicina per superare i periodi di crisi" [leaving is the only remedy for overcoming periods of crisis] and the only way to gain "un'altra terra . . . un'altra vita, *un'altra lingua*" (1992: 26; my emphasis) [another land . . . another life, *another language*]. Yet, for Melliti, as for other writers who resonate with more than one culture and language, it is not simply national languages that are acquired by living in another country, but figurative idioms that also take the form of confessions, songs, and poems.

Pantanella is loosely based on the 1991 violent round-up of immigrants from different parts of the world who for six months inhabited an abandoned and dilapidated pasta factory in a downtrodden area of the Italian capital.[16] There is no traditional plot, and the narrative structure revolves around four main characters. Voice and perspective shift from one to another and at times come from a disembodied figure, a *deus-ex-machina* presence that calls the reader's attention to a collective body as well as to each individual. As if to re-create the form of a *halqah* and thus draw attention once again to the very act of narration and performance, the protagonists are first seen sitting in a circle and in turn sing a "Maghrebi melody," a *maqāmāt*, dance, confess, or recite a poem. Insisting on the form of the circle, which expands over the course of the first few pages of the novel as the characters are presented, Melliti draws the reader into a narrative act that turns the private into public as more voices are added to the mix. In so doing, he makes language less an instrument of direct communication and more one of symbolic representation, a means of channeling suffering into art for a disparate group of people. To this effect one of the main protagonists, Ahmad, describes Pantanella as "uscita dalla mitologia greca . . . un teatro della vanità scritta da filosofi ambiziosi e anarchici" (1992: 136) [something out of Greek mythology . . .

a theatre of vanities written about by ambitious and anarchical philoso-
phers]. From the outset the "theatre of vanities" is marked by a babelic
chorus of voices and accents, from the character who answers a question
posed to him in Italian with "yes yes. Drink birra" (1992: 12) to the one
who Arabizes the pronunciation of the Italian word "soggiorno" to "sugiurno" in designating the *permesso di soggiorno* (a temporary residence
card), to the use of Arabic words such as *ghurba* and *muezzin* among
others. More importantly, unlike the stereotypical depictions of illiterate
immigrants commonly found among much of mainstream society and in
the media, Melliti paints the residents of Pantanella as educated and with
a masterful command of language(s); for Ahmad, "il mondo era formato
dalle parole scritte nei quaderni e nei libri" (1992: 54). [The world was
shaped by words written in journals and in books.] He reads Sartre and
Camus in an attempt to make sense of the alienation and absurdity that
characterize his life in Italy. He is clearly marked by a French colonial
heritage and uses its cultural capital—at a distance and by choice—to
make sense of his existential questioning.

Many of Melliti's techniques render his writing filmic; a diegesis composed of numerous dialogues, the use of multiple viewpoints, cross-
cutting, temporal discontinuities, ellipses and vivid descriptions of place.
This comes as no surprise as he is a filmmaker as well as a writer and is
increasingly turning towards film as his medium of expression. His feature film *Io, l'altro* came out in 2007, a decade after his last novel, and he is
currently working on a second film about the war in Afghanistan.[17] His
second novel *I bambini delle rose* (1995) was first conceived of as a screen-
play for Rachid Benhadj's film *I figli della notte* and was then turned into a
novel by Melliti himself. His is what could be called, after Hamid Naficy's cultural theory of accented cinema, an accented *literature*; for Naficy
"all exilic and diasporic films are accented. If in linguistics accent pertains
only to pronunciation, leaving grammar and vocabulary intact, exilic and
diasporic accent permeates the film's deep structure: its narrative, visual
style, characters, subject matter, theme, and plot" (2001: 23). Naficy's theory is useful in the context of this chapter as it offers a pertinent analytical
framework within which to read the *texts* I analyze, and upon which to
build. According to Naficy, accent subtends the deep structure of each
work, that is to say it is woven into the text in its entirety, appearing and
disappearing unpredictably. Accent does not only refer to an audible
enunciation (see above example of "soggiorno" versus "sugiurno") but is
a trope that modulates the aforementioned creative aspects of a work,
from technique to style to characters and plot.[18] Furthermore, autobiographical elements of the directors of "accented films" are acknowledged
as having a significant bearing on their works, and the fact that they
operate outside mainstream modes of production, often on the margins
of the society from which they speak, is repeatedly underscored.

Filmmakers of accented cinema emerge out of two distinct historical moments; the late 1950s to the mid-1970s and the 1980s to the 1990s, and are therefore "the products of this dual postcolonial displacement and postmodern or modern scattering" (2001: 11).[19] While it is deleterious to keep relegating such texts to the margins of Italian literary culture, Melliti's novels (unlike Amara Lakhous's, for example, discussed later in this chapter) have been published with difficulty and scarcely distributed before going out of print and, only in the case of his second novel, then being reprinted. His feature film, on the other hand, has benefited from greater attention and stars one of Italy's most famous actors, Raoul Bova.

Accented cinema typically features a series of "organizing centers" that Naficy calls narrative chronotopes or "time-space" nodes (after Bakhtin): open chronotopes most often correspond to an "idealized homeland" and incorporate images of nature, landscapes and iconic markers such as monuments, whereas closed chronotopes describe exilic and diasporic life, often under the modes of imprisonment and panic. Finally "third-space" chronotopes are situated in transitional and transnational sites such as borders, tunnels, seaports, airports, hotels, and transportation vehicles. Although this taxonomy may appear overly prescriptive here, it is useful in understanding the multiple languages, in the widest sense of the term, at work in accented texts. "Each film may contain a primary chronotope or multiple 'mutually inclusive' chronotopes, which may reinforce, coexist with, or contradict one another" (2001: 153). Melliti's works include all three of Naficy's chronotopes and at the same time lead us further to add to the theory of accented works the preponderance and significance of urban settings as spaces of self-affirmation of the exilic subject.[20] The transitional and transnational sites, or what the anthropologist Marc Augé would call non-places, that characterize Naficy's "third-space" chronotopes indeed most often correlate to city spaces. However, the city itself brings to accented works another interpretive frame through which to read key functions of language.

INCURSIONS AND EXCURSIONS

The language of self-examination, for example, comes from incursions into the city: wandering through the Roman city streets, Melliti's protagonist in *Pantanella* and those in his second novel *I bambini delle rose* (1995) bring out the significance of urban spaces for the *straniero* [the foreigner], and make marginal social types such as street-vendors and immigrants central.[21] In fact, much like for the authors themselves, it is not the spaces of the provinces or the countryside that hold interest and are productive but an urban life of (economic) possibilities and promises of better lives. In *Pantanella* Ahmad is a new type of flâneur who notes street names and places with a familiarity and a detachment that ultimately breeds much contempt as he is barred entry from a cheap hotel (what Naficy calls a "third space" chronotope), insulted, and in the end rejected by the formal institutional structures of the city.[22] Yet despite such marginalization he is not dissuaded from marking the city as his as he dances and makes music in some of the streets and piazzas of the capital: "loud incursions into the city represent a moment of loud, ebullient self-expression and of appropriation of the central spaces of the city to different marginal uses" (Burns 2002: 368). Alongside the "eternal city" exists the temporary "city" of Pantanella, the abandoned pasta factory and dwelling for Ahmad and his fellow foreigners.[23]

From the outset of the novel, Pantanella is referred to as a "città" in inverted commas, underscoring the possibilities of multiple semantic valences at work in Melliti's language but also "inscribing relentlessly the alternative, unsanctioned nature of this construction of a city. It is as if this typographical cordoning-off expresses essentially not only the marginalized, ghettoized existence of the migrant community, but also its parodic, unreal quality—its lack of substantiation and of substance" (Burns 2006: 363). Moving between a "ghettoized existence" and that of a new flâneur with his occasional loud incursions and appropriation of sanctioned spaces, Ahmad fights relegation to the margins. Pantanella, this city within a city and on its margins, dispels the binary logic of center and periphery. Both cities bear the accents of Naficy's open, closed and third space chronotopes and metaphorically bring to mind what is at the heart of this book, the avowedly shifting—or impermanent—characteristics of a Mediterranean ethos *and* its persistent presence.

The eternal return of this topos is exposed through the figure of the circle evoked earlier: stories in the "città," which is called a "centro di delinquenza" [a crime hub] by the media, are told sitting around a circle; the city of Rome figures as being in the center of the Mediterranean, which is described as circular, and Ahmad himself envisions himself as encircled. "Quella sera si sentiva come un pianeta illuminato, circondato da un oceano sconfinato nell'immensità dell'universo" (1992: 68). [That night he felt like a bright planet, surrounded by a limitless ocean in the vastness of the universe.] He also walks around Rome literally in circles, "cosi continuò a camminare finché si ritrovò al punto di partenza" (1992: 28). [So he continued to walk until he found himself back where he began.] If the city provides a stifling sense of going nowhere, zigzagging one's way across the Mediterranean provides a momentary way out, if only through the imagination. As one of the characters is walking in the Roman neighborhood of Trastevere he is reminded of his own North African city: "Quando cammino per Trastevere mi ritorna alla mente la mia città . . . Sotto l'effetto di questi pensieri e di queste sensazioni, le immagini cominciarono a confondersi, ad andare a zig zag e poi di nuovo dritte, danzando sulle acque del Mediterraneo" (1992: 20). [Walking around Trastevere reminds me of my city . . . With these thoughts and feelings, images began to blur together, zigzagging and then going straight again, dancing on the waters of the Mediterranean.][24] Just as Rome appears as foreign and exclusionary, at the same time it reminds the Maghrebi characters of their own cities. Again a circle is traced between home and Rome; stuck in the middle, though, many of the protagonists seek a way out. In the end, Melliti's novel is tragic: the "città" of Pantanella burns down as the city of Rome remains intact, and Ahmad ends his days—and the novel—by jumping from a bridge. His is a suicide reminiscent of a Camusian form of revolt as Ahmad puts an end to what he sees as the absurdity of his condition, such an act emphasizes the impossibility of integration even when Rome resembles home.

For this generation of writers—those who, like Melliti, began writing in the eighties and early nineties—the difficulty of being a foreigner in Italy is still at the forefront of their works. Their writing betrays the disillusionment of failed integration in language(s) that speak directly to those responsible for such failure. Yet unlike Francophone writers writing in France (Beur writers in particular), they do this without reference to historical precedents. Accented literature is situated and counter-hegemonic as it is not only produced in the margins—in this case by a very small publisher for a limited period of time—but also because it undermines prevailing ways of writing, while "reinterpreting narrative techniques" and reviving "an ability of narrative to enforce with almost cruel simplicity a re-appraisal of social conditions on the part of the reader" (Burns 2001: 179). Like the other authors discussed in this chapter, Melliti was a writer before he was a migrant, and hence inevitably challenges one of the most common denominations of this genre of writing, that of "letteratura della migrazione."[25] In fact, although *Pantanella* is centered on a group of foreigners in Italy, it is less about the experience of migration than it is about language, community and citizenship.

PIRATES AND PIROUETTES

Melliti's "accent" in *Pantanella* comes in part from the fact that the novel was originally written in Arabic and translated into Italian. Furthermore, the text reflects a concern for multilingualism by using words and phrases in Arabic and by reproducing other languages in the text.[26] Amara Lakhous, one of today's most popular and prolific Italophone novelists, presents a similar case, although the content and genre of his novels are starkly dissimilar. His first published work of fiction was a bilingual Italian and Arabic version of a novel that he had originally written solely in Arabic (Al-baq wal qursān). This edition quickly went out of print, however, and was rewritten by the author and republished in Italy in 2011 under the title *Un pirata piccolo piccolo*, after Lakhous had already gained notoriety in Italy and abroad. *Scontro di civiltà per un ascensore a*

Piazza Vittorio was also originally written in Arabic and published in Algeria and Lebanon in 2003, but again had a short shelf-life.[27] It was subsequently re-written by the author in Italian and appeared in 2006 to great acclaim. In between *Scontro* and *Un pirata*, *Divorzio all'islamica a Viale Marconi*[28] was published in 2010, originally written in Italian and rewritten by the author in Arabic (also published in 2010).

What do these pirouettes between languages reveal? First of all they indicate that Lakhous, unlike the other authors in this chapter, does not have a professional translator for his Italian and Arabic texts; rather than use a professional translator for *Scontro*, *Divorzio*, and *Un Pirata*, or even directly translate them himself, he re-writes his novels using an uncommon technique that will be discussed shortly. Second, by examining the trajectories of these novels we are able to see not only increased use of Italian rather than Arabic or French or any other language, but the author's investment in the languages of his works emerges clearly. Third, like Melliti and Smari, Lakhous was a writer before he was a "migrant," or more appropriately an emigrant, and therefore his works call into question the moniker of "migrant literature" and the linguistic dilemma that presumably afflicts many such writers. Lastly, the various publications and multiple editions of his works raise the issue of reception and marketing, a question that directly calls attention to reader expectations as they pertain to language.

Lakhous's method is one of self-pirating, as he takes elements from one work to transform them into another. He describes his method for the creation of *Scontro*:

> I took a filesheet, I divided it in two columns, the Arabic text on one side, the Italian on the other. Then I started re-writing it, and there I have a trace. For example, let's say my characters are at a bar having a coffee: I rewrite—in Arabic I write they are at the bar having a coffee then at some point I lose myself in the text. If a phrase comes to me I add it. While I re-write I see that there are things I want to add in the Italian text, I switch the keyboard of my computer from Arabic to Italian and I go to the Italian text. I then go back to the Arabic text and continue to work. These two texts, these two languages, look at each other. When I have reached the end, I separate them, you go your way, you go the other—and give them different titles. I changed a few of the characters' names, in Arabic they have one name, in Italian another. (Esposito: 6)

The technique of mirroring, of having Arabic and Italian "look at each other" suggests that, for Lakhous, the languages are on equal footing in a dialogue where neither is privileged. It also reflects how the writer Arabizes Italian and Italianizes Arabic, as he has stated in numerous interviews. In this way then, Lakhous undermines the Eurocentric ideal that would assume hierarchy of one (Western) language and attendant cultural norms over a non-Western language and set of norms. Furthermore, unlike with Melliti or numerous other early Maghrebi writers in Italy, Lakhous does not rely on an Italian co-author or translator. This too eliminates the possibility of reading Lakhous's texts as in any way dependent on a "stamp of approval" from mainstream Italy. Finally, this mode of writing eschews the relationship to French colonial power altogether; as Parati writes in describing general characteristics of Italophone literature, "The coloniser's language and literature are [therefore] displaced from their usual privileged position in order to become secondary to the appropriation and personalization of another culture" (1997: 174).

In *Scontro* Lakhous's attention to language is a focal point; the novel has often been compared to Carlo Gadda's 1957 *Quer pasticciaccio brutto di via Merulana*, a groundbreaking novel as it was the first to be written in multiple Italian dialects. *Scontro* is a highly polyphonic *roman parlé* or "spoken novel"; each chapter is a first-person narration or witness testimony of a different resident of a building in which a man was found murdered in the elevator. Suspicion about who committed the murder erroneously falls on one of the residents Amedeo (whom we find out later is really called Ahmed), who is missing from the building. Each witness testimony is narrated in a differently inflected Italian (Roman, Neapolitan, Milanese, Pakistani), and each chapter alternates with Amedeo's journal in which he records *his* perception of each resident of the building. The alternation of witness testimonies and Amedeo's journal produces an interesting juxtaposition between speech on the one hand (the oral testimonies) and writing on the other (the journal, a form that is traditionally scripted). Amedeo is missing, and his writing (or his journal) is thus haunted by absence, whereas the oral testimonies convey a palpable presence. The play of presence and absence, along with the dynamic juxtaposition of the different forms of Italian, suggest that beyond any political or cultural representations, any issues of national idioms, language itself is infinitely unstable, volatile, and changing.[29]

Scontro brings to the fore cultural layering; alongside the Italian novel to which it is often compared, echoes of traditional Arab folktales are evoked through the structure of shifting perspectives and multiple truths. In fact, the novel ends with several invocations to King Shahryar (Sherazade's husband from *A Thousand and One Nights*). Furthermore, the protagonist ends each journal entry with a howl or a ululation—spelled "Auuuuuu"—which along with being called the "eternal song of Orpheus" (2006: 185), recalls the *zagharid*, or the ululations common to women in the Maghreb. This language without words, so to speak, speaks its own truth just as each character tells his or her own version of what they deem to be the truth. Each chapter is entitled "the truth according to" and the character's name. Beyond the evident suggestion that there is no one truth to anything, above all to the egregious stereotypes purposely written for each character—Chinese people eat dogs, immigrants are criminals, for instance—each truth comes with its own language, in the widest sense of the term.

In *Divorzio all'islamica a Viale Marconi*, Lakhous draws on a classic of Italian cinema, the 1961 comedy by Pietro Germi, *Divorzio all'italiana* [Divorce, Italian Style]. The immediate connection between a cultural work that is quintessentially "Italian Style" and what is taken to be foreignness ("all'islamica") is striking and at the same time perfectly natural. "Italian style" has gone through sea changes since the 1960s to now include— although not always accept—non-Italian cultural constituents. Playing with language and cultural signifiers beginning with the very title, Lakhous continues to treat sensitive issues of an increasingly mixed nation with parody and satire. *Divorzio*, which bears most of the characteristics of a spy novel, revolves around, and is alternately narrated by, two main protagonists. Both of them—Christian/Issa and Safia/Sofia—have double names that reflect their mixed affiliations. Christian is a Sicilian, born to Tunisian immigrants in Italy and Safia is an Egyptian woman who has moved to Rome to follow her husband. Christian is a language enthusiast and a professional interpreter for the courts in Palermo but is hired by the Italian secret service anti-terrorism squad to infiltrate a presumed terror çell operating behind a call-center in Rome. There he meets Safia, who refers to him as the "Arab Marcello," after the Italian actor Marcello Mastroianni, and takes on the name Sofia, not only because it resembles her Arab name but because of her admiration for the actress Sofia Loren. The novel takes place entirely in Rome, in the neighborhood around Viale Marconi, an area that has seen increasing numbers of shops run by Africans, Middle Easterners and East Asians among others. The space of the city is a key player in the novel as the diasporic characters live in run-down apartment buildings, walk the streets and go in and out of the call center—the setting of much of the action—calling home or looking for business.

Italian is Cristian's mother tongue, although he also speaks Tunisian Arabic, thanks to his parents and to his upbringing in Mazara del Vallo (a fishing town in Sicily only a few kilometers from Tunisia), and Classical Arabic, as he studied it at the University of Palermo. For his undercover mission he is required to play the part of a Tunisian immigrant. Early in the novel he affirms that in order to be credible in his role: "L'ideale è parlare un italiano con una doppia cadenza: araba, perché sono tunisino, e siciliana, perché sono un immigrato che ha vissuto in Sicilia" (2010: 45). [The ideal is to speak an Italian with a dual cadence: Arab, because I'm Tunisian, and Sicilian, because I'm an immigrant who has lived in Sicily.] Instead of being torn and tormented by a diglossic or polyglossic schizophrenia, a condition frequently attributed to bi- or plurilingual subjects, Cristian/Issa lightheartedly shifts from one to the other as each situation presents itself. Lakhous accentuates Christian's speech with Sicilian dialect as well as Arabic sayings, and peppers his landlady's exclamations with Roman expressions. When Christian breaks the news to his fiancé that he will be away for a while she quizzes him on the "where, when, why, who and what" (in English in the Italian original), but he cannot tell her the truth about his undercover mission and thus lies, manipulating language to present one thing rather than another. As Christian reminds us, quoting the Italian filmmaker Nanni Moretti, "le parole sono importanti" (2010: 31) [words are important].[30] Given that the main character is acting a part, the multiple references to film are not surprising.

Cristian/Issa ironically remarks on his role as the "salvatore della nazione" (2010: 21) [savior of the nation], as he will presumably thwart a terrorist attack. Thus, Lakhous puts the "immigrant" (he plays a Tunisian immigrant for his mission) in the position of power. Duplicitous language and quid pro quos are intended to derail and detour and double-cross both the reader and the characters. The double names of the characters—not only Christian/Issa and Safia/Sofia but also her husband Said/Felice and Capitano Tassarotti/Giuda (Christian's boss)—accompany their double professions; Christian is an interpreter and secret agent, Safia is a clandestine hairdresser, Said/Felice was an architect in Egypt but a pizzamaker in Rome. Lakhous is didactic in leading readers to the conclusion that appearances are deceptive and fictions sometimes more believable than reality. But on another level, his method of writing hides more complex cultural questions. "My biggest discovery," he says, "is that writers have difficulties and blocks in explaining themselves in their own language. The example is Sofia, when she speaks of the Muslim paradise and asks the question: what awaits Muslim women in heaven? I'm sure that I couldn't have asked this question in Arabic directly. I needed another language to mediate it" (personal correspondence, 2012). With the concept of mediation, however, comes the imperative, or the expectation of impartiality. Does Lakhous imply, therefore, that the use of Italian is less risky, in some ways more neutral? Where might French fall in this spectrum?

Interestingly, Lakhous, whose signature style is to work between multiple languages, does not re-write his works into French: "By eclipsing the colonial language, the history of colonialism is parenthesized and the focus turns instead to the passage through languages, a mobility which is geographic as well as linguistic. Italian, in its perhaps 'neutral' status, allows the expressive and interpretative possibilities of writing in an acquired language to be stretched beyond the strictures established by history" (Burns 2010: 135). Italian, as Burns notes, might be considered post-postcolonial or acolonial for certain Maghrebis and thus more disengaged, evenhanded, permissive and open. To both author and local audience, Lakhous's *Scontro* and *Divorzio* sound both foreign and familiar chords.

The Italian is straightforward and the cultural references are easily recognizable, but the familiar sounds and words are inflected by a multiplicity of cadences and cultural references that sound "accented" in Italian. The accents emerge predictably in the frequent dialogues between the characters and more unpredictably elsewhere. For instance, one finds "Amico mio, bassato trobbo timbo. Chi biacere reviderti" (2010: 81) [My friend, too much time has bassed. What a bleasure to see you], stressing the lack of the letter "p" in Arabic and substituting it with a "b." Or else, in conformity with linguistic differences, the protagonist, who speaks Italian with a Sicilian accent, often inverts subject and verb. However, the novel is also marked by other "accents." Christian's co-protagonist Sofia quips, "Quando camminavo per le strade di Viale Marconi non ero mai sola. Ero sempre a braccetto con tanti accompagnatori fantasma: i loro nomi? Jihad, guerra santa, kamikaze, undici settembre, terrorismo, attentati, Iraq, Afghanistan . . . al-Qaeda, talebani . . . ero una sorta di Bin Laden travestito da donna!" (2010: 48) [In fact, when I walked through the neighborhood of Viale Marconi I was never alone. I was always arm in arm with a crowd of ghost companions: their names? Jihad, holy war, suicide bomber, September 11th, terrorism, attacks, Iraq, Afghanistan . . . Al Qaeda, Taliban . . . I was a sort of bin Laden disguised as a woman!] Here the accent is cultural, it reads as humorous criticism of the stereotyping and identitarian imprisonment of Arab subjects in Italy. The novels have the benefit of drawing the reader's attention to the fact that in today's Italy a Sicilian born to Tunisian parents, as in the case of the protagonist in *Divorzio*, might very well be the one to "save the nation." His ability to seamlessly weave in and out of overlapping cultural spaces in the heterogeneous cultural constellation that is increasingly at the forefront of Italian national culture sets an ambitious example for a politics of adaptation.

However, Lakhous is part of a generation of Maghrebi writers who aspire to privilege a new aesthetic rather than a new politics. And it is here that the question of language becomes thorny. For a long time the question posed to Maghrebi writers has been about their choice of French over Arabic. For most writers the question proved false as many revealed that French was really the only choice either because it was the language in which they were schooled (and therefore mastered better) or because they wanted to speak about certain taboo subjects. More than half a century after independence from France, with the colonial questions slightly more distant or removed, we can begin to ask "why are these authors not writing in French, like so many writers before them and of their generation?"

Lakhous, who speaks and writes Arabic and French fluently, claims that his choice of language is an aesthetic decision, not a political one. It is true that the political stakes behind language in these novels are attenuated as an aesthetics of play, common to the murder mystery and the spy genre, comes to the fore.[31] For instance, the central question of *Scontro* is a classic "whodunit," while in *Divorzio* there is a palpable crescendo of tension as the reader waits to find out whether the terrorist plot will be thwarted or successful. It is also true that in *Scontro* Lakhous cites some of the most politically engaged Algerian writers; aside from his reference to Kateb Yacine he quotes Tahar Djaout, "la gente felice non ha memoria" [happy people have no memory], a writer who was assassinated for his political beliefs and for writing in French. However, if the political aspect is present, it comes less in the form of a politics of denunciation, but rather as an incitation to adopt practices of recognition and inclusion of otherness.

Escaping the paradigmatic lens that underscores a (post)colonial burden, via language, on writers of Maghrebi origin, Lakhous sets the stage for new literary configurations to emerge. For many *other* writers the language of literary expression may not have implied a political choice either: in fact many reject the notion of political choice. Yet given the conflicted relationship to French in the Maghreb (seen as both burdensome and emancipatory), this issue has rarely been ignored in the criticism devoted to Maghrebi literature. For the Algerian writer Abdelmalek Smari, writing happens in all his languages, as he dexterously selects from his palette depending on the matter at hand.[32] Writing in Italian is both a self-imposed challenge and an evident choice, he affirms, given that he lives in Italy but also, he adds, given his sense of respect for those around him.[33] Smari is one of the least known Italophone writers and yet one of the most outspoken and prolific; although he has written but two novels and several unpublished plays[34] he has published hundreds of articles in Italian for the online magazine *El-Ghibli, rivista online della letteratura della migrazione*,[35] and in French and Arabic on his personal website "algérien, berbericus, arabicus, humanum.est."[36]

LITERATURE OF IMPACT

Smari's first novel *Fiamme in paradiso* was published in 2000, eight years after his arrival in Italy. Like Melliti's and Lakhous's first novels, *Fiamme in paradiso* was first written in Arabic. Smari then translated it into French (but never published it) and then, with assistance, translated it into Italian. The online magazine *El-Ghibli* houses an archive—with digital reproductions—of selections of the manuscript in Arabic, allowing a glimpse into the linguistic pirouettes and changes that the author has made.[37] Avowedly autobiographical, the novel follows Karim the young protagonist as he arrives in Italy from Algeria. The hardships of eking out a living, having neither a fixed domicile nor employment, and living under constant siege by police and hostile "hosts," are juxtaposed with the allure of being in an unfamiliar place. The novel sparks several interesting concerns related to language. Karim reflects upon the stratification and different functions of the languages at his disposal; French is formal but efficient, Classical Arabic is God's language, pretentious and best used for highbrow literature, colloquial Arabic is most consonant with daily life, and Berber is, he says, the language that Saint Augustine, "il primo immigrato algerino a Milano" (2000: 44) [the first Maghrebi immigrant to Italy], spoke in the streets of Milan. Whereas the protagonist classifies each language separately, the author combines them, stratifying the text and integrating each one (with the exception of Berber) into the novel. The novel takes place during Karim's first weeks in Italy when he does not yet have the linguistic tools to communicate in Italian and thus is taken advantage of by dishonest employers; preying on this weakness, he is recruited by a fundamentalist organization, which ultimately leads to self-sacrifice for the greater good as he blows himself up.

Critical of both Eurocentric hostility and Islamic extremism, Smari effects what Khatibi called a double-critique; in this case an exposition of both European traditions of hegemony and Arab traditions of theological unity, patriarchal positionings and victimization. He extends this to the realm of Arab letters which he labels *Letteratura d'impatto*; impatto, to Smari, refers to the negative impact of European imperialism and conquest on the Arab psyche and consequently on literary production. Boldly (and, in my view, mistakenly) claiming that there has been no original Arab literature in the last two centuries—only mere imitations of European traditions, with a few exceptions—Smari urges a reawakening and a *prise de conscience* for real innovation. What is interesting, along with the double-critique that he effects, however, is how the moniker a "literature of impact" misleads us into believing the opposite of what he intends, thanks to his own unique use of Italian. Rather than effect impact (as *d'impatto* would indicate), Smari designates a literature that was subjected to impact. Ironically perhaps, it is his literature, along with Lakhous's, for one, that is the subject rather than the object of impact, that is changing "Italian literature" and that is gaining purchase in the postcolonial Mediterranean.

Although Khatibi's *pensée autre*, as he calls this double-critique, was first elaborated in the context of decolonization (and therefore largely in relation to France), it gains new relevance in the twenty-first century as Smari's novels shift the focus of a still imperial Europe and an Italy in which marginalization, and objectification, of Maghrebi men and women is the norm. Khatibi stresses the importance of dialogue: "D'une part, il faut écouter le Maghreb résonner dans sa pluralité (linguistique, culturelle, politique), et d'autre part, seul le dehors repensé, décentré, subverti, détourné de ses déterminations dominantes, peut nous éloigner des identités et des différences informulées" (2008: 26). [On the one hand one must listen to the Maghreb resonating in all its plurality (linguistic, cultural, political). On the other, only the reconsidered, decentered, subverted, outside, itself diverted from its dominant determinants, can keep identities and unformulated differences at bay.] Through the prism of the

Mediterranean, Smari brings back to the Maghreb from that "dehors"—
the outside—the possibility of thinking plurilingualism in and around
Morocco, Tunisia and Algeria.

In his 2008 novel *L'Occidentalista*, Smari revisits a genealogy linked to
Renaissance Italy, devoting numerous pages to an interpretation of
Dante's role in the construction of a language and of a nation. The novel
takes the form of a posthumous narration by an Algerian man who dies
while living in Italy, a country to which he fled after being accused of
betraying his wife. Achronological and non-linear, the multiple story
lines are set in contemporary Milan, particularly around marginal figures
(prostitutes, homeless men, the mad) and in the urban spaces of parks
and bars. Samir's spectral viewpoint from beyond the grave points to a
time that is out of joint, at once of the past and seemingly current, both
ancient and modern. Samir (also an anagram of the authors' surname), an
Algerian exile living in Milan, remarks "Mi sono spesso chiesto i motivi
che fanno di Dante, Dante. Secondo me la sua importanza è più politico-
religiosa che puramente letteraria, nel senso che grazie alla Divina Commedia, egli riuscì a dare forma a una iper-nazione, cioè il cosiddetto
occidente, a una religione e, sopratutto a livello locale, a una lingua"
(2008: 89). [I have often asked myself what makes Dante, Dante. I think
his importance is more politico-religious than strictly literary, for thanks
to the Divine Comedy he was able to create a hyper-nation, that is to say
the so-called West—he created a religion, and above all, at a local level,
he created a language.] Smari points to the very constructedness of what
is called the Occident, and to the undeniable imbrication between literature and politics, especially when exile is a central preoccupation.[38] Furthermore the author also suggests that with each literary text comes a
singular language. Bridging past and present, Smari establishes a trans-
linguistic, transcultural and trans-temporal filiation. In *Eloge du Cosmopol-
itisme* Guy Scarpetta writes "L'aspect le plus 'moderne' de Dante . . . est
sans doute cette dimension de voyage, d'exil essentiel, de traversée des
localisations et des langages qu'il a inscrites dans sa Comédie" (1981:
116). [Dante's most "modern" side . . . is without a doubt the exploration
of the journey, of an essential exile, of transcending the boundaries of
places and languages that he embeds in his *Divine Comedy*.] Just as Dante
appeared modern, creating a new idiom by writing in Florentine rather
than in Latin, Smari deviates from writing exclusively in Arabic, in a
Berber language or in French, presumably logical choices for him, as
none appear adequate to his twenty-first-century Italy.

In fact, *L'Occidentalista*, although written in Italian, bears the marks of
other languages—Arabic in particular—ranging from the profusion of
verbal sentences to the use of sentence structures that, although gram-
matically correct, reflect an uncommon syntax in Italian. For instance,
Smari writes of someone answering the phone "'Pronto' s'incazzò la voce
rauca di un'altra donna" (2000: 121) ["Hello" pissed off the raspy voice of

another woman]. My translation in English demonstrates the unfamiliarity of Smari's language; a voice cannot piss off (as an intransitive verb) in English just as it cannot "incazzarsi" in Italian. Attention to language is rendered more explicit when Smari's protagonist evokes the eighth-century philologist and poet 'Abd ar-Rahman Khalīl ibn Ahmad al-Farāhidī, commonly known as al-Farāhidī. Al-Farāhidī is "known for the discovery of the rule-governed metrical systems used in pre-Islamic Arabic poetry" (Ryding 1998: xiii) and as the author of *Kitāb al-'ayn*, which is considered the first dictionary of the Arabic language. Comparing himself to al-Farāhidī, who Samir says set his poetry to the rhythm of the steps of his camel, the protagonist walks the streets of Milan as part of his job as an unskilled laborer, questioning the meaning of his existence in exile. When he momentarily loses his *carta d'identità* (his identity card), he also feels that he has lost the power of speech, and then ironically notices how he had been using the misnomer *carta d'esistenza* (existence card rather than identity card) to refer to the lost object. In the protagonist's use of a *sui generis* Italian, Smari underscores the impossibility of linguistic purity and situates his writing in a space akin to Meddeb's which, as Khatibi writes, is "loin de la violente contradiction du français et de l'arabe" (1985: 8) [removed from the violent contradiction between French and Arabic].

BEYOND *RESSENTIMENT*

One of the characteristics of early Italophone literature, according to Graziella Parati, one of its primary critics, is that it tends towards the autobiographical and/or towards the *mise-en-fiction*, or the fictionalizing, of the authors' life story. Both *L'Occidentalista* and *Scontro di civiltà* instead connect to a broader sociopolitical and analytical discourse, most immediately through their very titles. If *Scontro di civiltà* unequivocally echoes Samuel Huntington's infamous 1996 book *The Clash of Civilizations and the Remaking of World Order*, Smari's *L'Occidentalista* obliquely recalls Edward Saïd's *Orientalism* and the more recent *Occidentalism* by Ian Buruma and Avishai Margalit (2004). The wordplay in Smari and Lakhous's titles further accentuates the malleability and instability of language and also brings to the forefront one of the major characteristics of both these novels, that is the critique of stereotypes.[39] These works thus dialogue with the political and cultural context out of which they grow, and they do so critically by questioning and supplementing existing discourses on the constructedness of a Mediterranean divided between Orient and Occident as well as between North and South. Furthermore, as Azade Seyhan remarks, "Transnational writers who write outside the preserved and protected space of national literary paradigms in borrowed and adopted languages establish verbal and cultural bi- and multilingualism as the most equitable form of dialogic encounter" (2002: 63). Such encounters extend beyond France, Algeria, and Italy to form a transnational Mediterranean-in-literature that is in continual process.

Smari and Lakhous bring a new relevance to Khatibi's *pensée autre*: if, as Khatibi writes (citing Fanon), referring to colonial and postcolonial subjects, the very core of their being has been shaken, this must be seen as "Un événement inévitable, qui n'est ni désastre ni une bénédiction, mais la condition d'une responsabilité qui reste encore à prendre en charge, *au delà du ressentiment et de la conscience malheureuse*" (1983: 11; my emphasis) [an inevitable event, neither a blessing nor a curse, but the conditions of a responsibility that has [yet] to be assumed *beyond resentment and beyond an uneasy conscience*]. These two writers are manifestly removed from such resentment, not simply because they are not colonized subjects themselves, strictly speaking. They are removed from this resentment perhaps *because* they have managed to break away from the France/Algeria stranglehold. They are also removed from a Nietzschean *ressentiment* which, grounded in the inequality of the master-slave dialectic, envisions tension between "strong" and "weak" whereby the "weak" seek a form of—at times imaginary—revenge. Often this impetus leads to a creative form. If in (post)colonial arrangements of power the Maghreb and its artists have occupied the latter position, the case of these Italophone writers leads to an annulment of such a dialectic as they attempt to extricate themselves from such a relationship by deemphasizing the "strong."[40] Camus saw in the concept of *ressentiment* the potential, on the part of the "weak," to revolt, and while Smari and Lakhous's novels are not works of revolt they do retain a sense of defiance.

What traces of resentment exist in and through these works are negotiated in ways that afford agency and empowerment. At the very end of his novel, Lakhous's protagonist cites the famous expression by Kateb Yacine regarding the uncomfortable heteroglossia that came with the French occupation of Algeria.[41] Amedeo exclaims, "Non sono nella bocca del lupo, 'la gueule du loup,' come dice lo scrittore algerino Kateb Yacine. Eccomi fra le braccia della lupa per farmi allattare fino a saziarmi. Auuuuuu . . ." (2006: 185). [I am not in the mouth of the wolf "la gueule du loup" as the Algerian writer Kateb Yacine says. Here I am in the arms of the wolf, so that I may suckle until I am sated . . . Auuuuuu . . .].[42] By playing on the image of the wolf that nurtured the orphans Romulus and Remus as a symbol of Rome, Lakhous heeds Khatibi's hope "de transformer les souffrances et humiliations et dépressions dans la relation aux autres" [to transform suffering, humiliation and depression in relation to others and to the other]. Rather than be consumed by an oppressive "other," Lakhous on the contrary suggests something quite different; it is now his exiled Algerian protagonist who is able to find fulfillment. Otherness becomes less a synonym of suffering and more a catalyst for life. In this particular case the author is specifically departing from French and France (the metaphorical wolf in Kateb's statement) as he finds his place in Rome. However, as is the case with Smari's novel, there is no "happy end," no felicitous co-existence. For the ending invokes Shahrayar's[43] exhortation to narrate again and again because, as Khatibi writes in *Maghreb Pluriel* (in 1983 but the same can be said today) "tout reste à penser" [everything remains to be thought]; the linguistic situation of Maghrebi writers is still very much in movement. In the case of Lakhous and Smari it is with full awareness, *en connaissance de cause*, and free from an uneasy conscience, that writing in Italian takes place. As Smari affirms:

> "La conoscenza di più lingue non porta alla schizofrenia come certi deboli menti o cattive lingue vogliono farci credere, ma bensì ad un verosimile super linguaggio dove le differenze originariamente diverse e date per incompatibili diventano dei fratelli sinonimi, modi di dire e una foresta di sintassi e paradigmi suggestivi, ricchi di poesia e di senso, forti ed invincibili, refrattari all'opacità del mondo e della realtà, della mistificazione della storia e del nostro egoismo, dai limiti e dalla *bêtise* umani . . . (personal correspondence, 2012)

> [Knowing several languages does not lead to schizophrenia as certain weak minds or rumormongers would like us to believe. Rather, it leads to a veritable super-language where differences that are presumed incompatible become synonymous. It leads to different ways of speaking and to a forest of syntaxes and suggestive paradigms, that are poetical and rich, strong and invincible, resistant to the opacity of the world and of reality, resistant to the mystification of history and to the opacity of our egotism, to limits and to human *bêtise*.]

Smari and Lakhous belong to a new time-space in which the famous schism between the language in which authors write and the language in which they speak is attenuated. The anxiety which characterized this divide is transferred into different concerns, ones that although still tied to a certain postcolonial configuration, underscore the parodic, the counter-hegemonic, and the accented.

SEA CHANGES, OR NEW MAGHREBI LITERATURES

In explaining how he learned Italian so quickly Smari says: "Se ce l'avevo fatta in così poco tempo, era grazie appunto a questa maledetta lingua amata e temuta nello stesso momento, questa lingua dai paradossi tremendi, combattuta tra un Camus o un Sartre civili ed umani ed un De Gobineau funesto e cafone. Questa lingua che gli scrittori algerini in lingua francese considerano come l'unico bottino di guerra . . ." [If I learned so quickly it was thanks to this cursed language that is at the same time loved and feared. It is a language of tremendous paradoxes, embattled between the civilized and humane Camus and Sartre, and a loutish and deadly Gobineau. This language that Algerian Francophone writers see as the only spoil of war.][44] Smari's words, like Lakhous's, hark back once again to Kateb's famous description of the French language as a "butin de guerre" [spoil of war]. But they also indicate the degree to which French and its cultural referents still linger in the background of Italophone literature. Rather than draw the latter back to Italy and its national identity, then, one must not exclude reading such texts alongside other literatures written in French. Drawing such connections means reinventing a history of different contacts, ones that are horizontal rather than vertical.

As the Algerian Italophone writer Tahar Lamri concurs, writing in French affords a larger readership and has the advantage of eliciting debates around the world—including with other Algerians of course—but, he adds, to write in Italian means writing about oneself more intimately and to a specific group or immediate community. In a country where numerous media outlets are still controlled by conservative Berlusconi enthusiasts and where, unlike France or Great Britain, debates around immigration, nationalism, and multiculturalism are still relatively new, these works forge a space of necessary awareness and dialogue in and beyond the nation. As the writer and documentarian Daniela Padoan writes in early 2012:

> L'attribuzione di una piena cittadinanza linguistica agli scrittori di origine straniera—una sorta di *ius soli* per chi abbia avuto nascita alla scrittura nella nostra lingua—sembra l'ultimo tabù della nostra globalizzazione; la loro opera non ha ancora una nominazione condivisa, e le definizioni più usate ("letteratura migrante in lingua italiana," "letteratura transnazionale," "letteratura italofona," "letteratura postcoloniale") si tengono in un'ambiguità tra riconoscimento di valore letterario, giudizio politico e sguardo antropologico.[45]

> [The attribution of full linguistic citizenship to foreign writers—a sort of *ius soli* for those who first started writing in our language—seems to be the last taboo of our being globalized; their works still do not have a common denomination, and the most frequently used definitions (migrant literature in Italian, transnational literature, Italophone literature, postcolonial literature) retain a certain ambiguity that hovers between a recognition of literary value, political judgment and an anthropological gaze.]

The problem of nomenclature evoked at the beginning of this chapter reflects a still uncomfortable situation in which we can read the need to further become more global, in the most positive and affirmative sense of the word. Returning to Melliti's works, for instance, it is clear how his urban-centered localized space of the Pantanella warehouse is one where Italy is directly interpellated, and in which its readers are required to recognize the multilingualism of the nation. Lakhous and Smari remain equally within a distinctly Italian context and thus also speak to an Italian audience, yet their works bring together multiple cultural spaces of the Mediterranean in ways that conserve a universal openness that is less political than aesthetic.

ENDNOTES

1. Shohat and Stam sustain that Eurocentrism "sanitizes Western history while patronizing and even demonizing the non-West. It thinks of itself in terms of its noblest achievements—science, progress, humanism—but of the non-West in terms of its deficiencies, real or imagined" (1994: 3).

2. Hereafter referred to as *Scontro.*

3. See Parati (1999, 2005), Gnisci (2003).

4. http://www.iom.int/jahia/Jahia/activities/pid/835. Accessed June 24, 2012.

5. Abdelmalek Smari claims that he will only accept this designation (Italian literature of migration) when first-world immigrants (American and British, for instance) will fall into the same category. Otherwise it just as well may be called third world literature. http://www.el-ghibli.provincia.bologna.it/index.php?id=2&issue=09_36&sezione=7&testo=6. Accessed October 6, 2012.

6. For an interesting discussion on nomenclature see Margherita Ganeri, "The Broadening of the Concept of 'Migration Literature' in Contemporary Italy."

7. See in particular *Italian Colonialism.* (2008) Ed. Mia Fuller, and Ruth Ben-Ghiat. And *Postcolonial Italy.* (2012) Ed. Cristina Lombardi-Diop and Caterina Romeo.

8. See Teresa Fiore, "The Emigrant Post-'Colonia.'" In *Postcolonial Italy*, Ed Cristina Lombardi-Diop and Caterina Romeo. (2012).

9. Along with Khatibi, Jacques Derrida analyzes in detail the question of monolingualism and plurilingualism in *Le monolinguisme de l'autre (ou la prothèse d'origine)* (2006).

10. I will use the term *Italophone* for recognition purposes and fully cognizant—although not partial to—the fact that it sets up a false distinction between literatures written in Italian.

11. Some examples include Pap Khouma's *Io venditore di elefanti* (1990), Salah Methnani's *Immigrato* (1990) and Saidou Moussa Ba's *La promessa di Hamadi* (1991).

12. According to critic Raffaele Taddeo there are five-hundred "migrant writers" in Italy today. http://www.malikamin.net/article-letteratura-e-letteratura-isbn-e-passaporto-2-fine-101274384.html. Accessed July 6, 2012.

13. Gnisci sees the collaboration as a positive move towards dialogue. Jennifer Burns (2001) argues that if these writers make an effort to write, it is to elicit a response form a language-specific community, and collaboration is an instrumental means of access into such communities.

14. Examples of authorial disagreements involve and include the collaboration between Salah Methnani and Mario Fortunato as well as between Tahar Ben Jelloun and Egi Volterrani, among others.

15. Personal correspondence, June 2012.

16. In his preface to the novel, the well-known writer Rachid Boudjedra goes to great lengths to insist on the fact that Melliti's novel is in fact a novel, and of the most writerly sort. He begins his introduction, "Questo primo romanzo si distingue sopratutto perché è un romanzo! Molti scrittori emergenti, infatti, ci hanno abituato a pubblicazioni, erroneamente chiamate (*sic*) romanzi, he non hanno niente a che fare con la letteratura" (1992: 7). [This first novel stands out above all because it is a novel! Many emergent writers have in fact gotten us used to publications that are mistakenly called novels when they have nothing to do with literature.] In his short two-page introduction he also writes that he discovered a style that was not at all didactic: "durante l'esplorazione di questo testo letterario (e sottolineo letterario) . . ." (1992: 8) [as I explored this literary text (and I stress literary) . . .]. Finally he affirms that the reader

comes away from this novel with something "extra" that "noi della scrittura chiamiamo passione letteraria" (1992: 9) [we who write call literary passion]. Rather than convince the reader that this novel is so unusually "novelistic," the effect of such repetition evokes suspicion on the part of the reader, as if Boudjedra were self-righteously defending his friend from anticipated criticism.

17. Personal correspondence, June 2012.

18. "Accent emanates not so much from the accented speech of the diegetic characters as from the displacement of the filmmakers and their artisanal production modes" (Naficy 2001: 4).

19. Published in 2001, Naficy's book stops at the 1990s.

20. The open chronotope is evident in the nostalgic reminiscing (referred to in the novel as *ghurba*) of a homeland, whereas the closed chronotope manifests itself in the panic and sense of imprisonment felt given the lack of opportunity and stasis that many of the characters suffer from. Third-space chronotopes instead appear in the form of the recurrent image of the train station, and one might even argue in the very space of the Pantanella warehouse itself given its temporary and makeshift nature.

21. His short novel *I bambini delle rose*, written in Italian subsequent to more than a decade spent in Italy, manifests significant attention to language. Melliti does not emphasize conventional bilingualism but adopts a register used by children, which includes occasional semantic play; the children become fascinated with Mao Tse Tung—calling him Miao—and Che Guevara. Again the city of Rome plays a prominent role as the two protagonists, a Chinese girl (Ly) and a Serbian boy (Nico) map out their existence through the city streets as they meander from piazza to piazza and restaurant to restaurant selling roses. Set over a week, the topography of Rome is detailed through the eyes of these two insider-outsiders, depictions that represent Rome both as gritty and bourgeois.

22. For analysis on the role of the city in *Pantanella* see Burns (2002).

23. Ahmad remarks, "La 'città' era diventato un centro importantissimo per gli stranieri" (75). [The "città" had become a very important center for foreigners.]

24. It bears noting that "mi ritorna *in* mente" rather than "mi ritorna *alla* mente" is the expression in Italian.

25. Before leaving Tunisia he wrote poetry and articles (Personal correspondence 2013).

26. This phenomenon has already been studied elsewhere. See Burns (2001).

27. In Algeria it was published by Al-Ikhtilef and in Lebanon by Dar Al-Arabia.

28. Hereafter referred to as *Divorzio*.

29. This also recalls influences of orality in literature of Maghrebi origin.

30. Aside from the title, there are several links to Italian cinema: there are references to actors Marcello Mastroianni and Sofia Loren, as well as to Nanni Moretti and Carlo Verdone, both of whom double as directors and actors.

31. The critic Carlin Romano asks whether in Lakhous we have "another Camus" (2008). Given the importance of Camus to this book, uncovering such a connection was inviting; there are, however, no significant philosophical, stylistic or thematic similarities.

32. For example, when asked about his relationship to his multiple languages, to French in particular, he responded with an email playfully entitled "delle muse, non dei musi" [of muses, not grudges]. In Italian the two words *muse* (muse) and *muso* (colloquial for grudge) resemble each other. The essence of his remark was that he held no grudge against French and that it was his muse that dictated which language he chose to write in.

33. Personal correspondence, November 2012.

34. *Il poeta si diverte* and *L'asino sulla terrazza*. For more on these plays see http://www.el-ghibli.provincia.bologna.it/index.php?id=2&issue=09_36&sezione=0. He is also writing a third novel.

35. http://www.el-ghibli.provincia.bologna.it/.

36. www.malikamin.net

37. See previous note for website address.

38. Dante lived in exile for twenty years, and some scholars maintain that exile is the principal theme of the *Divine Comedy*.

39. There are numerous deliberate stereotypical or caricatural characters and situations in both these works.

40. Smari goes so far as to say "non voglio incolpare l'Occidente, anzi, ormai mi sono reso conto che la colpa della nostra arretratezza è solo nostra." [I don't want to blame the West. On the contrary, I have now realized that we are the only ones to blame for our backwardness.] http://www.el-ghibli.provincia.bologna.it/index.php?id=6&sezione=4&idrecensioni=62

41. In *Le polygone étoilé*, Kateb Yacine writes that going to a French school and learning French was like being thrown into "la gueule du loup" (1966: 181) [the mouth of the wolf, or the lion's den].

42. Interestingly, Lakhous's original title in Arabic was *How to Be Suckled by the Wolf without Getting Bit*.

43. The king in *A Thousand and One Nights*.

44. http://www.el-ghibli.provincia.bologna.it/index.php?id=2&issue=09_36&sezione=8&testo=0

45. "Razzismo letterario: scrivi in italiano e non vinci mai." *Il fatto quotidiano*, 16 January, 2012.

Conclusion: Reflections on a Future

In her autobiographical work *Cruises and Caravans*, Ella Maillart writes, "No sooner had I left to cruise the Mediterranean than the following question preoccupied me: How far does one kill a journey by making it become real?" (1944: 48) Maillart's question raises an important issue; along with querying the division between imagined worlds and "real" experiences, she calls forth the opacity that is inherent in all writing. Writing, or putting an experience into words, overwhelms and potentially suppresses the experiences it purportedly describes. The exigencies of writing, autobiographical and other, place us in a state of continual inquiry and interpretation. The challenges of writing on the Mediterranean are numerous and multifarious, and they continue to come into question as this book moves towards completion. Rather than coming to a neat conclusion, new questions have emerged, entering into dialogue with the earlier ones, and thus urge an ending somewhere in a middle ground of further investigation. This is not to say that the conclusions of this book have always arisen in the form of questions, but rather it is an acknowledgement of the fact that some of the thornier partially resolved issues persist: does not the very idea of the Mediterranean tend towards essentialism? Is the notion of a Mediterranean ethos reductive, idealistic, "utopic"? Is, and if so in what way, ethos connected to ethics and to morals? Is not the literary Mediterranean a fundamentally nostalgic reminiscence of times past, or what in French is called *passéisme*? And finally, how does the question of literature in French or in Italian fit into such a space?

To be sure, these would not be conclusions at all if there were no hypothetical answers. Beginning with the question of essentialism, the Mediterranean might indeed be seen as such in a framework that posits the space as homogeneous and unified. Critics such as Horden and Purcell, and Fernand Braudel himself have posited the unity of Mediterranean countries around similarities that range from olive trees, to courtyards and from "characteristic" qualifiers of honor and shame to those of fate and destiny. While these claims have their own legitimacy, they tend to place the emphasis on similarity rather than difference. As I have noted throughout the book, distinct similarities between different Mediterranean constituencies are evident, however this has not been my overall approach. Seen through the medium of literature—and specifically of texts by writers who are at the very least bilingual and/or bicultural—

163

homogeneity is impossible from the outset. Not only because the writing subjects themselves are in perpetual translation and in-between languages and places but also because there can be no "purity" of idioms, of positionings, of values, transmitted through the works of writers who privilege alternate histories, transculturalism, the baroque and unfixed notions of gender. A Mediterranean ethos risks being reductive if read as a stable continuum. My study has not set out to prove that there is a single Mediterranean ethos forcibly built around the abovementioned notions, but that these ideas, these chronotopes, have emerged at a distinct time, in a distinct place, for a distinct reason.

In this sense, it should be clear that the Mediterranean has served both as an analytical tool and a heuristic device and, as such, has significant future potential.[1] For, at a time when the ideals of national literature are increasingly incommensurate with nations themselves, it may indeed be more fruitful to examine the links and connections among and within nations instead of seeking a presumable coherence. If, as Benedict Anderson put it more than a decade ago, nineteenth-century technology (of the printing press and the steamboat, for instance) was largely responsible for the national idea and the ensuing identification to such a construct, we might resume that line of thought to say that a new engagement with national time and space is upon us. With the now expanded use of new technologies (the Internet in particular), imagined communities are more pervasive and wide-ranging than ever and they often do not include the nation.

In an article tellingly entitled "Mediterranean Thinking: From Netizen to Medizen," Miriam Cooke suggests thinking the Mediterranean metaphorically, through the Internet, and draws on analogous terms used in both domains (navigation, port, network, surfing). Netizen and Medizen, instead, are neologisms for "citizens" of the Internet and of the Mediterranean. For Cooke, cyberepistemology, like a Mediterranean epistemology, is about a process as much as it is about a place or space. She calls this process radical networking, and sustains that, as such, it destabilizes the meaning of place paradigms that are structured as core and periphery. She takes, as an example, islands that are not typically seen as centers of power but that are geographically central to the Mediterranean. Cooke writes, "The meaning attached to their location will depend on the subject-position of the speaker, which in turn determines where the perimeter of the Mediterranean is drawn" (1999: 297). Places, then, shift with time and perspective so that "today's Greek citizen [for example] has a double consciousness of being marginal today but central yesterday, and is seen as such" (1999: 297). Cooke sees this as a coming together of fluidity and fixity, of past and present, of land and water, and defines the Mediterranean subject as being akin to a "Netizen," a term she borrows from the sociologists Barney Warf and John Grimes who define it as someone "who may occupy numerous, even contradictory social positions and inhabit multiple, overlapping communities simultaneously" (1999: 298). The example of Greece indeed points to the unceasing changes that have taken place in the Mediterranean over time: the physical place has stayed the same but mentalities, practices and ways of being have not remained constant.

There is no mention, however, of the troubles that Mediterranean thinking and cyberepistemology, since this is the analogy that Cooke draws, might generate. Might we not see the Internet's abundance of information and infinite connectivity as productive of an excess so criticized by the writers in this study? Although hardly comparable to the political terms that Camus, for example, associated with the notion of excess, it nevertheless points to a *dépassement* of the measures of man. If the possibilities of connectivity are unending, constantly being "updated" and changed, might this not be as psychologically damaging as it is enriching? If earlier I asked whether a Mediterranean ethos is not idealistic or utopic, it was precisely with this conundrum in mind, for my own elaboration relies on similar enabling notions of connectivity and infinite renewal.

This sense of *dépassement* may very well explain why on numerous occasions during the research for this book I came across the word *schizophrenic*, in reference to the Mediterranean and its inhabitants. The historians Gérard Chastagnaret and Robert Ilbert maintain that it is the contrast between the memory of a past Andalusia, which is seen as exemplary of peaceful coexistence between monotheisms, and today's boat people, which epitomizes the divide between the northern and southern shores of the Mediterranean, and results in schizophrenia. More weighty still is the political scientist Bruno Etienne's claim that "les Méditerranéens sont *ontologiquement* schizophrènes" (2000: 115; my emphasis). [Mediterranean people are ontologically schizophrenic.] Jean Déjeux uses the adjective "névrosé" [neurotic], and Emily Apter writes of the schizophrenia of French Algeria. Perhaps, as is often the case, the word has been used loosely, but perhaps there is something to investigate, a responsibility that must be taken, in order to come to terms with such solemn allegations.

Might there be, as I asked earlier, a moral dimension to a Mediterranean ethos? Unlike Horden and Purcell who see the codes of honor and shame as being so pervasive in the Mediterranean, this book does not draw conclusions as to any moral component. Unless we read the writers in this study as propounding the imperatives to take a stand against intolerance and divisiveness as *moral*, then I would venture to say that there is no such thing as a "Mediterranean moral." There is, however, something quite sinister about the recent cooptation of the Mediterranean by Nicolas Sarkozy. In an attempt to quell controversy over admitting Turkey into the European Union, and as a strategy to garner votes for the presidency, Sarkozy suggested creating a Mediterranean Union that would be similar to the EU, but whose purpose would be to combat terrorism and organized crime. This catch-all shared judicial area, whose purpose seems motivated by vehement national, rather than transnational, sentiment, would erect even greater barriers within the Mediterranean and build up Fortress Europe to become even more restrictive and intolerant.[2] Given the current climate of a post-9/11-predicted "Eurabia," that is to say a Europe driven by predominantly right-wing fears of a hostile Islamic takeover of the continent, this book underscores the degree to which it is imperative, now more than ever, to expose some of the fallacies surrounding issues of national purity and identity formation in the Mediterranean.

Binebine's *Cannibales* and Ben Jelloun's *Partir* remind us, in no uncertain terms, of the effects of such policies, and point to the near inevitability of the presence of politics in literatures of the Mediterranean, in particular, when that literature is written in French. France's relationship with the Mediterranean is undoubtedly one of the most complex and politically charged. Its history is long-standing, and its defining events controversial. Today, just over a decade after recognizing the Algerian War as a veritable war, and not just a series of events, the France-Mediterranean nexus still appears tenuous. In a campaign speech, Sarkozy acknowledged France's ties with Algeria, claiming the need to recognize and "repay" a debt of honor to the harkis and pied-noirs who fought on France's side. In almost the same breath he prided the country on never having committed crimes against humanity, and as having "made mistakes." Human rights groups have long been investigating allegations of torture and crimes committed in Algeria that were more than simply war crimes, but regardless, the systematic atrocities carried out on Algerian soil are now well-known.[3] The future of *this* Mediterranean appears highly compromised. It was also the same Sarkozy who, in response to the *Pour une littérature monde* manifesto cited in my introduction, affirmed with assurance that "la francophonie n'est pas un concept colonial" (*Pour*: 1). [Francophonie is not a colonial concept.] The disavowal of how French even came to be spoken in North Africa in the first place, for instance, is blatant. Perhaps the schizophrenia lies here, then.

Might this brand of nationalism, which has been building steadily in France, explain why a number of French-speaking Maghrebi writers have chosen to live and write in other countries such as Italy, for instance, a choice that appears unusual considering that they are faced with learning and writing a new language? Whereas the question usually—and now somewhat tiresomely—posed to Francophone writers is why they write in French instead of in their native language, it might now be shifted to why do they not write in French? Why write in Italian, for instance? When framed within a transnational Mediterranean literary landscape the hegemony of the French language is displaced and no longer occupies the center of the debate. Why *not* write in Italian might be a better question. To speak of Maghrebi literature, then, means to speak about it *also* in Italian.[4]

The "journey" between the "real" and the fictional, to borrow Ella Maillart's words cited at the beginning of this conclusion, comes in and out of focus in the texts considered in this book. Multiplicity and difference are primordial concerns in the Mediterranean, beginning with the simple polyvalence of the word itself, through which we witness writers who have been moved to *méditer* on the *me*, on the *dit*, on the earth (the *terra*), on the *errance* that characterizes their words, their *iter*ations, on the fact that *éditer*, to write, also means to immortalize, to be in perpetual regeneration.

ENDNOTES

1. In particular, the Mediterranean may stand as a fertile area of study and provide fruitful frameworks of comparison with Edouard Glissant's and Paul Gilroy's oceanic and transnational models. It also points to the continual evolution and value of maritime models as analytical devices.

2. The union appears highly ineffectual given the problems that ensued after the creation of Euromed in 1995, a group of Mediterranean nations committed to working together to strengthen ties in the region. After this initial meeting, the project was carried ahead with significant difficulty.

3. Following the confession of General Aussauresses, a former French general in the Algerian War, who owned up to having tortured and assassinated Algerian prisoners, France has undertaken investigations into French complicity involving crimes against humanity. General Papon, who was convicted for such crimes against Jews in France, was a prefect in Algeria during the Algerian War. He was also responsible for a large-scale massacre of peaceful Algerian demonstrators in Paris in 1961. General Messmer was also accused of crimes against humanity against the harkis. For a more detailed analysis see Bickerton (2006).

4. As previously stated, Italian is but one case among many other Mediterranean languages.

Bibliography

Abderrezak, Hakim. "Burning the Sea: Clandestine Migration Across the Strait of Gibraltar in Francophone Moroccan 'Illitérature,'" *Contemporary French and Francophone Studies* 13.4 (2009): 461–69.

Agamben, Giorgio. *Infanzia e storia: distruzione dell'esperienza e origine della storia.* Torino: Einaudi, 1978.

Albera, Dionigi, ed. *L'anthropologie de la Méditerrannée.* Paris: Maisonneuve et Larose, 2001.

Aldrich, Robert. *The Seduction of the Mediterranean: Writing, Art and Homosexual Fantasy.* London: Routledge, 1993.

Allen, Beverly, and Mary Russo, eds. *Revisioning Italy: National Identity and Global Culture.* Minneapolis: University of Minnesota Press, 1997.

Ancelovici, Marcos, and Francis Dupuis-Déri. *L'archipel identitaire.* Québec: Boréal, 1997.

Andall, J., and D. Duncan. *National Belongings: Hybridity in Italian Colonial and Postcolonial Cultures.* New York: Peter Lang, 2010.

Appadurai, Arjun. "Theory in Anthropology: Center and Periphery." In *Comparative Studies in Society and History,* 28 (1986): 356–361.

Apter, Emily. "Out of Character: Albert Camus's Algerian Subjects." *MLN* 112.4 (1997): 499–516.

Archambault, Paul. *Camus' Hellenic Sources.* Chapel Hill: University of North Carolina Press, 1972.

Aresu, Bernard. "Tahar Ben Jelloun." *CELFAN Monographs.* Special Issue, 1996.

Argand, Catherine. "Entretien avec Tahar Ben Jelloun." *Lire,* mars 1999.

Arkoun, Mohamed. *Actualité d'une culture méditerranéenne.* Tampere: TAPRI, 1990.

Audiso, Gabriel. "Documents sur l'esprit méditerranéen." *Cahiers du Sud* 181 (March 1936).

Barrouhi, Abdelaziz. "Les damnés de la mer." *Jeune Afrique* n.2510, 17 February, 2009: 24–25.

Bartfeld, Fernande, and David Ohana, eds. *Perspectives. Albert Camus: Parcours Méditerranéens. Actes du Colloque de Jérusalem 10–13 Novembre 1997.* Jerusalem: The Hebrew University, 1998.

Behdad, Ali. *Belated Travelers: Orientalism in the Age of Colonial Dissolution.* Durham : Duke University Press, 1994.

Bekri, Tahar. *Littératures de Tunisie et du Maghreb.* Paris: L'Harmattan, 1994.

Ben Jelloun, Tahar. *L'ange aveugle.* Paris: Seuil, 1992.

———. *L'auberge des pauvres.* Paris: Seuil, 2000.

———. "Don Quichotte à Tanger." *Le Monde Diplomatique,* August 2005.

———. "*En attendant les barbares!*" *Libération,* 21 January, 2005.

———. *L'enfant de sable.* Paris: Editions du Seuil, 1985.

———. *Ignorances mutuelles.* Conférence du séminaire international sur Ibn Khaldun. www.taharbenjelloun.org.

———. *Le labyrinthe des sentiments.* Paris: Seuil, 2001.

———. *Leaving Tangier.* Trans. Linda Coverdale. New York: Penguin Books, 2009.

———. *Moha le fou, Moha le sage.* Paris: Gallimard, 1978.

———. *Partir.* Paris: Gallimard, 2006.

———. *State of Absence.* Trans. James Kirkup. London: Quartet Books, 1994.

169

Bensmaïa, Réda. "La langue de l'étranger ou la Francophonie barrée." *Rue Descartes: Revue du Collège International de Philosophie* 37 (2002): 65–73.

Berry, Ellen, and Mikhail Epstein, eds. *Transcultural Experiments.* New York: St. Martin's Press, 1999.

Bey, Maïssa. *La langue française vue de la Méditerranée.* Ed. P. Martin. Paris: Zellige, 2009.

Bhabha, Homi. *The Location of Culture.* 1994. London: Routledge, 2004.

———. *Nation and Narration.* London: Routledge, 1990.

Bickerton, Chris. "France's History Wars." *Le Monde diplomatique,* February 2006.

Binebine, Mahi. *Cannibales.* Paris: Éditions de l'Aube, 2005 (first published, 1999).

———. *Welcome to Paradise.* Trans. Lulu Norman. Portland: Tin House Books, 2012.

Bivona, Rosalia. "Nina Bouraoui: un sintomo della letteratura migrante nell'area franco-magrebina." Diss., University of Palermo. http://www.limag.refer.org/Theses/Bivona.PDF.

Blumenfeld-Kosinski, Renate, Louise Von Flotow and Daniel Russel, eds. *The Politics of Translation in the Middle Ages.* Tempe: Arizona Center for Medieval and Renaissance Studies, 2001.

Bonn, Charles. *Paysages littéraires algériens des années 90: témoigner d'une tragédie?* Paris: L'Harmattan, 1999.

Borthwick, Fiona. "Olfaction and Taste: Invasive Odours and Disappearing Objects-Critical Essay." *Australian Journal of Anthropology* 11:2 (2000): 127–40.

Bouraoui, Nina. *L'âge blessé.* Paris: Fayard, 1998.

———. "Ecrire c'est retrouver ses fantômes." Interview with Dominique Simonnet, *L'Express* 31 May 2004.

———. *Forbidden Vision.* Trans. Melissa Marcus. Barrytown: Station Hill Press, 1998.

———. *Garçon manqué.* Paris: Stock, 2000.

———. *Le jour du séisme.* Paris: Stock, 1999.

———. *Mes mauvaises pensées.* Paris: Stock, 2005.

———. *Poupée Bella.* Paris: Stock, 2004.

———. *Tomboy.* Trans. Marjorie Salvodon and Jehanne-Marie Gavarini. Lincoln: University of Nebraska Press, 2007.

———. *La vie heureuse.* Paris: Stock, 2002.

———. *La voyeuse interdite.* Paris: Gallimard, 1991.

Bourdé, Guy, and Hervé Martin. *Les écoles historiques.* Paris: Seuil, 1983.

Braudel, Fernand. *The Mediterranean and the Mediterranean World in the Age of Philip II.* Trans. Siân Reynolds. New York: Harper and Row, 1972.

———. *Memory and the Mediterranean.* Trans. Siân Reynolds. New York: Knopf, 2001.

Buci-Glucksmann, Christine. *Baroque Reason: The Aesthetics of Modernity.* Trans. Bryan S. Turner. London: Sage Publications, 1994.

———. *Folie du voir: de l'esthétique baroque.* Paris: Galilée, 1986.

Burns, Jennifer. "Exile within Italy: Interactions Between Past and Present 'Homes' in Texts in Italian by Migrant Writers." *Annali d'Italianistica* 20 (2002): 369–83.

———. "Figurations of Rome in Recent Italophone Writing" in *Imagining the City.* Ed. C. Emden. Oxford: Peter Lang, 1996. 360–72.

———. *Fragments of Impegno.* Leeds: Northern Universities Press, 2001.

———. "Language and its Alternatives in Italophone Migrant Writing" in *National Belongings.* Eds. J. Andall and D. Duncan. New York: Peter Lang, 2010.

Buruma, Ian and Avishai Margalit. *Occidentalism.* London: Atlantic Books, 2004.

Butler, Judith. *Subjects of Desire: Hegelian Reflections in Twentieth-Century France.* New York: Columbia University Press, 1987.

Camus, Albert. *Carnets. 3 vol.* Paris: Gallimard, 1962–1989.

———. *Correspondance: 1932–1960 / Albert Camus, Jean Grenier.* Paris: Gallimard, 1981.

———. *Discours de Suède.* Paris: Gallimard, 1958.

———. *Essais.* Paris: Gallimard, 1965.

———. *L'étranger.* Paris: Gallimard, 1946.

———. *L'homme revolté.* Paris: Gallimard, 1951.

———. *Lyrical and Critical Essays.* Trans. Ellen Conroy Kennedy. New York: Vintage Books, 1970.

———. *The Myth of Sisyphus.* Trans. Justin O'Brien. New York: Vintage Books, 1955.

———. *Noces, suivi deL'été.* Paris: Gallimard, 1959.

———. *Le premier homme.* Paris: Gallimard, 1994.

———. *The Rebel.* Trans. Anthony Bower. New York: Vintage, 1956.

———. *The First Man.* Trans. David Hapgood. New York: Knopf, 1995.

Carroll, David. "Camus's Algeria: Birthrights, Colonial Injustice and the Fiction of a French-Algerian People." *MLN* 112.4 (1997): 517–49.

Casanova, Pascale. *La république mondiale des lettres.* Paris: Seuil, 2000.

Cassano, Franco. *Il pensiero meridiano.* Roma: Laterza, 1996.

———. "Il pensiero meridiano oggi: Intervista e dialoghi con Franco Cassano." Interview with Claudio Fogu. *California Italian Studies* 1.1 (2010).

———. "Il Sud può spostare il centro del mondo." *La Gazzetta del Mezzogiorno*, 11 July 2011. http://www.lagazzettadelmezzogiorno.it/GdM_le_analisi_NOTIZIA.php?IDNotizia=440497&IDCategoria=2682. Accessed April 12, 2013.

Chabot, Jacques. *Albert Camus "la pensée de midi."* Aix-en-Provence: Edisud, 2002.

Chambers, Iain. *Culture After Humanism: History, Culture, Subjectivity.* London: Routledge, 2001.

———. *Migrancy, Culture, Identity.* London: Routledge, 1994.

———. *Mediterranean Crossings.* Durham and London: Duke University Press, 2008.

———. "Off the Map: A Mediterranean Journey." *Comparative Literature Studies* 42.4 (2005): 312–27.

Chastagneret, Gérard, and Robert Ilbert. "Quelle Méditerranée." *Vingtième Siècle* 32 (1991): 3–5

Chebel, Malek. *L'esprit du sérail: mythes et pratiques sexuels au Maghreb.* Paris: Payot, 2003.

Cooke, Miriam. "Mediterranean Thinking: From Netizen to Medizen." *The Geographical Review* 89.2 (1999): 290–300.

Corbin, Alain. *Le territoire du vide. L'Occident et le désir de rivage, 1750–1840.* Paris: Flammarion, 1990.

———. *The Foul and the Fragrant.* Cambridge: Harvard University Press, 1986.

Costa Ragusa, Giuliana. *Figure e miti della Sicilia e del Mediterraneo nelle letterature europee moderne.* Palermo: Flaccovio, 2001.

Crang, Mike, and Nigel Thrift, eds. *Thinking Space.* London: Routledge, 2000.

Cruickshank, John. *Albert Camus and the Literature of Revolt.* London: Oxford University Press, 1968.

Daoud, Zakya. *Gibraltar croisée des mondes: d'Hercule à Boabdil.* Paris: Séguier, 2002.

Déjeux, Jean. *La literature féminine de langue française au Maghreb.* Paris: Karthala, 1994.

Deleuze, Gilles, and Félix Guattari. *Essays Critical and Clinical.* Trans. Daniel W. Smith and Michael A. Greco. Minneapolis: University of Minnesota Press, 1997.

———. *Kafka: Pour une littérature mineure.* Paris: Éditions de Minuit, 1975.

———. *A Thousand Plateaus: Capitalism and Schizophrenia.* Trans. Brian Massumi. Minneapolis: University of Minnesota Press, 1988.

———. *What Is Philosophy?* Trans. Hugh Tomlinson and Graham Burchell. New York: Columbia University Press, 1994.

Derrida, Jacques. *Geneses, Genealogies, Genres and Genius.* New York: Columbia University Press, 2008.

———. *Of Grammatology.* Trans. Gayatri Spivak. Baltimore: The Johns Hopkins University Press, 1974.

———. *The Other Heading: Reflections on Today's Europe.* Bloomington: Indiana University Press, 1992.

Dib, Mohamed. *Qui se souvient de la mer.* Paris: Seuil, 1962.

Di Maio, Alessandra. "Salah Methnani's Immigrato: Portrait of a Migrant as a Young Man." *Expressions maghrébines* 11.2 (Winter 2012).

Djebar, Assia. *Women of Algiers in Their Apartment.* Charlottesville: University Press of Virginia, 1992.

Donadey, Anne and Adlai Murdoch. *Postcolonial Theory and Francophone Literary Studies.* Gainesville: University Press of Florida, 2005.

Doray, Jocelyne, and Julian Samuel, eds. *The Raft of the Medusa: Five Voices on Colonies, Nations and Histories.* Montreal: Black Rose Books, 1993.

Dotoli, Giovanni. *Le récit méditerranéen d'expression française 1945–1990.* Paris: Schena-Didier, 1997.

Duby, Georges. *An 1000, an 2000: Sur les traces de nos peurs.* Paris: Textuel, 1995.

———. ed. *Gli ideali del Mediterraneo: storia, filosofia e letteratura nella cultura europea.* Messina: Mesogea, 2000.

Dunwoodie, Peter. *Writing French Algeria.* Oxford : Oxford University Press, 1998.

El-Ghibli, rivista online della letteratura della migrazione. http://www.el-ghibli.provincia.bologna.it.

Epstein, Mikhail. *After the Future: The Paradoxes of Postmodernism and Contemporary Russian Culture.* Trans. A. Miller-Pogacar. Amherst: University of Massachusetts Press, 1995.

Esposito, Claudia. "Literature is Language: Interview with Amara Lakhous," *Journal of Postcolonial Writing* Vol 48 (4) 2012. 418–430.

Etienne, Bruno. "Une grenade entrouverte." Interview with Thierry Fabre and Bertrand Millet. *La pensée de midi* 1 (2000): 114–19.

Fabre, Thierry. *La Méditerranée créatrice.* Paris: Editions de l'Aube, 1994.

———. *Rappresentare il Mediterraneo: lo sguardo francese.* Catania: Mesogea, 2000.

Felman, Shoshana and Dori Laub. *Testimony: Crises of Witnessing in Literature, Psychoanalysis and History.* New York: Routledge, 1992.

Ferrini, Costanza. *Venature mediterranee.* Messina: Mesogea, 1999.

Fogu, Claudio. "From Mare Nostrum to Mare Aliorum: Mediterranean Theory and Mediterraneanism in Contemporary Italian Thought." *California Italian Studies* 1.1 (2010).

———. "Il pensiero meridiano oggi: Intervista e dialoghi con Franco Cassano." *California Italian Studies* 1.1 (2010).

Forsdick, Charles, and David Murphy. *Francophone Postcolonial Studies: A Critical Introduction.* London: Arnold Publishers, 2003.

Foucault, Michel. "Nietzsche, Genealogy, History." *Language, Counter-Memory, Practice: Selected Essays and Interviews.* Ed. and Trans. Donald F. Bouchard. Ithaca: Cornell University Press, 1997.

———. *The Order of Things: An Archeology of the Human Sciences.* New York: Vintage Books, 1973.

Freud, Sigmund. *Civilization and Its Discontents.* New York: Norton, 1962.

Fukuyama, Francis. *The End of History and the Last Man.* New York: Free Press, 1992.

Ganeri, Margherita. "The Broadening of the Concept of 'Migration Literature' in Contemporary Italy." *Forum Italicum* 44.2 (2010).

Gay-Crosier, Raymond. "Les enjeux de la pensée de midi." *Albert Camus: Parcours méditerranéens. Actes du Colloque de Jérusalem Novembre 1997.* Jérusalem: Editions Magnès, 1998.

Giddens, Anthony. *Modernity and Self-Identity: Self and Society in the Late Modern Age.* Stanford: Stanford University Press, 1992.

Giono, Jean. *Provence.* Paris: Hachette, 1954.

Glissant, Edouard. *Introduction à une poétique du divers.* Paris: Gallimard, 1995.

Gnisci, Armando. *Creolizzare l'Europa.* Roma: Meltemi, 2003.

———. *La letteratura del mondo nel XXI secolo.* Milano: Mondadori, 2010.

Gontard, Marc. *Le moi étrange: littérature marocaine de langue française.* Paris: L'Harmattan, 1993.

Gonzales, Jean-Jacques. "Dissonance de Camus." *Albert Camus et les écritures algériennes. Quelles traces?* Paris: Edisud, 2004.

————. *La violence du texte: Etude sur la littérature marocaine de langue française.* Paris: L'Harmattan, 1981.

Graebner, Seth. *History's Place: Nostalgia and the City in French Algerian Literature.* Lanham: Lexington Books, 2007.

Grenier, Roger. *Albert Camus Soleil et Ombre.* Paris: Gallimard, 1987.

Haddour, Azzedine. *Colonial Myths: History and Narrative.* Manchester: Manchester University Press, 2000.

Hall, Stuart. "Cultural Identity and Diaspora." *Identity: Community, Culture, Difference.* Ed. Jonathan Ruterford. London: Lawrench and Wishart, 1990.

————. "Minimal Selves." In Ed. H. Baker, M. Diawara, and B. Lindeborg. *Black British Cultural Studies: A Reader.* Chicago: University of Chicago Press, 1996. 114-19.

Hargreaves, Alec. "Writers of Maghrebian Origin in France" in *African Francophone Writing.* Ed. L. Ibnlfassi, and N. Hitchcott. Oxford: Berg, 1996.

Harris, W. V., ed. *Rethinking the Mediterranean.* Oxford: Oxford University Press, 2005.

Hayes, Jarrod. *Queer Nations: Marginal Sexualities in the Maghreb.* Chicago: University of Chicago Press, 2000.

Hegel, Georg Wilhelm Friedrich. *Æsthetics: Lectures on Fine Art, vol. II.* Oxford: Clarendon Press, 1975.

Herzfeld, Michael. "Practical Mediterraneanism: Excuses for Everything from Epistemology to Eating." *Rethinking the Mediterranean.* Ed. V. W. Harris. Oxford: Oxford University Press, 2005. 45–63.

Horden, Peregrine, and Nicholas Purcell. *The Corrupting Sea: A Study of Mediterranean History.* Oxford: Blackwell, 2000.

Hughes, Edward, J. "Building the Colonial Archive: The Case of Camus's *Le premier homme.*" *Research in African Literatures* 30.3 (1999): 176–93.

Huntington, Samuel. *The Clash of Civilizations and the Remaking of World Order.* New York: Simon and Schuster, 1996.

Hutcheon, Linda. *A Poetics of Postmodernism: History, Theory, Fiction.* New York: Routledge, 1998.

Jackson, Peter, Philip Crang, and Claire Dwyer, eds. *Transnational Spaces.* London: Routledge, 2004.

Jourde, Pierre. *Géographies imaginaires.* Paris: José Corti, 1991.

Khair-Eddine, Mohammed. *Le déterreur.* Paris: Seuil, 1973.

Khatibi, Abdelkébir. "Incipits" in *Du bilinguisme.* Ed. J. Bennani. Paris: Denoel, 1985.

————. *Œuvres d'Albdelkébir Khatibi. 3 vol.* Paris: Editions de la différence, 2008.

————. *Le Maghreb pluriel.* Paris: Denoel, 1983.

————. *L'œuvre de Abdelkébir Khatibi (préliminaire).* Rabat: Marsam, 1997.

Kinoshita, Sharon. "Medieval Mediterranean Literature." Forum on Theories and Methodologies in Medieval Literary Studies. *PMLA* 124:2 (2009): 600–8.

Kouchner, Bernard. "Europe: L'avenir passe par la Méditerranée." *Le Monde* 10 July, 2008.

Laacher, Smaïn. *Le peuple de clandestins.* Paris: Calmann-Levy, 2007.

Lakhous, Amara. *Clash of Civilizations Over an Elevator in Piazza Vittorio.* Trans. Ann Goldstein. New York: Europa Editions, 2008.

————. *Divorce Islamic Style.* Trans. Ann Goldstein. New York: Europa Editions, 2012.

————. *Divorzio all'islamica a Viale Marconi.* Roma: Edizioni E/0, 2010.

————. *Un pirata piccolo piccolo.* Roma: Edizioni E/0, 2011.

————. *Scontro di civiltà per un ascensore a Piazza Vittorio.* Roma: Edizioni E/0, 2006.

————. Personal Correspondence, 2012.

Lamri, Tahar. "E della mia presenza; solo il mio silenzio." In *Parole Oltre I Confini.* Ed. Roberta Sangiorgi. Santarcangelo di Romagna: Fara Editore, 1999.

Laroui, Fouad. *Le drame linguistique marocain.* Léchelle: Zellige, 2011.

Law, John and Kevin Hetherington. "Allegory and Interference: Representation in Sociology." http://www.lancs.ac.uk/fss/sociology/papers/law-hetherington-allegory-interference.pdf. Accessed November 2011.

Le centenaire de l'Algérie française. Programme, Alger, numéro spécial de la "Presse nord-africaine," 10 décembre 1929.

Leparulo, William. *L'Italia nell'opera di Albert Camus.* Pisa: Giardini, 1975.

Lionnet, Françoise, and Shu-Mei Shih. *Minor Transnationalism.* Durham: Duke University Press, 2005.

Lismonde, Pascale. *Le goût de Naples.* Paris: Mercure de France, 2003.

Maalouf, Amin. *In the Name of Identity: Violence and the Need to Belong.* Trans. Barbara Bray. New York: Penguin, 2003.

———. *Les croisades vu par les Arabes.* Paris: LGF, 1983.

———. *Les identités meurtrières.* Paris: Grasset, 1998.

———. *Léon l'africain.* Paris: Editions Lattès, 1986.

———. *Le périple de Baldassare.* Paris: Grasset, 2000.

———. *Le premier siècle après Béatrice.* Paris: Grasset, 1992.

Majumdar, Margaret. "La méditerranéité: identités et discours." *Aire regionale méditerranée.* Paris: UNESCO, 2001.

Malkin, Irad, ed. *La France et la Méditerranée: vingt-sept siècles d'interdépendance.* Leiden: Brill, 1990.

Manifeste des 44. "Pour une 'littérature monde' en français." *Le Monde,* 16 April, 2007.

Marshall, Brenda. *Teaching the Postmodern.* London: Routledge, 1992.

Matvejevic, Predrag. *Il Mediterraneo e l'Europa.* Roma: Garzanti, 1998.

McIlvanney, Siobhan. "Double Vision: The Role of the Visual and the Visionary in Nina Bouraoui's *La voyeuse interdite* (Forbidden Vision)." *Research in African Literatures* 35 (2004): 105–20.

Mechakra, Yamina. *La grotte éclatée.* Alger: Entreprise nationale du livre, 1979.

Meddeb, Abdelwahab. *L'exil occidental.* Paris:Albin Michel, 2005.

Mellah, Fawzi. *Elissa la reine vagabonde.* Paris: Seuil, 1998.

———. *Clandestin en Méditerranée.* Paris: Editions du Cherche Midi, 2000.

Melliti, Mohsen. *I bambini delle rose.* Roma: Edizioni Lavoro, 1995.

———. *Pantanella. Canto lungo la strada.* Roma: Edizioni Lavoro, 1992.

———. Personal correspondence, 2012.

Memmi, Albert. *The Colonizer and the Colonized.* Boston: Beacon Press, 1965.

———. *Portrait du Colonisé* précédé du *Portrait du Colonisateur.* Paris: Editions Buchet Chastel, 1957.

———. *Le nomade immobile.* Paris: Arléa, 2003.

Mengara, Daniel, ed. *Images of Africa: Stereotypes and Realities.* Trenton: Africa World Press, 2001.

Merleau-Ponty, Maurice. *Phénoménologie de la perception.* Paris: Gallimard, 1945.

———. *The Visible and the Invisible.* Trans. Alphonso Lingis. Evanston: Northwestern University Press, 1968.

Moran, Dermot. *Introduction to Phenomenology.* London: Routledge, 2000.

Mouillaud-Fraisse, Geneviève. *Les fous cartographes.* Paris: L'Harmattan, 1995.

Moussaoui, Rosa. "Le récit colonial n'a été pris en charge ni par les partis politiques ni par l'école." (Interview with Benjamin Stora). *L'Humanité,* July 26, 2006, http://www.humanite.fr/node/94536. Accessed March 28, 2013.

Murdoch, Adlai H., and Anne Donadey. *Postcolonial Theory and Francophone Literary Studies.* Gainesville: University Press of Florida, 2005.

Naficy, Hamid. *An Accented Cinema: Exilic and Diasporic Filmmaking.* Princeton: Princeton University Press, 2001.

Neggaz, Soumaya. *Amin Maalouf: le voyage initiatique dans Léon l'Africain, Samarcande et Le rocher de Tanios.* Paris: L'Harmattan, 2005.

Negri, Antonio. "Italy, Exile Country." *Revisioning Italy: National Identity and Global Culture.* Ed. Beverly Allen and Mary Russo. Minneapolis: University of Minnesota Press, 1997. 43–51.

Nelle, Marie. "Harraga: La jeunesse désenchantée d'Algérie." *Le Monde,* 7 April, 2009.

Nietzsche, Friedrich. *On the Genealogy of Morals.* New York: Vintage Books, 1969.

O'Brien, Conor Cruise. *Albert Camus of Europe and Africa.* New York: Viking Press, 1970.

Orlando, Valérie. *Nomadic Voices of Exile.* Athens: Ohio University Press, 1999.

Pacquot, Thierry, ed. *La Bibliothèque des deux rives.* Paris: Lieu Commun, 1992.

Padoan, Daniela. "Razzismo letterario: scrivi in italiano e non vinci mai." *Il fatto quotidiano*, 16 January, 2012.

Parati, Graziella. *Migration Italy: The Art of Talking Back in a Destination Culture.* Toronto: University of Toronto Press, 2005.

Pieprzak, Katarzyna. "Bodies on the Beach: Youssef Elalamy and Moroccan Landscapes of the Clandestine." In Eds., M. Compan and K. Pieprzak. *Land and Landscape in Francographic Literature.* Cambridge: Cambridge Scholars Publishing, 2007.

Ponzanesi, Sandra. *Paradoxes of Postcolonial Culture: Contemporary Women Writers of the Indian and Afro-Italian Diaspora.* Albany: SUNY Press, 2004.

Quilliot, Roger. *The Sea and Prisons.* Alabama: University of Alabama Press, 1970.

Redouane, Najid, Ed. *Clandestins dans le texte maghrébin de langue française.* Paris: L'Harmattan, 2008.

Renan, Ernest. *Qu'est-ce qu'une nation?* Paris: Mille et une nuits, 1997.

Ricœur, Paul. *Du texte à l'action.* Paris: Seuil, 1986.

———. *Oneself as Another.* Trans. Kathleen Blamey. Chicago: University of Chicago Press, 1992.

Robin, Régine. "Un Québec pluriel" in Eds, Claude Duchet and Stéphane Vachon. *La recherche littéraire: objets et methodes.* Montréal: XYZ, 1998.

Roche, Anne. "Regards échangés ou comment lire les romans du Maghreb" in *La bibliothèque des deux rives. Sur la Méditerranée Occidentale.* Ed. Thierry Pacquot. Paris: Le lieu commun, 1992. p.115–125.

Romano, Carlin. "Clash of Civilizations over an Elevator in Piazza Vittorio." *The Philadelphia Inquirer*, 29 October 2008. Online http://www.popmatters.com/pm/review/clash-of-civilizations-over-an-elevator-in-piazza-vittorio/ Accessed January 2013.

Rosello, Mireille. *France and the Maghreb: Performative Encounters.* Gainesville: University Press of Florida, 2005.

Rousset, Jean. *La littérature de l'âge baroque en France: Circé et le paon.* Paris: José Corti, 1953.

Rushdie, Salman. *Step across This Line: Collected Non-Fiction 1992–2002.* New York: Random House, 2002.

Ryding, Karen, Ed. *Early Medieval Arabic: Studies on Al-Khalil Ibn Ahmad.* Washington, DC: Georgetown University Press, 1998.

Saïd, Edward. *Culture and Imperialism.* New York: Knopf, 1993.

———. *Humanism and Democratic Criticism.* New York: Columbia University Press, 2004.

———. *Orientalism.* New York: Vintage Books, 1978.

Sarkozy, Nicolas. Discours. *Caen*, 9 mars 2007. http://www.ump-lehavre.org/discours/discours_sarkozy_caen_mars_2007.pdf.

———. "Pour une francophonie vivante et populaire." *Le Figaro* 22 mars 2007. http://www.lefigaro.fr/debats/20070322.FIG000000021_pour_une_francophonie_vivante_et_populaire.html.

Sartre, Jean-Paul. *Huis clos.* Paris: Gallimard, 1947.

———. "Réponse à Albert Camus." *Les Temps Modernes* 82 (Août 1952): 334–53.

Scarpetta, Guy. *Eloge du cosmopolitanisme.* Paris: Grasset, 1981.

Schaeffer, Jean-Marie. *Pourquoi la fiction?* Paris: Seuil, 1999.

———. Interview with Alexandre Prstojevic *Vox Poetica*, http://www.vox-poetica.org/entretiens/intSchaeffer.html. Accessed 5 November 2012.

Schnapper, Dominique. *Community of Citizens: on the Modern Idea of Nationality.* Trans. Séverine Rosée. New Brunswick: Transaction Publishers, 1986.

Sellars, John. "The Point of View of the Cosmos: Deleuze, Romanticism, Stoicism." *Pli* 8 (1999): 1–24.

Semprun, Jorge. *L'écriture ou la vie.* Paris: Gallimard, 1994.

Seyhan, Azade. "Linguistic Difference and Cultural Translatability." *ADFL Bulletin* 33.2 (Winter 2002): 59–63.

Shohat, Ella. "Notes on the Postcolonial." *Social Text* 31/32 (1992): 99–113.

———. and Robert Stam. *Unthinking Eurocentrism.* New York: Routledge, 1994.

Silverstein, Paul. "France's Mare Nostrum: Colonial and Post-Colonial Constructions of the French Mediterranean." *Journal of North African Studies* 7.4 (2002): 1–22.

Smari, Abdelmalek. *Fiamme in paradiso.* Milano: Il Saggiatore, 2000.

———. *L'occidentalista.* Milano: Libribianchi, 2008.

———. Personal Correspondence, 2012.

Southgate, Beverley. *What Is History For?* London: Routledge, 2005.

Sprintzen, David, ed. *Sartre and Camus: A Historic Confrontation.* New York: Humanity Books, 2004.

Stétié, Salah. "La Méditerranée entre les deux consciences." In *La Méditerranée Créatrice.* Ed. Thierry Fabre. Paris: Editions de l'Aube, 1994.

Stora, Benjamin. *La gangrène et l'oubli: la mémoire de la guerre d'Algérie.* Paris: Editions de la découverte, 1991. Accessed 28 May, 2013.

Tamalet Talbayev, Edwige. "The Languages of Translocality: What Plurilingualism Means in a Maghrebi Context," *Expressions maghrébines* 11.2 (Winter 2012): 9–25.

Témime, Emile. *Un rêve méditerranéen.* Paris: Actes Sud, 2002.

Tillion, Germaine. *Le harem et les cousins.* Paris: Editions du Seuil, 1996.

Valéry, Paul. *Inspirations Méditerranéennes dans Œuvres complètes I.* Paris: Gallimard, 1957.

———. *The Collected Works of Paul Valéry* Vol 10. Tr. Marthiel and Jackson Mathews. Princeton: Princeton University Press, 1975.

Van Zuylen, Marina. "Maghreb and Melancholy: A Reading of Nina Bouraoui." *Research in African Literatures* 34.3 (Fall 2003): 84–99.

Verdicchio, Pasquale. "The Preclusion of Postcolonial Discourse in Southern Italy." In *Revisioning Italy: National Identity and Global Culture.* Ed. Beverly Allen and Mary Russo Minneapolis: University of Minnesota Press, 1997. 191–212.

Vermorel, Henri. *Sigmund Freud et Romain Rolland: correspondance 1923–1936: de la sensation océanique au trouble du souvenir sur l'Acropole.* Paris: Presses Universitaires de France, 1993.

Vidal-Beneyto, José and Gérard De Puymège. *La Méditerranée: Modernité Plurielle.* Paris: Editions Unesco, 2000.

Wallerstein, Immanuel. *The Modern World-System, Vol II.* New York: Academic Press, 1974.

White, Hayden. *The Content of the Form.* Baltimore: Johns Hopkins University Press, 1987.

———. *Metahistory.* Baltimore: Johns Hopkins University Press, 1973.

Woodull, Winifred. "Postcolonial Thought and Culture in Francophone North Africa." In *Francophone Postcolonial Studies: A Critical Introduction.* Ed. Charles Forsdick and David Murphy. London: Arnold Publishers, 2003. 211–20.

———. *Transfigurations of the Maghreb: Feminism, Decolonization and Literatures in French.* Minneapolis: University of Minnesota Press, 1993.

Yelles, Mourad. "Centralité et métissage. D'un baroque méditerranéen." In *Aire régionale méditerranéen.* Paris: UNESCO, 2001.

Zhiri, Oumelbanine. "Leo Africanus, Translated and Betrayed." In *The Politics of Translation in the Middle Ages.* Ed. Renate Blumenfeld-Kosinski, Louise Von Flotow and Daniel Russel. Ottawa, Canada: University of Ottawa Press, 2001. 161–74.

Index

About the Author

Claudia Esposito is assistant professor of French at the University of Massachusetts, Boston.

Her research interests focus on translation, migration, urban geographies and transcultural crossings in Maghrebi and French literature and film. Her articles on Albert Memmi, Tahar Ben Jelloun and Abdellatif Kechiche have appeared in several journals, including *Studies in French Cinema*, *Expressions Maghrébines*, *Journal of Postcolonial Writing*, and *The French Review*, among others.

www.ingramcontent.com/pod-product-compliance
Lightning Source LLC
Chambersburg PA
CBHW030646110726
47901CB00002B/586